HEARING A FILM, SEEING A SERMON

Preaching and Popular Movies

Timothy B. Cargal

Westminster John Knox Press
LOUISVILLE • LONDON

Scripture quotations, unless otherwise indicated, are from the New Revised Standard Version of the Bible, copyright © 1989 by the Division of Christian Education of the National Council of the Churches of Christ in the U.S.A., and used by permission.

Portions of chapter 4 were first published as "A Share of the Spirit," *Emphasis: A Preaching Journal for the Parish Pastor* 34, no. 1 (May–June 2004), 58–61. Portions of chapter 5 were first published as "What Makes a King?" *Emphasis* 33, no. 6 (March–April 2004), 36–39. Portions of chapter 6 were first published as "Spirit-Person," *Emphasis* 33, no. 1 (May–June 2003), 40–43. Used by permission from CSS Publishing Company, 517 S. Main Street, Lima, Ohio 45804.

Book design by Sharon Adams
Cover design and illustration by RD Studio

First edition
Published by Westminster John Knox Press
Louisville, Kentucky

This book is printed on acid-free paper that meets the American National Standards Institute Z39.48 standard. ♾

PRINTED IN THE UNITED STATES OF AMERICA

07 08 09 10 11 12 13 14 15 16 — 10 9 8 7 6 5 4 3 2 1

Library of Congress Cataloging-in-Publication Data

Cargal, Timothy B. (Timothy Boyd)
   Hearing a film, seeing a sermon : preaching and popular movies / Timothy B. Cargal.
— 1st ed.
       p. cm.
    Includes bibliographical references.
    ISBN 978-0-664-22951-1 (alk. paper)
    1. Motion pictures—Homiletical use. 2. Motion pictures—Religious aspects—Christianity—Sermons. 3. Sermons, American—21st century. 4. Presbyterian Church—Sermons. I. Title.

   BV4235.M68C37 2007
   261.5'7—dc22

                                                                            2007003345

For
Sherri, Eric, and Larissa Cargal,
who remind me always to "see" my sermons in life around me,
and
Daniel Patte,
who taught me to "hear" all "texts" both critically and respectfully

Contents

Acknowledgments   vii
Introduction—Preaching to a "Cinemate" Culture   1

1. Hearing a Film—Film Interpretation for the Seminary Trained   13
2. Seeing a Sermon—The Homiletics of Dialogue with Cinema   37
3. "Heaven's Light"—*The Hunchback of Notre Dame*   65
4. "Time to Get On with It"—*Bruce Almighty*   77
5. "The Return of the King"—*The Lord of the Rings: The Return of the King*   89
6. Dialogues with Two Superheroes—*Spider-Man* and *Superman Returns*   103
7. "Better Days Ahead"—*Pleasantville*   117
8. "In His Shoes"—*In Her Shoes*   129
9. Hearing More than Just the Film—*The Passion of the Christ, Atlantis,* and *Million Dollar Baby / The Sea Inside*   141

Conclusion—Opening the Preacher's Eyes and Ears   153
Notes   157

Acknowledgments

This book has a long history. As I look back over almost two decades of ordained ministry, I can see where the engagement with popular culture through movies has figured prominently at some key points along the way. Even before my ordination, I was invited to give the "senior sermon" at the commencement exercises of the denominational college I attended. That sermon had as one of its illustrations a discussion of the film *Chariots of Fire*. More than a decade later, having by then changed to the denomination that is now my context of ministry, I preached a sermon drawing on themes from Disney's *Hunchback of Notre Dame*, which was heard by the pulpit nominating committee that eventually extended the invitation to serve the church where I have been pastor for another decade. While in this call, I have been blessed with opportunities both formal and informal to reflect on films theologically and to incorporate them into my homiletical craft. Consequently, there are many to be acknowledged here.

The suggestion that I should consider compiling a book of some of my sermons dealing with movies originated with my clergy colleagues in a weekly lectionary discussion group. Over the years its membership has changed as folks have come in and gone out as they received new opportunities for ministry, so I won't try to name them all here. They know who they are, and they know their support and encouragement of my ministry goes far beyond this project.

The opportunity to try out this basic approach to analyzing films and sermons first came while I was a fellow of the Pastor-Theologian Program, funded by the Lilly Endowment, at the Center of Theological Inquiry in Princeton, New Jersey. During the second year of my three-year term our topic was "Theology, Worship, and the Arts." My paper for that year became the basis for the chapter here dealing with *The Hunchback of Notre Dame*. My thanks to Wallace Alston, director of the center at the time, for the invitation to participate in the program, and to Kathi Morley, the center administrator, whose hospitality knows no bounds; and special thanks to the members of the mid-Atlantic region group from Fall 2001 to Spring 2004, with whom I shared so much rich theological discussion and even richer fellowship.

Just as my involvement with the Pastor-Theologian Program was ending, Northwood Presbyterian Church in Silver Spring, Maryland, where I have the privilege of serving as pastor, provided me with a three-month sabbatical for spiritual, professional, and personal renewal. The professional part of that time was spent beginning work on this book, and during that sabbatical about the first third of it was drafted. I am deeply grateful to them for their crucial support in launching this project. It was in and for this community of faith that virtually all of the dialogue with Scripture and culture presented in these pages first took shape.

For six weeks of that sabbatical, I was privileged to be a fellow of the College of Preachers (now Cathedral College) at the Washington National Cathedral. I spent my weeks living at the college facilities (and my weekends at home), reading film criticism and homiletical theory and completing the initial drafts of chapters 1 and 2. My thanks to James Fenhagen, warden of the college then, and Dean McDonald, director of the Cathedral College of Preachers, for accepting my application to become a fellow and for their ongoing encouragement; and to Lucy Lind Hogan, professor of preaching and worship at Wesley Theological Seminary, who served as my advisor for the project. My affiliation with the College of Preachers extends over almost the whole time that I have been in the capital area, and whatever preacher I am today I owe in significant measure to them. Special thanks to David Schlafer, who earlier supervised my work in the college's core-curriculum program, and to Bill Hague, who taught me much about the art of delivering sermons and with whom I am now privileged to serve on the associate faculty. Thanks also to Shelagh Casey Brown, associate warden; Joan Roberts, conference registrar; and Kim Gilliam, director of operations; they are the people first in my mind when I think of the college's legendary hospitality.

The College of Preachers invited Edward McNulty and me to lead a conference in the fall of 2005 on preaching in dialogue with films that shared the title of this book. During that time many of both the theoretical and practical ideas in this book received an important trial run. My thanks to Ed and to the conferees for sharing their love for films and love for preaching with me, encouraging and strengthening this project in the process.

I also wish to thank Jon Berquist of Westminster John Knox Press, whom

I have known since our days as graduate students at Vanderbilt University. When demands of the parish, family responsibilities, and all manner of other things kept pushing this book further down on the tyrannical list of the urgent, he exhibited tremendous patience and understanding.

Finally, and by far most importantly, I want to thank my family: Sherri, Eric, and Larissa. Since my vocation is pastor and adjunct professor of biblical studies, every minute of the time spent in writing a book on preaching and film ultimately came at their expense. They, too, have exhibited extraordinary patience with the writing of this book, but in a very different way. They have patiently waited for me to return from fellowship meetings, conference presentations, and even my home office so that I could engage in the only dialogues with films that may in the end prove of lasting importance: our family's Friday "pizza and movie" nights. They are the ones with whom, through whom, and for whom I see movies, so this book is foremost dedicated to them. It is also dedicated to Daniel Patte, my *Doktorvater* (if one may use that German title of a *Français*) at Vanderbilt University, who introduced me to the world of semiotics and gave me the tools to interpret respectfully texts of many kinds and who over the many years since has always encouraged my various research efforts.

Introduction

Preaching to a "Cinemate" Culture

Preaching is one of the great bastions of oral culture. It is in its very essence an oral form of communication. Sermons—the content of what is preached—may either originate as written texts or subsequently be transcribed into written texts, but preaching itself is an oral event (and the best preaching bears this constantly in mind from the beginning of preparation through the performance, the preaching event itself). The preacher may even incorporate body language or the use of props (thankfully only rarely) into preaching, but the fact that even those instances of preaching usually lose little when experienced as strictly audio recordings underscores the essential orality of preaching.

Leaving aside technical definitions derived from studies of the Greek word *kerygma*, the long history of discussions about theological oratory, and so on, a pragmatic definition of preaching that would be immediately acceptable to folks in the pews might be that "preaching" is oral communication intended to shape a person's religious understanding of the world and to motivate behavior in accord with that religious understanding. It had its beginnings in culturally recognized religious contexts by persons acknowledged to have particular authority within such settings. (The colloquial use of the word for an unwelcome harangue, such as when a teenager tells a parent, "Don't preach to me!" is a subsequent development.) The world's first preachers were those who told the stories and traditions that made sense of life in this universe.

For centuries certainly and perhaps for millennia, there was an essential fit between the sources for preaching and preaching itself. The preacher drew on a repository of oral traditions to find ideas, stories, and images that had already shaped people's understanding of the world and their actions in it. The preacher might challenge those understandings or people's self-conceptions about how

1

well their lives reflected them—like the earliest prophets of Israel who used the traditions about slavery in Egypt to confront injustices within their own societies—but oral traditions provided the grist for the oral preaching mill.

By the time that specifically Christian preaching emerged, the fundamental connection between the sources of preaching and preaching itself had begun to change. First-century societies in the Mediterranean basin were in the midst of a transition from primarily oral cultures into increasingly literate ones. Determining how far this change had permeated those societies (filtering down from higher socioeconomic levels to lower ones) is an academic debate the details of which need not concern us here. Our concern is with preaching as understood in pragmatic terms, and at this level the implications are clear. Preachers as we encounter them in Acts draw not only on distinct stories and summaries of traditions as in preliterate, oral cultures (so Stephen in Acts 7:2–50); they also specifically quote texts (as Peter cites Joel 2:28–32 and Pss. 16:8–11 and 110:1 in his sermon in Acts 2:14–36, and Paul cites Epimenides and Aratus in his sermon in Acts 17:22–31). Preaching continued in its oral form,[1] but it began to draw on the sources of a literate culture.

Because the cultural history of the West has been predominately one of literate societies, it is hardly surprising that preaching in the West has continued to draw on written sources. Indeed, most people now probably think of preaching as *oral* exposition of sacred *texts*. Preaching as we know it thus combines preliterate and literate cultures. Written communication has borne fundamental authority while oral forms like preaching held derivative authority as expressions of written truths. Yet as we have entered the twenty-first century, social commentators, particularly in America, have been suggesting that we are becoming a "postliterate" society. The label does not intend to assert that we have become illiterate (though certainly some would sound those alarm bells), but rather that literate discourse—what is written and subsequently read—may be losing its hegemony for communicating important ideas about how we view the world and should act within it.

Just as preaching maintained its oral form even while adapting its sources in the move from preliterate to literate cultures, it only stands to reason that preaching will have to adjust as well to a postliterate society. Simply being "literate" (able to read, interpret, and converse about written texts) is no longer enough for preachers. Fluency in the multiple forms of media in which discourse now takes place will increasingly be required. An exceptionally prominent and increasingly important form of that media in America over the past century has been film,[2] so much so that one film-studies scholar suggests the term *cinemate* to describe people who have developed a fluency in the ability to interpret the meanings created in films by the juxtaposition of images, words, music, and sound.

FILMS AS CONTEMPORARY CULTURAL DISCOURSE

Cinemate was coined by James Monaco,[3] who draws parallels between film and language. He rightly insists that film is only "*like* a language" since it does not have all the features of complete language systems, whether conversational (as with English, Spanish, or Chinese) or symbolic (as with mathematics). To understand films in themselves does not require knowledge of a specific vocabulary, although knowledge of some film terms can be helpful for discussing films either orally or in writing (which is, when you stop to think about it, a matter of translating film into other forms of discourse). With regard to making a movie, says Monaco, "it's impossible to be ungrammatical in film" since it does not have rigid rules of syntax that must be adhered to for meaning to be properly conveyed. Yet film does have specific conventions that serve as a kind of syntax in constructing meaning. Consequently, he observes, "people who are highly experienced in film—highly literate visually (or should we say 'cinemate'?)—see more and hear more than people who seldom go to the movies. An education in the quasi-language of film opens up greater potential meaning for the observer."

Providing a brief introduction to some of this "quasi-language of film" will be a chief concern of the next chapter, but for the moment I want to discuss another way in which film functions as a kind of language. Several writers have discussed the cultural prominence and importance of film by describing it as a "*lingua franca*" or "'cultural currency' in which discussions about life and death (and life and depth) issues are conducted."[4] It is increasingly through film (particularly as more broadly construed to include other recent visual-media narrative forms, including television) that our culture analyzes and discusses life's most important questions.[5]

Although some have debated whether movies portray popular culture or seek to create it, Brian Godawa has correctly noted that they do both.[6] Following Michael Medved's argument that Hollywood not only does influence culture but specifically intends to do so,[7] Godawa noted the disingenuousness of film producers who deny their movies can influence cultural trends even as they charge companies millions of dollars for prominent placements of their products in those movies. But tempering Medved's critique, he acknowledged "that much entertainment meets an already existing demand in the audience." As a general rule, it is probably correct to say that movies more often become blockbusters by resonating with some segment of the culture than by running counter to all cultural streams. In fact, as Marsh observed, "the popularity of a film may, indeed, be an indication of its importance."[8] Consequently the study of films can be a powerful tool for the study of the culture in which they were produced.[9]

Movies can become the megaphones that make ideas more widely discussed. A seemingly unlikely influence in the emergence of modern environ-
mentalism may well have been Walt Disney's *Bambi*, which sparked a more
than 80 percent drop in the deer-hunting business in the year following its
release in 1942, from $5.7 million to $1 million.[10] More recently three
actresses—Jessica Lange, Sissy Spacek, and Sally Field—were invited to testify before Congress about family farm issues in 1984 because of roles they
played in the films *Country*, *The River*, and *Places in the Heart* that were released
that year.[11] No doubt millions more people had their thinking about capital
punishment shaped by the film *Dead Man Walking* than by reading Sister
Helen Prejean's book on which it was based. Sometimes films mirror attitudes
in the society and even create catchphrases for expressing them, as with the
line "Greed is good" from *Wall Street*. They can present interpretations of key
moments in our history and spark vigorous debate about the adequacy of their
particular interpretations, as with Oliver Stone's films *Platoon* and *JFK*. Over
time the development of film genres can even express our changing cultural
attitudes. Consider the transformation in thinking about the role of violence
in the settlement of the American West and its appropriateness for dealing
with modern social problems portrayed in the classical movie westerns of the
1950s and 1960s as compared with Clint Eastwood's *Unforgiven*.

The cultural power of movies has spawned a growing interest in the relationship between theology and film. Indeed, some writers insist that theology
must engage film if it is also to engage contemporary culture.[12] Christian theology has a fundamental narrative quality that requires a dialogue between
God's story and our stories,[13] so as films become a dominant way for relating
our stories, they will in some ways set the limits for what it will be possible to
say to our culture.[14] At the heart of the Christian theological narrative is the
conviction that God is at work in the world, not only in distant "Bible times"
but in the present as well, speaking to us by the Spirit through all of life.
Engaging films and other forms of popular culture opens us to what God may
be saying to both the world and the church and reminds us of the public
dimension of theology.[15] Since we encounter God through both word and
image, films serve to remind theology that it must speak not only to the mind
but also to the emotional and aesthetic aspects of life.[16] If theology cannot
escape these imperatives, neither can preaching.

THE RELATIONSHIP BETWEEN PREACHING AND FILM

Despite all the changes from preliterate to literate to postliterate cultures, the
fundamental purposes of preaching remain to shape a person's religious

understanding of the world and to motivate behavior in accord with that religious understanding. Now, if you closely compare that statement with the working, pragmatic definition of "preaching" that I gave earlier, you will notice that part of it has dropped out in this restatement. This time I have not restricted the definition of preaching to "oral communication." My reason for doing so is not to introduce "visual communication" to preaching (either through the orthographic systems of writing or the images of films and related media, or even the physical aspects of nonverbal communication in the preacher's performance of a sermon). Rather, it is that "*oral* communication" oversimplifies even preaching as an act of speech. One of the changes in our understanding of all speaking is that we are increasingly aware that it is not simply oral communication but also "aural" communication. That is to say, preaching is not only what comes out of the preacher's mouth; it is also what happens when it is received and processed by those who hear it. Genuine communication requires that attention be given to the one originating the communication (here, the preacher), to the recipients (those who are listening), and to the medium of communication (for our purposes in this book, we will focus on the sources from which the preacher draws).[17]

Shaping people's understanding of the world and their actions requires persuasion, and persuasion depends on moving people from where they are to where you wish them to be. If you misjudge what people already know, how they feel about things, or what personal investments they may already have, then you will not succeed in persuading them—especially if your goal is persuading them to make real changes in outlook or behavior rather than the more modest, yet still-sometimes-daunting, task of persuading them to continue in what you think they already believe and how they act on that belief.

At its most rudimentary, this means preaching must be done in the language understood by those who hear it. No matter how good my sermon, it will be lost on people who speak only Spanish, or Chinese, or a host of other languages about which I know little or nothing. I don't speak those languages and so cannot preach in them. But that is such a ridiculously obvious point that it should hardly require making. I raise it, however, to point out once again that "languages" are not simply demarcated by linguistic groups like Spanish or Chinese. Perhaps you have heard the quip "The Americans and the British are one people separated by a common language." Or maybe in learning a foreign language you have been reminded by your teacher, as my son has in his Spanish classes in high school, that even a single language can legitimately be spoken in quite distinct ways (as the differences between European and Central American Spanish illustrate). Regional idioms and even slang may be simply rather than ridiculously obvious, yet they are markers leading to something less obvious precisely because it is in some ways beneath notice. Understanding between a preacher and those who listen is just as dependent on shared cultural references. The oral part of preaching must be done in the cultural language or idiom of the hearers if its aural component is to succeed as well.

With regard to preaching, key components of those "shared cultural references" are obviously the sacred texts and religious teachings and traditions within which the preacher and listeners gather. As preachers, however, we are constantly reminded that we must exercise caution with regard to what we assume is encompassed by those "*shared* references." As overall biblical literacy declines, preachers have to be very careful with passing references to biblical stories. Years of seminary training and ministry experience may have fixed the relationship between Hosea and Gomer in our minds, but there are many for whom "Gomer" will conjure only recollections of a lovable, bumbling, Marine Corps private in a sitcom recalled from years past or encountered in the outer reaches of the cable television spectrum. But even for those who may recall the story of Hosea and Gomer, we are mindful that we must bridge the historical-cultural gulf that separates prostitution in its ancient Middle Eastern setting from our conceptions of it in contemporary American society. A tried-and-true means of building such bridges between the biblical and modern worlds in preaching—of creating analogies between what the listeners are presumed to know from their own lives and what we assume they may not know about that historically and geographically distant setting—is the use of illustrations.

Preachers have mined the movies for illustrations almost since Edison invented the medium.[18] Their interests have generally been more confined to single scenes or perhaps to the narrative arc traced by a brief series of scenes and not to films as a whole. In this regard the use of films as source material was perhaps not that different from any other type of sermon illustration. The illustrations served to develop and reinforce a point in the sermon, often by shifting the tone, or especially the temporal frame of reference, in an attempt to create or maintain interest as much as to assist understanding. They were examples of what the preacher was speaking about and were not necessarily concerned with what the movie from which they were taken was really all about.

Such "illustrative scene" approaches to incorporating cinematic art into worship are problematic in at least two ways. As viewed over against the more thorough thematic evaluations of movies that are now appearing in studies of film and theology,[19] such approaches are unfair to the films from which they draw. Like any proof text, isolated scenes can be wrested from their context and thus misrepresent the intention of the film. And just as we as preachers are quick to call our colleagues on proof-texting from the Scriptures that is misleading with regard to the biblical and historical context, the cinemate members of congregations will similarly call preachers on their misuse of films. Credibility will thus be undermined regarding one's status not only as an interpreter of films but also as an interpreter of culture, morality, and even the scriptural and theological tradition.

As viewed from recent homiletic discussion, such isolated scenes, like any isolated illustration, can be more disruptive than illuminative. The greatest power of images and illustrations is also their greatest liability: they engage the listener in the process of meaning production in the preaching event by evoking associations from her or him. Consequently, the preacher must simultaneously call forth the full evocative potential of an image while limiting and focusing its associations to increase the likelihood that the hearers' responses will reinforce the preacher's purposes in the sermon rather than undermine them. Preachers tend to choose movie illustrations because they have evocative power (especially for those who have seen the films and can call forth the visual, musical, and other cues as well as the words of the dialogue). At a minimum, however, the illustration will bring with it associations with other scenes from the same film and, given the cinematic conventions of borrowing techniques and images from other films, potentially associations from other movies as well. Having interpreted the film—and not just the scene(s)—thus becomes one important component of the preacher's ability to maintain some control over the associations evoked by the cinematic image.

PREACHING AS INTERPRETATION
OF SCRIPTURE, FILM, AND CULTURE

This book provides an introduction to the hermeneutics for interpreting the theology of films and shows how these interpretations can be used as homiletical devices for preaching in worship. I have specifically tried to address the following questions: How can the theological themes in these films be used to elucidate/illustrate the theological themes of biblical texts? Given the fact that popular films achieve their success at least in part because of their resonance with the broader culture, how can films be used to make explicit those cultural assumptions so that they may be brought into dialogue with Scripture and the Christian faith? When employing a film as a dialogue partner in preaching, how do we keep the film from running away with the sermon? That is, how do we avoid preaching on the film rather than on the scriptural text? How do we orally relate such visual media as cinema when not all listeners will have seen the film? Preaching that attempts to engage the hearers by exegeting both scriptural text and modern culture must be able to dialogue with film.

Preaching must also engage in this dialogue while avoiding the two pitfalls identified at the end of the previous section: it must respect the integrity of the movies engaged by interpreting them in cinemate ways, and it must carry on the dialogue in a means that is appropriate to the particular context of preaching. That is to say, when the preacher chooses to enter into dialogue with cinema, that engagement must be both legitimate in terms of the methods and concerns of film criticism and homiletically appropriate. Without becoming either a textbook in film criticism or a fully delineated homiletical method, this book encourages the preacher both to engage in such dialogues and to avoid falling into these two traps.

Even preachers who may not wish to enter into formal dialogue with particular films but who might still want to slip in an illustration taken from a movie will be helped by this study. In most instances, such illustrations would be affected little by dropping any reference to the movie from which it was taken. One could easily talk about Eric Liddell's refusing to run in an Olympics 100-meter heat because it was scheduled on a Sunday without ever mentioning that the source for the illustration was the film *Chariots of Fire*. The same holds true for scenes from original screenplays not based on real events. The preacher could refer to the relationship between the Jack Nicholson and Diane Keaton characters in *Something's Gotta Give* simply by telling a story about an aging music producer who falls in love with the middle-aged mother of the young woman he is dating. To mention the movie titles or even the fact that these stories are taken from films is little more than footnoting if one's purpose is simply to work in a brief scene or bit of dialogue to support a point in a sermon. Nevertheless, the more one understands about how movies communicate and how film critics translate films into other modes of discourse, the better able one will be to treat cinematic material in preaching.

The first chapter will assist preachers in becoming more cinemate by introducing some concepts of critical film interpretation. Following a discussion of why "dialogue" is the right metaphor or model for engaging films in preaching, I will offer a scheme that seeks to relate the language and concerns of film studies with the exegetical methods and interpretative approaches to Scripture that most pastors learned in their seminary training. Films need to be interpreted in as disciplined and critical a manner as the scriptural texts themselves before one turns to the issue of incorporating them into the homily.[20] Like the various literary genres contained in Scripture that must be learned and respected in biblical interpretation, films have their own conventions for constructing and communicating meanings that must be learned and respected.

Consequently, preachers who wish to engage cinematic media seriously as a dialogue partner are going to have to do their homework in the area of "film studies." Many of the tools and habits of mind developed over years of interpreting literary media such as Scripture will be helpful, particularly the more recent critical approaches employing sociological and ideological theory (e.g., feminist and liberationist approaches) as compared with the historical-critical approaches. But film interpretation does have its own tools, and the preacher needs to know how to use them. As Johnston has commented, "If theologians, both amateur and professional, are to avoid reading into movies what is not there, they must learn something of the craft of viewing and reflecting; they must develop their critical skills."[21] It may be useful to take a course in film studies at a local college or university or, at a minimum, to work through one of the standard textbooks in the field.[22] This book does not provide a substitute for such study but instead offers encouragement that it will be more akin to learning a new dialect rather than a wholly foreign language.

Chapter 2 will address homiletical issues, both pragmatic and theoretical. The pragmatic concerns relate to how we incorporate cinemate interpretations of films into preaching for cinemate congregations while basically employing sermon models and structures that we may already have. How much of the movie can and should you divulge within the limited amount of time that you can devote to it in a sermon? Where can we look for help and examples in how to do this? If one decides to focus on a particular scene because it captures the theme of the film, what are the pros and cons of interrupting the oral/aural communication of preaching by actually showing a clip to your congregation?

At a more theoretical level, we need to consider what might be the implications of the prominence of cinema in popular culture for the adequacy of sermon models and structures developed prior to the emergence of a post-literate culture. What underlying cultural shift is revealed by the fact that video narrative (whether cinema, television, or other emerging media, such as computer role-playing games) has become a fundamental way that our culture discusses important life questions? One answer is that ours is an increasingly narrative culture, one that shapes and expresses its understanding of the world through stories. The causal relationship here is subject to much debate. Was the culture already shifting away from logical syllogism toward narrative logic, assisting the rapid rise of visual narrative forms to cultural prominence? Or was it the influence of visual narrative forms that pushed the culture away from syllogism toward story? Regarding the preaching task, resolving that debate is of less importance than recognizing the need to develop sermon forms that favor narrative structures of persuasion over logical ones. Preaching may need to go beyond simply enhancing the incorporation of movies as illustrative material and adopt some of the methods used by films to persuade audiences through narrative. Some homileticians have begun explicitly using "filming" as a metaphor for describing the process of sermon development. Paul Scott Wilson uses this image to discuss the importance of "showing" things to those who listen to sermons rather than "telling" them things,[23] and Thomas Troeger has suggested employing screenwriting techniques in preaching a biblical story.[24]

Following these more methodological chapters, I present a series of examples of this approach to preaching in dialogue with popular movies. These chapters present an extended theological interpretation of a film (or in one case, two films) followed by the actual sermons I have preached to my congregation over the past several years. Some of these films will have been in release for sufficient time that there are published analyses bringing them into dialogue with Scripture; in other cases the films are more recent. In each case, however, the sermons themselves were first delivered before such extended analyses were available. The reason for this approach is both to help preachers develop skills of detailed film analysis and to illustrate that such is not the prerequisite to dialoguing with film in sermons. Just as seminaries train students to produce exegetical research papers but pastors do not write such formal analyses of every passage before they preach on it, so it is possible through the study of theologically sensitive film criticism to develop a mind-set for viewing films that will provide resources for preaching.

The examples chosen present three different types of films: 1) movies with a clear and explicit religious theme or character, 2) films with clear ethical and/or moral concerns but without a particular religious context, and 3) films with themes related to important cultural issues that are not obviously developed in a religious or ethical context (which is not to say that they do not themselves use symbols that developed in religious contexts).

Each type of film has two chapters that provide examples of sermons related to them. Beginning with films that have clear and explicit religious themes or elements, I will enter into dialogue with Disney's *The Hunchback of Notre Dame* and the comedy *Bruce Almighty*. Next, two of the all-time-most-successful movies at the American box office will provide examples of films with clear ethical and/or moral concerns: *The Lord of the Rings: The Return of the King* and *Spider-Man*. The chapter engaging the movie *Spider-Man* will be joined with an analysis of *Superman Returns* and will include two sermons. Finally, analyses of *Pleasantville* and *In Her Shoes* will address films without obvious religious or ethical context.

In the methodological chapters I discuss ways that films might be engaged homiletically other than by thematic analysis—methods that are suggested by other forms of critical film studies. Often movie reviewers and other commentators will look specifically at the impact a film may be having on society or at how a particular film fits into an actor's or director's overall body of work. So a final chapter will present three sermons as examples of these types of engagement with films. The first sermon is a dialogue with *The Passion of the Christ*, looking at how it relates to ideas about redemption found in several of Mel Gibson's films. The next example reflects on the notion of empire as expressed by Disney's *Atlantis: The Lost Empire* and on the debate about America's role in the world as well as concerns about how to respond to the diminished role of the church in Western societies. The final sermon engages how the Academy Awards presented to *Million Dollar Baby* and *The Sea Inside* fit into widespread discussion in American society at that time about assisted suicide. These sermons will be introduced only by brief discussions of why I chose to treat these films in particular ways in my preaching rather than by extended analysis of the movies themselves.

If you compare this selection to the films often treated in books on theology and film, one uniting characteristic becomes clear. All are what may be considered "popular movies" rather than "art house films."[25] That choice is both considered and deliberate. The purpose of this book, as already noted, arises from the need of preaching to respond to the power of cinema as both a culture-shaping force and a lens through which to examine our culture. *Babette's Feast* is both an excellent film and one that is theologically profoundly evocative,[26] but despite having won the "best foreign film" Oscar for 1987, it did not shape our culture or enter into the "cultural discourse" or lingua franca of American society broadly considered. Films (and other potential illustrations or images from "high culture") should not be brought into sermons to demonstrate the sophistication of the preacher or to raise the cultural level of the congregation. They should serve as "parallel stories in the contemporary world that resonate with the stories" in and/or behind the biblical text.[27] "Art films" are not necessarily ruled out as preaching dialogue partners, but they are more difficult both for the preacher to use and for the congregation to engage precisely because their use is likely to introduce a second, unfamiliar case rather than to provide a shared cultural experience to engage an already unfamiliar one.

With regard to all of the films presented in this book, in only one case did I go to the theater to see the film with the intention of using it as a dialogue partner in a sermon. That movie was *The Lord of the Rings: The Return of the King*. My congregation had asked me for two years whether I was going to "preach on" the film trilogy of Tolkien's epic fantasy. Wanting to be able to treat the themes of the whole work, I had planned to use it in a sermon even before I saw it. I also anticipated the possibility of using three of the other films in sermons even before seeing them, but was not sure I would. Those films were *The Passion of the Christ* (I knew I would teach about it in an adult education setting but was undecided about whether to engage it in preaching), *Superman Returns* (because of a particular line in the trailers that I discuss in that chapter), and *Atlantis*.

No doubt that final film will come as something of a surprise. Over the years, however, I have engaged enough Disney animated films in my preaching (beginning with *The Hunchback of Notre Dame*, which is also included here) that some members in my congregation would ask me when a certain year's "Disney sermon" would come. The commercial success of Disney animated films demonstrates their resonance with the culture,[28] and the company's effective influence on culture is often criticized (especially by non-U.S. cultures and some religious conservatives) but never questioned. Although I have let some Disney animated films slip by, I have often found them to be prime examples of the potential of films to both express and shape the culture so profoundly that they enter the "cultural discourse" in ways that may be fruitfully engaged theologically and homiletically.

My point is that very seldom do I go to see a film looking for sermon fodder. Rather, like many folks in my congregation, I at times when watching a film either have a "God-moment" (a sudden and unexpected awareness of God's gracious action in the world) or a flash of cultural insight. As I subsequently study the Scriptures in the process of sermon preparation, something in the text will trigger within me a sympathetic resonance that will call to mind that experience or insight. Or conversely, while working on a sermon I will see a film that resonates with what I am encountering in the text. Such resonances are both signs that I am a citizen of a cinemate culture with opportunities to engage my congregation in a postliterate dialogue about the Scriptures and the world in which they live.

A moment of resonance is but the beginning of my work as a preacher, however. I still need to test my interpretation of both the film and Scripture. I still need to translate that multisensory communication through film and that literary communication through the Bible into the oral communication of preaching. This book is an introduction to how to go about this necessary work in preaching to a cinemate culture.

1

Hearing a Film

Film Interpretation for the Seminary Trained

It did not take long after the development of motion-picture technology before some within the church recognized that preaching would have to take films into account. Already in 1911, Herbert A. Jump advised that one response to what was even then considered a declining interest in Christian worship among the American population was to engage this new visual medium.

> The growing possibility of the motion picture . . . is its usefulness to the preacher as he [or she] proclaims the moral truth. It will provide the element of illustration for his [or her] discourse far better than it can be provided by the spoken word. It will make his [or her] gospel vivid, pictorial, dramatic, and above all, interesting.[1]

At the same time others were advocating that motion-picture projection devices had "actually become a part of the equipment of the up-to-date church . . . almost as necessary as a janitor, an organ, or the heavy and depressing looking pews of oak."[2] The more things change. . . .

Yet while these voices seem extremely prescient a century later, one reason for their current timeliness is precisely that much of the church—especially but not exclusively its conservative segments—did not readily embrace this new technology and indeed were often quite hostile toward it. I still recall the amusement of the student body at the conservative denominational college I attended when the promoter of the film *Jesus*,[3] who had been invited to speak about it in a morning chapel service, offered us all free passes to see the movie at the local cinema. He apparently did not know the school's student conduct code prohibited going to movie theaters. Somewhat trapped, the administration waived the prohibition for only this particular case.

Now even conservative Christian critics of much of the Hollywood film industry have given up such head-in-the-sand responses to this cultural juggernaut. Echoing Paul's advice to the Corinthians to stay engaged with the culture (1 Cor. 5:9–13a), either from sheer necessity or perhaps to evangelize it, Godawa notes that "those who would completely withdraw from culture because of its imperfections suffer a decreasing capacity to interact redemptively with that culture"—and would also miss out on some instances in films of what would be considered, even from such conservative theological vantage points, positive influences.[4] But given the long and sometimes strained relationship between the church and the film industry in America,[5] it is hardly surprising that there is disagreement about how the church should engage films. At one level these differing views about Christian responses to film are nothing other than a specific example of attitudes toward culture generally, as described by H. Richard Niebuhr's now-classic study *Christ and Culture*.[6] Simplifying his scheme somewhat, these basic approaches can be described as "Christ against culture," "Christ in critical dialogue with culture,"[7] and "Christ of culture" (that is to say, "immersed in culture").

Although Godawa talks about the need to engage cinema in its own terms in order to understand it and the culture it reflects and shapes, his conservative theology finds much more to be leery of than to embrace. His concern is fundamentally to help viewers uncover what he considers the faulty worldviews present in most movies,[8] so his stance finally is one of "Christ against culture." The same is true for Margaret Miles, even though both her theological starting point and methodological means are almost precisely opposite Godawa's. Operating from a liberal theological perspective, the concerns Miles had with the values presented and reinforced by popular films relate to race, gender, class, and a tendency to view religious experience either skeptically or too much from a Christian-centric perspective. Given these specific concerns she chose a cultural studies approach to studying films,[9] and viewing movies primarily through these ethical and ideological lenses she also finds much more to be concerned about than to embrace.[10]

At the other end of the spectrum are some interpreters of religion and film who have adopted something of a "Christ immersed in culture" attitude.[11] These writers operate with a view similar to that espoused by Tillich: "Everything that expresses ultimate reality expresses God whether it intends to do so or not."[12] Johnston has labeled this view "divine encounter" and describes it as the conviction that "movies have, at times, a sacramental capacity to provide the viewer an experience of transcendence."[13] Certainly I have had such an experience both in the cinema and in the theater, a "God-moment" that was unanticipated and for that reason all the more gracious. Yet not all such experiences were even remotely the intention of the filmmakers, and we need to exercise caution in "baptizing" or Christianizing films themselves, or even ascribing to them a "religious" or "religion-like" quality.[14]

What is required, then, is an approach toward films that is neither overly hostile nor overly accepting. What is needed is a critical stance that would allow for movies to be engaged in preaching even when their themes do not warrant attack or denunciation, on the one hand, or when they roll back the curtains of the transcendent, on the other. Such an approach has been often referred to as "dialogue."

WHAT IS A "DIALOGUE" WITH FILM?

The first thing to emphasize in discussing my desire to see preaching enter into dialogue with cinema is that "dialogue" here serves as a metaphor. That needs to be stressed because dialogue has become a stock metaphor in contemporary discourse, one that is used so commonly and in such diverse contexts that it begins to lose it metaphorical quality. This development into stock metaphor is the central stage in a progression from new metaphorical expression that opens fresh insights, to common turn of phrase, and ultimately to cliché. The danger with stock metaphors is that they can collapse into simple statements of "what is" and lose that vital quality that invites one to play in the space between the thing the metaphor seeks to elucidate and the ways that thing is both like and unlike the metaphorical image. The problem, for example, with the metaphor "God the Father" after two millennia of Christian discourse is that it has become a stock metaphor that no longer invites us to imagine how the Divine is both like and unlike the human fathers we have known.

The danger with dialogue as a stock metaphor within this present context is that it too will collapse into a simple statement of "what is." Dialogue with film in preaching becomes nothing more than "talking about" movies from time to time in our sermons. In that sense, a dialogue has occurred every time a preacher describes a scene in a movie. But as I have already indicated in the introduction, I am calling on those of us who preach to do much more than just "talk about" movies in our sermons because our listeners seem to enjoy it when we do.

In order to revitalize this stock metaphor, let me begin by substituting a synonymous metaphor for dialogue, namely, "conversation." As Bernard Brandon Scott observed, "The advantage of conversation is that as metaphor it suggests mutuality, a common seeking for truth while recognizing the ambiguity and the plurality of our common situation."[15] Conversation is open-ended and at its best not driven by a desire for resolution. Scott was himself building on David Tracy's development of the metaphor of conversation. For Tracy, conversation "is not a confrontation. It is not a debate. It is not an exam. It is questioning itself. It is a willingness to follow the question wherever it may go. It is dia-logue."[16] Conversation is full of give-and-take and recognizes that both parties bring something essential to the endeavor.

So why not just use conversation as the metaphor for incorporating film into preaching? Like all synonyms, there are connotations that shade the specific denotations that distinguish the words *conversation* and *dialogue*. One connotation between these words is that *dialogue* has the nuance of being more serious and considered than *conversation*, which can often be characterized as "casual" or even "frivolous." If movies were nothing more than entertainment, then perhaps preachers would be justified in spicing up their sermons with a bit of frivolous talk about movies to capture the listeners' attention. But when movies become part of the cultural discourse, a prime means by which a society shapes and expresses its fundamental values, then something more serious and considered is needed. Robert Jewett described his preferred approach to films as "valid conversation partners" by the phrase "dialogue in a prophetic mode."[17] While one may have "casual *conversations*," one can only have "prophetic *dialogue*."

What conversation and dialogue share is that they only genuinely occur when both parties to the endeavor are allowed to have their say. Neither side can be permitted to speak for the other. Now, at one level, that observation might suggest that dialogue with film in preaching is therefore impossible. To let the film truly have its own say, the film would need to be viewed in its entirety as part of the dialogue. Such would certainly be ideal (but still not sufficient for reasons I will return to shortly), but I would suggest that it is not necessary or essential. Listeners who have seen the film will no doubt gain more from a dialogue with it in preaching than those who have not (just as those who have read the novel, seen the play, heard the song, seen the painting, or have otherwise personally engaged the countless other things preachers draw on for illustrations benefit more than those who have not).[18] There are ways, as we know from reading about films in other media, to represent "their say" fairly even in the summary fashion required in preaching.

I will turn to the means of conveying a film's "say" in preaching in the next chapter, but here I want to stress that what will be the necessary and essential element to genuine dialogue with film in preaching is for the preacher to present fairly and accurately what is true of the film as a whole, and not simply provide a technically accurate description of the details of a particular scene. A "willful suspension of disbelief" is required, a giving of oneself over totally and completely to the filmmakers in order to live for the duration of the movie in their world, just as the old proverb admonishes "walking in another's shoes." Johnston described this attitude as follows:

> In a sense, the real world must for a time "stand still." Moviegoers must give to the screen their "as-if" assent and enter wholeheartedly into the movie's imaginative world, or the experience risks being still-born. With motion pictures, moreover, this happens naturally, as the darkness of the theater and the community of viewers, not to mention the surround sound and oversized screen, combine with the images and story to capture the audience's attention.[19]

It is precisely this "willful suspension of disbelief" that makes critics of the power of cinema on both the left and the right so nervous. But one can only dialogue with a film (as with any interlocutor) if one is willing, at least "for the sake of argument," to take on its mind-set and risk that one's own understanding of the world will be changed in the process. What Marsh has observed as true of Christian theology in a postliterate age is equally true of preaching:

> Christian theology cannot . . . simply quarry film for good illustrative material. It looks for confirmations of its own content, but also expects to be challenged and even radically questioned in the process. For this to happen, theology and culture must be understood as in dialog: existing in a critical, dialectical relationship. . . . Christian theology will bring its grasp of truth and be reluctant to give ground when, for example, the content of a film presents a challenge to it. But if it is unwilling to be questioned, and reluctant to consider the possibility of change, then it has ceased to live as theology.[20]

To gain the benefits of drawing on the sources of a multimedia culture both for ourselves as preachers and for our congregations as listeners, we have to be willing to risk that our preconceived notions not only of that culture but also of our own Scriptures might be changed.[21]

Johnston has suggested the label "appropriation" for those whose "goal in relating theology and film is not, first of all, to render moral judgments . . . but to achieve greater insight."[22] Having gained such insights by entering into the film, they then, and only then, "bring their outside theological perspective . . . into the conversation."[23] He summarized "appropriation" this way:

> Those who would seek to appropriate a movie's vision of life recognize that movies can offer insight to the Christian viewer about the nature of the human. There is something new that a movie can provide a Christian. More than dialogue is called for. The theologian must be receptive to encountering spirit in a new guise and only then turn to respond from the viewer's own theological point of view.[24]

Why, then, isn't appropriation the best metaphor for describing the relationship between film and preaching? After all, doesn't its nuance of "use" better describe what it is in fact that preachers would be doing—using films as a source for their sermons? One reason I resist this metaphor is that standing on its own, in isolation from the way that Johnston carefully delineates its relationship to other theological approaches to film, it conveys too much the idea of "use" and too little the idea of first entering the film on its own terms. It is too quick to "baptize" the film put to a positive use or to "demonize" the film used as a negative example. His discussion of "appropriation" makes it clear that Johnston is himself aware of this problem.

But there is another reason that I prefer the metaphor of dialogue to appropriation. As a metaphor, dialogue keeps in play the oral/aural dimension that I have insisted is an essential characteristic of preaching. Dialogue is seriously listening to and hearing another so that one can in turn seriously speak what one has to say in response (whether "Amen" or "Not so fast . . ."). Dialogue keeps before us that our purpose is communication, and its seriousness as compared to casual conversation reminds us that interpretation will be an integral part of the process. As Graham commented, "As with any other example of communication, [a film's] information has to be interpreted. It is the interpretative process which results in what one 'hears' or 'sees,' which is why there can be so many different interpretations or 'readings' of any texts, including film."[25] Fairly "hearing" what a film has to say requires interpretation.

What a film has to say is not limited to how it goes about saying it. As with other forms of artistic expression, the meaning conveyed goes beyond the material means of representation. The work of interpretation is the drawing out of this meaning of the whole, what I will call the "theme." At one level, it is the ultimate reason that a film which has not been viewed can still have its say as long as its theme has been properly interpreted and accurately conveyed through the new medium (be it a movie review in a newspaper, a technical analysis in a work of film study, or a portion of a sermon). But of course, the theme can only be discerned by a careful analysis of the film's material means of representation. Again there is a certain common-sense aspect to this observation, but it is nonetheless why the theme of one movie is different from another. This point holds even with regard to remakes of the so-called "same" movie. For example, the theme of the original *Planet of the Apes* (dir. Franklin J. Schaffner, 1968) may be different from that of Tim Burton's remake (2001), and indeed both may have different themes than Pierre Boulle's novel[26] on which the movies are in some sense based. Nor is this meant to suggest that there is only one correct theme that can be drawn from a film; nevertheless, the particulars of a film do proscribe certain limits on what others will accept as fair.[27] At its best, interpretation is a move through a hermeneutical spiral that improves understanding of the relationship between the theme(s) of the whole and the particulars of expression; and at its worst, it degenerates into a vicious circle.

So at what point are we able to enter into the path of this hermeneutical spiral so that we can "hear a film" in such a way as to dialogue with it? In the case of movies, suggests John May, that entrance would be the story:

> My principal assumption about film is the unassailable one, I think, that all feature films are stories. Story in cinema, I . . . suggest, must be discerned in terms of film's unique formal elements—photography, composition, sound, movement, and editing, especially the latter two, which set film apart from all the other arts—rather than simply in terms of those formal structures that film shares with literature; namely, setting, character, dialogue, dramatic tension, plot, and theme.[28]

This is not to discount "those formal structures that film shares with [narrative] literature," but it is to insist that film has its own means and conventions for presenting even those shared structures. And so it is to an overview of those conventions that I now turn.

ANALYZING THE CONVENTIONS OF FILM

Despite the fact that even very young children can watch, understand, and emotionally respond to movies, the intellectual process of "hearing a film" is one of the most complex communication endeavors in which we as human beings engage. To appreciate why that is the case, consider the expression of an idea—say, a young child's desire to rise to a parent's position of power and authority—written out as words on a page. Now imagine those words being expressed through somewhat poetic language so that there are images and associations that play off one another, deepening the expression of the idea. Next, rather than silently reading those words, imagine that you are listening to an audio recording of them being read by someone else, who thus brings additional layers of meaning through tone and inflexion. Take another step, where the poetic words are set to music and become a song that is performed, adding even more nuances of mood and expression to the idea, first through the a cappella voice but then further deepened by instrumental accompaniment. Now imagine listening to and watching a simple video of the singer performing in the recording studio, where you now see and are influenced by his or her facial expression and body language. Move that song performance out of the studio, and watch as it is not only sung but acted out as part of a larger narrative portrayed in a realistic setting, where the surroundings look normal in terms of color, size proportionality, appropriateness, and so on. This sense of realism is itself another layering of meaning. Finally, place that singer in other settings where the colors, backgrounds, and behaviors are not at all realistic but yet comport with the overall effect of what has come before and so seem appropriate and add significantly to the meaning of what you are experiencing.

What we have just built up, layer upon layer, is not a description of some intensely complex scene from an avant-garde art-house film but the song "I Just Can't Wait to Be King" from Disney's *The Lion King*.[29] Young children can "hear" this bit of film in the sense that they get it. They understand the words, the playfulness of the language, the joy of the music, the exuberance of the movement, the transition from reality to imagination. Could they describe the discrete elements of what they are watching and hearing, and how those elements work together to create the meaning of the scene? No, no more than they could diagram the grammatical structure of the sentences in the preceding paragraph. But just as surely as there are conventions of language (word definitions, grammar, punctuation, spelling, orthography, etc.) in that paragraph that enable it to communicate, there are similar conventions of filmmaking that enable the scene to work. The more you know the conventions, the more meaning you interpret from the experience. For example, as an adult watching that scene you will probably see in the portrayal of the dancing ostriches allusions to fan dancers that (hopefully) are lost on five-year-olds and add another dimension of meaning to what awaits the child in adulthood.[30]

All that I can really do in this context is to make explicit some conventions of filmmaking,[31] not all areas of which were even drawn out in the preceding discussion of the scene from *The Lion King*. When we are truly engaged in any artistic experience, we are seldom aware of the conventions that are at work to create that experience. It is only as we reflect on the experience, trying consciously to make sense of it either to ourselves or to others, that the implicit conventions begin to come explicitly to the fore. In some cases we may remember having been taught the techniques of a particular convention, and in other cases we will simply have imbibed them through the many and varied processes of enculturation and education. The work of interpretation begins with the identification of the conventions at work in what is being interpreted—perhaps even implicitly rather than explicitly for the creator(s) of the work itself—and considering the meanings evoked by those conventions. With a text, those most basic conventions might be the definitions of words and the grammatical conventions for relating those words to one another through the rules of syntax. Movies that employ dialogue (whether between characters or by voice-over narration) will likewise employ such conventions along with many others.

Many film conventions are heavily indebted to the techniques of other artistic forms.[32] Indeed, were it not for our familiarity with the use of such conventions in other settings, it would be much more difficult to "make sense" of the cinematic experience. The narrative conventions of plot, setting, and character from storytelling and literature; the visual conventions of composition and color from painting and photography; the staging conventions from dramatic and comedic theater; the tonal and rhythmic conventions from vocal and instrumental music—all these things and more have been adopted and adapted by cinema. For future generations, perhaps living in cultures even more dominated by film than our own, the use of such conventions in film will inform their experiences of these other art forms.

But in the very process of adopting these conventions from other artistic forms, films have adapted them as well. Consider the relationship, for example, between the conventions of characterization in storytelling (whether oral or written) and in movies. To develop a character in a story, the one relating the story can freely employ the convention of omniscience to tell us what the character is thinking, feeling, or in other ways responding to what is happening. But unless the film likewise adopts the convention of omniscient narration (either by means of voice-over or graphical impositions of commentary on the screen), it must show a character's thoughts, feelings, and responses through actions. The same would of course be true of live theater, but the conventions of stage acting and film acting are necessarily different because film can bring us so much closer to the actors and can control and change our angles of view. The action of what happens can be controlled and augmented in myriad ways. There might be a sudden or dramatic stop in the action by means of a "freeze frame," dramatic music or other sudden changes in the soundtrack, or changes in the light levels, or color saturations (more or less intense), or color values (shifted toward more reds, perhaps). A certain combination of conventions might express joyful surprise—or even death. Obviously then, conventions are neither self-contained nor static with fixed, definite meanings. There can be no magic decoder ring. The simultaneous presence of other conventions affects the meanings they convey.

For our present purposes, then, I will limit the examples discussed to some specific conventions that are either particular to film or are shared conventions with other forms of expression that are altered in fundamental ways by film. The skills we have developed for identifying the raw materials, as it were, used in interpreting stories generally will apply to films as well, although film will also have some particular ways of relating stories that may not be available to other forms of expression. For example, film can have true simultaneity by showing multiple things at once whereas spoken language is resolutely linear, able to deal with only one thing at a time, even as it may endeavor to have the hearer/reader hold other things consciously in mind as that one thing is related. Again, the purpose is to show that film interpretation is akin to learning a new dialect, not an entirely new language.

The two general categories of conventions that in some ways define filmmaking in terms of its artistic means are mise-en-scène (originally a French expression meaning "placed in the scene") and montage (again from French, expressing the idea of "putting together"). These terms describe the ability of film to control both "space" (what it is that we see) and "time" (the order and duration in which we see it) in ways not available to other artistic forms.[33] Thus while painting and photography may control what we see, they have little or no control *in themselves* over the order or duration in which we see it. Similarly, audio performances (whether live or recorded) may control the order and duration of the experience but have little or no control *in themselves* over what we hear. The point of stressing "in themselves" with regard to these other artistic forms is that their presentation within certain venues may introduce elements of these types of control by the one(s) providing the presentation (the museum curator of visual images, the stage manager of a musical performance), but these presentations bring additional conventions to those of the art form itself. In the case of film, these controls are intrinsic to the medium.[34]

Mise-en-scène refers to the visual presentation of film—what is seen and how it is seen. It includes "four distinct formal elements: (1) the staging of the action, (2) the physical setting and decor, (3) the manner in which these materials are framed, and (4) the manner in which they are photographed."[35] Staging involves not only the acting but things such as the movement within the frame and/or the movement of the field of vision within the frame to follow the action. Costumes, set design and decoration, props—whether directly involved in the staging of the action or less directly in creating the space in which the action takes place—are all elements of setting. Framing has a number of components. What is the aspect ratio of the image—that is, its overall width relative to its height (usually either 1.33:1, much like a traditional television screen; 1.85:1, the standard for most contemporary films; or 2.35:1, which is called "widescreen")? Is the action tightly packed within the frame, perhaps with significant features spilling out of view at the edges of the image, or is the action minimized in a small portion of the overall view? Is the dominant feature of the image close up or far away? Or is it presented in closed-in proportions in terms of the overall image yet still made to seem far away due to the depth of field, an affect created by including out-of-focus objects in the foreground space? Framing thus overlaps with photography, which also includes features created by the use of filters (to shift colors or affect the perception of light sources); the angle of vision on the scene (from above, below, neutral "eye-level," and/or skewed relative to the natural horizon); and the overall focus of the image (sharp and clear, or soft and blurred).

Giannetti identified fifteen "visual principles" that can be used to analyze just the image of a single frame of film without even delving into aspects of mise-en-scène related to costume, set design, or the action that progresses across a sequence of individual frames.[36] Every aspect of mise-en-scène can be used as a convention for conveying meaning to the viewer. For example, in the Disney film *Brother Bear*, the filmmakers mark the transformation in Kenai's view of the world from that of a human to that of a bear by widening the aspect ratio from 1.85:1 to 2.35:1 and brightening the color intensity of the images. In *Schindler's List* Steven Spielberg uses the somewhat counterintuitive move of photographing most of the film in black-and-white to *increase* the sense of reality, because as viewers we are accustomed to seeing the actual events surrounding World War II in black-and-white newsreel footage. The same technique—black-and-white photography—was used to exactly the opposite effect, however, in Mel Brooks's *Young Frankenstein* to associate it not with the newsreels of an earlier period but with the classic horror films of the 1930s and 1940s, the conventions of which Brooks's film is satirizing.

Montage involves arranging and relating to one another the individual "shots" that are the concern of mise-en-scène. Whether one thinks of this process as one of "cutting" down and "editing" together the shots (the dominant metaphors among American filmmakers) or of building up the finished film (the dominant metaphor among European filmmakers) may say a lot about one's attitudes toward filmmaking more generally.[37] Obviously the options here are more limited than in constructing scenes, but they are nevertheless complex in and of themselves, and the distinctions that film scholars draw to distinguish among the various options for creating these relationships can be fine and hard to grasp.[38] The conventions themselves, however, can be related to two concerns: (1) the physical relationship between the shots (i.e., does one image transition to another by the use of some photographic technique such as a fade or multiple exposure, or do the images simply exist side by side as sequential frames in the film, creating a "cut" or "jump"?); and (2) the chronological and/or symbolic relationships that exist between the shots (i.e., are they simultaneous, sequential, or in reversed order—a "flashback"— in terms of the film's narrative time, or do they relate to one another in some nonchronological fashion?).

As is true with all forms of artistic expression, the varieties and sheer numbers of conventions employed in films simply defy complete analysis. Far and away most of them wash over us in the experience of watching a film without our even being aware of them, much less consciously analyzing their discrete effects on us as viewers. Yet when pressed to explain how we arrived at such and such an expression of meaning for a film, we will have to appeal ultimately to the evidence expressed through these conventions. Consequently, the best way to describe these conventions and their meaning-producing effects is by employing them as evidence for interpretations of specific films (which is why most of this book is devoted to such case studies). But two points must be emphasized about the role of identification and analysis of conventions in movie interpretation.

First, like all conventions of expression, the "rules" regarding their use and meaning are not set down in advance but rather arise from the trial-and-error processes of communication. Filmmakers, like novelists and painters, have tried numerous things to communicate meaning with their audiences. Those that have worked are picked up and used again; those that don't are generally discarded. But the usage in the particular case is always determinative; that is why the same convention can potentially be used both to increase a sense of realism or to place us in a completely imaginary place. There is nothing automatic, then, between identifying a convention and analyzing its meaning effect in a film. It is a broad awareness of both the conventions of filmmaking generally and focused attention to the interplay of conventions within the particular film that define a cinemate viewer.

Second, the identification and analysis of conventions would usually be considered a logical precursor to the types of interpretation that normally concern us as movie watchers generally and as preachers seeking to dialogue with film more particularly. Just as your Bible professor in seminary would not have been satisfied with an "exegesis" of a scriptural passage that did nothing more than parse the verbs, decline the nouns, and diagram the grammatical relationships, so knowledge of cinematic conventions is not the end goal of film study. It is the foundation on which "higher criticism" is built. So we turn now to considering some of these more inclusive and productive forms of film criticism and interpretation.

FOUR APPROACHES TO FILM INTERPRETATION

To encourage those with a theological interest in cinema to become film critics themselves, Robert Johnston has summarized the many concerns of film criticism into four interrelated approaches to analyzing a movie: "*Genre criticism* examines the common form and mythic shape of film; *auteur criticism* attends to the author; *thematic criticism* compares film texts; and *cultural criticism* focuses on a film's social context."[39] He emphasizes that each aspect of film criticism broadly conceived is related to and ultimately leads into the others at certain points; nevertheless, there are distinct differences among them that can help newcomers find their way through the array of different analyses that can be made of even a single film.

One particular benefit of Johnston's scheme is that it can be easily correlated to the various concerns and exegetical methods of biblical studies. Just as we have seen that the identification and analysis of film conventions can be likened to what were once called the "lower criticism" concerns of textual criticism and grammatical exegesis, we can in the same way compare each of these approaches to film criticism to what was once called "higher criticism" in biblical studies. What a film scholar calls genre criticism is closely analogous to the concerns of form criticism that ministers studied in seminary. Auteur criticism, because of the complexity of the notion of "authorship" in such a collaborative endeavor as filmmaking, corresponds not only to such "biblical introduction" concerns as identifying the author and the date and place of composition but also to tradition-criticism approaches to the vast majority of the Scripture corpus that likewise does not have a single author in the way we typically use that word. A review of the methods of thematic criticism in film studies will illustrate that this approach to film analysis is closely akin to the use of redaction criticism in biblical studies. And finally the most recent of the concerns in film studies, cultural criticism, corresponds to the most recent additions to biblical studies as well, namely, the various forms of ideological criticism (feminism, liberation theology, etc.) and sociological analysis. Let's explore each of these analogous approaches to interpretation.

Genre Criticism and Form Criticism

Of the four approaches to film studies, the one most closely related to the identification and analysis of conventions is genre criticism.[40] *Genre* can indeed be defined as the use of a set of particular conventions. For example, as children we learn to associate the opening phrase "Once upon a time . . ." with fairy tales, and that generic marker arouses certain expectations about both the conventions that will be employed in relating the story (for example, the rules about reality in normal daily life need not apply—wolves can talk to girls in red capes; pigs can construct houses, etc.) and the purposes for telling the story (not only to entertain but to teach some lesson about life or social values). Other genres of film and literature are characterized by conventions of setting and plot. Science fiction, like fairy tales, suspends the expectations of what we consider normal life but is often more constrained in what it can allow (for instance, there must be technological jargon or some extension of accepted scientific theory that grants some measure of plausibility, however slight, to faster-than-light travel). Genres of course can be combined. Thus, when George Lucas began his *Star Wars* films by writing across a black screen the words "A long time ago in a galaxy far, far away . . . ," he signaled both his intention to employ the conventions of science fiction (but with a bit more freedom than, say, Isaac Asimov would allow) and the moral purpose of exploring good and evil found in fairy tales.

If viewers of film fail to identify the genre of a film, they will not be able to interpret it properly. It makes no sense to criticize the shaky scientific underpinnings of "hyperdrive" or the symbionic relationship between humans and "mitochlorians" (whatever they may be) that enables Jedi knights to tap into the power of "the Force." Lucas's films are science-fiction fairy tales located far away in a mythical past; they are not a vision of our technological future. But at the same time filmmakers are free to reshape and even violate the conventions of the genre of their films for artistic reasons. Genres such as satire depend on subverting the conventions of other genres, but at times the variations on conventional expectation are subtle—like the romance where the boy doesn't get the girl. Run counter to too many generic conventions, however, and the audience will simply be left confused.

Because genres determine the expectations of what viewers will accept in a particular film, they can also shape people's understandings of the meaning of their own lives outside the world of the movie. The expectations for the heroine in the romance to live happily-ever-after with a handsome and loving "prince" become the young girl's expectations in her own life. The exploits of the action hero that resolve all the dislocations in life wrought by evil set up a role model for young boys of the "real man" who always succeeds in making things right. Unmasking these social expectations and showing their breakdown within the confines of a film can become a way for filmmakers to challenge views of the real world held by viewers. And as society itself changes over time, its own expectations of genres change as well. The conventions of the film westerns of the 1940s and 1950s seem too quaint for most people today, not only because our moral view of the world is more complex than that of white-hatted-good-guys and black-hatted-bad-guys but also because the film conventions of westerns themselves have admitted this moral confusion, with films like *True Grit* in 1969 and Clint Eastwood's more-recent *Unforgiven*. Genres give pattern to films and to life.

This two-fold aspect of genre—setting up expectations regarding both the conventions to be used and the purposes of the film in terms of its meaning—correspond to the concerns of form criticism in biblical studies. Form critics emphasize that identifying the particular form employed in a scriptural passage not only defines the appropriate ways to interpret the textual details but also provides insight into the author's purposes in writing. Recognizing the genre of apocalypse reveals to the reader that the conventions of realism in terms of normal life do not apply. Jesus can ride a white horse into battle wearing a robe dipped in blood in order to slay his adversaries with "the sword that came from his mouth" (Rev. 19:11–21), but this description cannot be taken literally, as if the event will eventually come to pass, precisely as described, at a future time on the plains of Megiddo in modern Israel. An apocalypse also presents a view of the world that sees a struggle between supernatural forces of good and evil inveighing against each other behind the superficial forms of normal life, until the time when God's sure victory is manifest to all. To read the conventions and purposes of either an apocalypse as if it were historical narrative or a historical narrative as if it were an apocalypse is to fall victim to fundamental misunderstanding.

Interpreters of both film and Scripture must be literate in the conventions and purposes of a wide variety of genres. They must also be sensitive to the ways that both filmmakers and Scripture writers might play with generic expectations to achieve their purposes within specific contexts, and so avoid boilerplate interpretations. Failing to respect the genre of a film in dialoguing with it in preaching will undo a preacher's credibility with cinemate listeners as quickly as failing to properly identify the form will undercut a preacher's handling of the Scriptures with biblical scholars. But properly recognizing the genres of film and text can open new vistas to how each sees the world.

Auteur Criticism and Tradition Criticism

Authorship is one of the most-contested ideas in film studies.[41] At a practical level it is easy to understand why. Filmmaking is such a collaborative process, who is to say who finally is the author of a film? Is it the director (perhaps the most common identification of the auteur), the producer, the actors, the cinematographers, or the editors? These are just the most obvious flesh-and-blood contenders to lay claim to some aspect of the authorship of a film. But film theorists also argue for some non-flesh-and-blood claimants as well, such as "author as effect of the text" and "author in production institutions." Some film scholars even wonder if there is any point at all in continuing to talk about authorship.[42]

Yet fans and critics still find it meaningful to speak of "Steven Spielberg films," even when recognizing the diversity of films such a description would encompass (e.g., the animated biblical epic *The Prince of Egypt*; *Splash!*, the romantic comedy about mermaids; the action-adventure films of the *Indiana Jones* trilogy; such film adaptations of contemporary literature as *The Color Purple*; and historical dramas like *Schindler's List*). Moreover, he has had different roles in the production of his films as director, producer, or both. Films can also be grouped according to their actors rather than their directors. An

"Arnold Schwarzenegger" or "Steven Segal film" conjures particular associations for people familiar with movies; a "Tom Hanks film" would evoke different and likely more diverse associations. Auteur criticism seeks to explore these personal influences on a film.

The tools for doing auteur criticism may begin with certain conventions especially associated with the particular author in view (for example, the use of animation in a Disney—itself a designation originally of a personal but now an institutional auteur—film), but quickly move out to take in concerns beyond the film itself. Such critics "explore the biographies of directors, as well as their own interpretation and commentary on their work, in the hope of uncovering the cultural and ideological context of the films,"[43] in the process indicating how these interests anticipate the concerns of cultural criticism and underscoring the interrelatedness of all these approaches to film criticism.

To the extent that auteur theory focuses on the collaborative process of filmmaking, it can be related to the analysis of scriptural texts in the older analyses of source criticism or the more recent developments in tradition criticism. These tools remind us that neither films nor Scripture, for the most part, are products of a single author. They reflect both the effort of many contributors and the complexity that must naturally arise from such diverse production. To the extent that auteur criticism chooses one particular collaborator to explore how her or his contribution to the project is shaped by specific biographical or cultural influences, its concerns are similar to attempts in biblical scholarship to identify the author, date, and setting of the text under study. Very often in Scripture the identification of the author can proceed no further than to the type of individual described by social and cultural characteristics that could have been capable of writing the text, rather than to a specific historical person.

Although it is possible to conceive of using auteur criticism in the context of a sermon, it is fair to say that it would be far and away the most difficult approach to dialoguing with film in preaching. In order to be convincing, the preacher would have to make the case for how the characterization of the designated author's work is supported by the corpus of his or her work. The practical constraints on how much of a sermon can be given over to the exposition of the cinematic dialogue partner (as will be discussed in the next chapter) provide little opportunity for such extensive development. Passing references to "Arnold Schwarzenegger films" to describe cultural fascination with violence don't qualify as genuine dialogue. More likely familiarity with auteur criticism in film studies may provide help in sustaining one's interpretation of a particular film. If one's understanding of a film runs completely counter to the well-established reputations of the filmmakers, it should give one pause about that interpretation. It would not be decisive evidence against it, however, since directors, producers, and actors often undertake a wide range of films during their careers.

Thematic Criticism and Redaction Criticism

As every seminarian learns in Homiletics 101, the theme of a sermon is the central point that the sermon is all about (i.e., "the sermon in a sentence"). It serves as the selection criteria for all that goes into the sermon: whatever supports and develops the theme stays in; whatever distracts or detracts from it needs to be cut out. Themes serve the same purpose in films.[44] Listen to the director's comments accompanying the "deleted scenes" on a DVD, and you will hear again and again that while the scenes in themselves may have been favorites in shooting the film, the reason they were ultimately deleted from the final version of the movie is that they didn't advance the story or aid in the development of the theme.

To say that the theme is what a movie is all about is not to make it synonymous with the plot, the sequence of events in the film's unfolding narrative. Themes determine why it is that viewers should care to follow through the unfolding of the plot. As Jon Boorstin observed,

> Movies can be made without themes. They're made all the time by producers who don't believe they need an emotional line to their film. They think a film can be about the greatest train robbery of all time or about saving the Super Bowl from terrorists. But I can't think of a movie that works that hasn't had a theme.[45]

Films that have only a story line but no theme are unlikely to engage you as a film viewer and so are even less likely to suggest themselves to you as a preacher as productive dialogue partners for sermons.

So, how does one go about analyzing a film's theme? Once again, attention is directed to the particular details of the film in the way it chooses and uses its conventions. The genre of the film may also provide important clues, but the determinative evidence must be the film itself. Johnston notes that once film critics have a sense of the movie's theme, they work to elucidate it by comparison with other films considered to have similar themes. He then argues that this intertextual approach means that "there is no reason that a film might also be compared, for example, to the novel or play from which it is adapted."[46] It is this methodology that raises the analogy with redaction criticism.

Most commonly associated with the Gospels, redaction criticism makes a careful, side-by-side comparison of two or more texts (particularly when the text under study appears to depend directly on the other text) in an effort to identify patterns for the differences that exist between them. If, to take a well-known example, Matthew consistently changes Mark's expression "kingdom of God" to "kingdom of heaven," that pattern reveals a particular characteristic of Matthew's theology (usually taken as a sign of a Jewish religious preference of avoiding direct reference to God to avert the possibility of using the divine name "in vain") and a possible clue to an important theme of that Gospel. There need not, of course, be a relationship of direct literary dependence between the texts; one can learn much about Mark as well from these careful comparisons with Matthew.

In a similar way one can analyze how the film under study uses and changes conventions as compared to other films within the same genre that treat similar themes. Trends in the way filmmakers choose and modify these conventions can provide evidence of the work's theme. Especially helpful can be a study of what is selected, omitted, and changed when a film has been adapted from another artistic form. How does the screenplay differ from the novel on which it is based? What, if anything, has the director chosen to bring over from the staging of the play into the filming of the movie? Care must be taken, however, not to impose the themes of these comparative works on the film, even when the film is clearly and explicitly "based" on the other work. The filmmakers may have chosen to play up a subtheme of the novel, or they may have used the plot for a wholly different purpose and consequently developed an unrelated theme. Yet it is precisely the act of making the comparison that will make the difference clear.

Consider, for example, the relationship between Michael Crichton's two novels *Jurassic Park* and *The Lost World* and the movies based on them. One of the themes of Crichton's *Jurassic Park* was an exploration of the implications of chaos theory (i.e., complex systems have too many variables to predict confidently the outcomes of their interactions) for genetic manipulation of life forms. To explore that theme, the novel describes an attempt to use genetic manipulation to reintroduce dinosaurs into the modern world within the context of a zoological park. Not surprisingly (at least to everyone other than the industrialist behind the effort), chaos wins out in the end, and everyone is forced to flee the island preserve. Steven Spielberg's film of *Jurassic Park*, also not surprisingly, places more emphasis on the action of the story and the opportunities for stunning, special-effects dinosaurs than on the discourses on chaos theory by the character Ian Malcolm (Jeff Goldblum), a mathematician who specializes in the application of chaos theory to complex equations. But enough elements of this theme are carried forward from the novel to the film that it is still clearly recognizable.

The example of *The Lost World* is quite different, however, even though Crichton wrote the novel to serve as the basis for a film sequel. Rather than revisit the earlier theme, Crichton brings a new theme to the second novel, namely, debates in evolutionary biology about mass extinctions and species survivability (i.e., how is it that dinosaurs genetically engineered to be unable to reproduce and to be dependent physiologically on their human tenders for an enzyme not available in their habitat nevertheless survive and thrive once abandoned on their isolated island?). This theme is absent from the film,[47] which substitutes themes related to greed and the human desire to dominate nature (i.e., man, the greatest predator of our eon, hunts a *Tyrannosaurus rex*, the greatest predator of the age of the dinosaurs), but what really seems to drive the film is the plot's desire to turn the *T-rex* loose on a major city (San Diego). The confusion and ultimate loss of thematic focus diminishes the effectiveness of this film as compared to its predecessor.[48]

Cultural Criticism and Ideological Criticism

At one level, the cultural criticism approach[49] to film analysis is what this book is all about. As discussed in the introduction, it is because the cinema so effectively reflects and shapes the culture that it is important to engage it as a dialogue partner in preaching. Cultural criticism in film studies looks beyond the movies in themselves to consider the dynamic relationship they have with the broader culture. It analyzes "the life cycle of a film from production to distribution to reception . . . to know what effect a movie has on its viewers, whether in attitude, emotions, or behavior . . . [and] also considers whether the differing social situations or competencies of an audience give to the movie experience a different viewing."[50]

As a method of film analysis and interpretation, cultural criticism draws on such ideological approaches as feminism; gender studies; racial and ethnic studies; economic and class systems theories, such as Marxism; psychoanalysis; and sociological analysis. These same tools and concerns have also been much in evidence in biblical studies over the past several decades. They are also obviously quite diverse in their particularities. Consequently, there is not space to provide specific examples of each ideological approach. Instead, let me draw on one example from a book that applies cultural criticism from a theological perspective to explore the treatment of religion, race, gender, sexuality, and class in film: Margaret Miles's *Seeing and Believing: Religion and Values in the Movies.*

Miles applied feminist theory to offer a challenge to interpretations of the film *Thelma and Louise* that identified it as "the first feminist buddy-film, or at least the first one that matters."[51] True to the form of this method of analysis, Miles draws heavily on the published comments of the filmmakers and reviewers about the film as well as those of social commentators on cultural concerns raised by the film. She quotes Callie Khouri, the screenwriter, who argues that the theme of women's friendship would have been even stronger in the film had the director, Ridley Scott, not "cut scenes that portrayed the close friendship between the two title characters" and added images—"the huge trucks, the giant cacti and a chemical-spewing plane"—that reinforced phallocentrism.[52]

Miles's criticism of the film from her feminist perspective had two major emphases. First, while she acknowledged "many women enjoyed *Thelma and Louise*'s depiction of powerful women holding the gun," Miles believed the film's violence "carried another, more dangerous, cultural message." By buying into the cultural sanctioning of violence the female leads in the film are as likely to confirm the view of some violent men (particularly domestic abusers) "that women are out to get them and suggest that nothing but preemptory male violence will keep women in their place." Rather than producing a "fear of retaliation" that might inhibit male violence, the effect is to actually increase the likelihood of male attacks on women.[53]

Second, Miles criticized the film for "its adherence to Hollywood conventions by representing . . . casual, unsafe sex as exhilarating, fun, and the best revenge on a sexist society." Even though the character Thelma (Geena Davis) is a victim of attempted rape early in the film, she only really finds her energy and selfhood after having a casual sexual encounter with a man the women meet while on the run. Miles considered that convention problematic not only because it promotes the idea that "sex is essential" but also because it is inherently dangerous in a time of AIDS. Rather than using its cultural influence to promote safe sexual practices, "Hollywood film, pornography, television, and the recording industry continue to represent casual, unsafe sex as exciting and unproblematic."[54] Summing up her analysis of the film, Miles concluded, "In a society characterized by violence and a backlash against feminism, and threatened by AIDS, the film fails to communicate an empowering vision of women's freedom and responsibility."[55]

As film analysis, Miles's cultural-studies approach has not been without its critics. In commenting on her work in a review article on books dealing with religion and film, John May asks, "Is it fair or reasonable to conclude, for example, that neither *Thelma and Louise* or *The Piano* 'succeed' because they fail to address some feminist issues that were being debated at the time of their release? . . . Certainly the very model itself is doomed if it expects to critique some other film than the one that was actually made."[56] I would agree with May in the restricted context of film studies—even theologically informed and directed film studies—but would be less convinced in the context of dialoguing with movies in preaching where the concerns are ultimately about the culture rather than the film (which serves to exemplify or illustrate a cultural value). Nevertheless, May's point does direct attention to a specific pitfall that must be avoided in preaching to cinemate congregations. The analysis of the film must be fair to the movie itself even if the sermon criticizes the particular values the movie may espouse. That is to say, we should not say that a movie "fails" because it does not support our theological vision of the world that God intends. But having expressed the movie's particular answer to a question (here, Khouri's response to the "passive role of women" in film and society by crafting a film where women "drive the story because they were . . . driving the car"[57]), it is fair to go on to challenge that cultural answer by means of a theological answer expressive of God's just vision for the world. Isn't there a better way for women (and men) to drive the car than one that ultimately sends them careening off a cliff?

The apparent congruity between ideological criticism of film and Scripture leads me to a second potential pitfall in using cultural-studies approaches as means to analyze films for preaching. Even here there are only *similarities* between the ways that biblical scholars have applied these tools to interpreting Scripture and the ways film scholars have used them to analyze movies. Just because a preacher feels comfortable using form criticism, redaction criticism, and even feminist and liberationist criticism in studying the Bible does not alleviate the need to become more cinemate through the study of film criticism that employs similar tools. Seminary training means that preachers need not be intimidated by the prospects of developing the skills necessary to interpret films critically, but it doesn't give them a free pass from doing their homework in this field.

"THOSE WITH EARS TO HEAR, LET THEM HEAR"

Having discussed our need as preachers to hear what films are saying to us and to our congregations about life in our culture, and having reviewed some tools available to make us critical listeners rather than passive ones, we need to consider briefly how we might go about the process. Staying with our comparison to seminary training, we need to lay out something of an "exegetical method" for interpreting films to be used as dialogue partners in preaching. And just as there are exegetical guides and handbooks that intend to help aspiring biblical interpreters develop a disciplined method of interpretation, so there are handbooks for aspiring film critics that walk through the steps of producing movie reviews and film studies. They, too, may prove useful reading as you develop your skills as a cinemate preacher.[58]

As I discussed at the close of the introduction, very seldom will it be the case as a preacher that you will go to a film cold, as it were, with the express goal of deciding how to incorporate it into a sermon. In the vast majority of instances you will have formed an idea about how the film could be homiletically useful either from having already seen the movie or perhaps having read reviews or heard informal discussions about it. You will in such cases have already formed an idea regarding what the film is about and how it relates to what the sermon will be about. What next needs to be done is to test that idea.

Once more, the analogy with scriptural interpretation in the process of sermon development is helpful. Most homileticians emphasize the importance of the preacher's reading and entering into the texts forming the basis for the sermon *before* turning to the commentaries. The point is to allow the texts themselves to speak to us (and, dare we say it, for the Spirit to speak to us through the texts) before we allow the biblical scholars to speak for the text. (I say that advisedly as one whose formal postgraduate education was in the field of biblical studies.) This ordering of the tasks is not an excuse for exegetical laziness, but rather the opening up of space for the preacher to play with possible themes within the text that can be developed homiletically. When the preacher has an idea of the theme, *then* it is time to test that understanding of the theme against the available scholarship. In this way the preacher not only is reassured that the interpretation of the conventions and details of the text can legitimately support the theme but also gains greater insight into that theme by seeing the evidence marshaled in support of it by others.

In terms of film interpretation, the first step in testing your statement of the theme—what the film is about and the point at which you wish to engage it in dialogue—will be to go back and watch the movie again. Hopefully this will consolidate the formulation of the theme in your mind by reinforcing your memory of certain details of the film that developed the theme and perhaps drawing your attention to additional details that may not have seemed as significant on a first viewing. This *re*-viewing of the film must be more disciplined and critical than the first because your purpose is not to be entertained or informed in a general sense but, in essence, to *review* the movie. Instead of sitting munching popcorn, you will be sitting there with notepad and booklight so that you can go about your work. If the film is still in theatrical release, it will mean going back to the cineplex; if it has been released to video, then you can review it in the privacy of your own home (for lots of reasons—some specific ones I will mention shortly—DVD is to be preferred to VHS). Also, as a consideration to others, if you are going to the cinema for the viewing, try to go to a showing where the audience will be smaller, and sit away from other viewers in the auditorium so your working doesn't distract them.

Beyond these general guidelines, John Moscowitz has offered a checklist for how to be an active, critical viewer of a film[59]:

Make a formal determination of the setting, tone, and genre as early in the viewing of the film as possible.

Understand the interactions and interrelationships among the characters of the film and how they each relate to the plot.

Make written notes about everything that seems important in the film (not just those things that may seem to confirm the understanding of the theme you are testing).

Be sure you have gathered information from the opening and closing credits, movie posters, and so forth, that may prove useful. Is the film based on a work in another form (a book, play, or historical events)? Who directed the film? Who played leading and supporting roles in the cast?

The primary things to watch for are patterns that emerge in the film from repetition of visual or symbolic elements that affect the story line and thus develop the theme. But don't ignore nonvisual aspects such as the music and sound track that will do much to establish the tone of the movie. Moscowitz stresses that in a critical viewing, one's attitude "should be interrogatory. You must keep questioning the meaning of what you see and jot down these interrogations."[60]

To this point, you have identified and begun to analyze the conventions used by the film and have drawn some conclusions about the genre based on this identification and analysis—the "lower criticism" aspect of your work. Now you can turn to the "higher criticism" tasks associated with genre, auteur, theme, and culture. As with biblical exegesis, it is probably at this point that you will be most inclined to study what others have had to say about the film. How long a film has been in release and how popular and/or controversial it has proven to be will have a great impact on how much analysis is available. If the movie has been released to video, the DVD may well have a director's commentary track that could provide you with useful information (or, frankly, just a lot of the director's and/or producer's navel gazing). Look for reviews and interviews in print media as well. If it has been out for several years, there may be treatments of the film available in books on the relationship between theology and film.

Keep in mind that what you are looking for is *critical* analysis of the movie. Just as preachers would be wary but not dismissive of popular scriptural interpretations, they should have similar attitudes toward film reviews that appear in the popular press. Some of the major reviewers have had formal training in film criticism, but others are simply journalists who happen to be film buffs—and this is certainly no less true of those who review films in Christian periodicals. Popular reviews can still be insightful and certainly provide information about how the movie may be received by the general public. And much can be learned from them about how to summarize a film concisely (particularly from the usually quite brief reviews in the weekly news magazines, such as *Time* and *Newsweek*).

Especially if the testing of your proposed theme will require the use of auteur, thematic, and/or cultural criticism, you will also want to draw on scholarly resources beyond those bearing directly on the film under analysis. How is this film like or dislike other films by the same director? How faithful has it been to the sources on which it might be based? How might people who are not within its primary anticipated audience in terms of race, ethnicity, class, and/or age group experience the film?

Hopefully through this careful and critical analysis you will have "heard the film" on its own terms and have had your initial understanding of its theme confirmed and deepened. Even if the analysis has tended to disconfirm your preliminary statement of the theme, it may still have provided you with a homiletically beneficial point of dialogue. After all, there was something about the film that resonated with you even if your first attempts at enunciating just what it was may not have been successful.

Now you have the raw material about the film you need to begin actually crafting the sermonic dialogue with the movie. Just as you would not simply drop the exegetical notes on the scriptural passage for your sermon (you can't neglect that aspect of your preparation work either!) directly into your homily, so you cannot just drop in your film-analysis notes either. How to shape the dialogue itself within the sermon is the focus of the next chapter.

2

Seeing a Sermon

The Homiletics of Dialogue with Cinema

When I took my first course in homiletics more than twenty years ago, my professor stressed to us the importance of "tactile preaching." Everyone in the class struggled to comprehend just how the oral event of preaching could be "tactile." We understood the phrase was not to be taken literally, but we were also quite sure that we had not fully unpacked the metaphor in the way the professor intended. The point was basically that the images employed in preaching had to be so vivid in their expression and so substantive in their purpose that the congregation would be able to "grasp" and "hold on to" them long after the preaching event had ended. Yet no matter how much time we spent in crafting vivid and substantive illustrations, his response to our sermons seemed to indicate that we had not quite truly "caught on" to "tactile preaching."

I am convinced that the problem was with the metaphor itself. The oral and aural nature of preaching is just too far removed from the tactile sense of touch for the comparison to be illuminating. Probably there will be some who will lodge the same complaint against my metaphor of "seeing a sermon," for as with "dialogue" in the previous chapter, I want to stress the metaphorical aspect of that statement. By "seeing a sermon," I am not referring to the visual aspects of preaching (i.e., body language, religious or secular attire, location in architectural space, etc.), nor am I promoting the display of film or video clips within preaching (though I will discuss what I think are the key issues to be addressed in considering that practice). Rather I am using the term *seeing* to describe how words are used to construct the oral/aural aspect of communication in preaching.

Like my first homiletics professor, I intend by this metaphor that the images employed in preaching must be both vivid and substantive *and* something more than that. Preaching must "show" what it intends to communicate to its listeners, not just "tell" them. It must create a world that the listeners can enter into and inhabit, a world that will at times be as familiar as the very space in which they gather to hear the sermon and at other times as foreign as George Lucas's galaxy long ago and far, far away. It must be able to create a hopeful, alternative reality as convincing and even more compelling than the world of day-to-day living.

As difficult as that may seem, it is the same task that feature filmmakers of all genres take on with each new production. Sometimes their goal is to create such close correspondence between the world in the film and the world of the audience that the screen is little more than a magnifying glass that focuses our view on what might otherwise pass unseen,[1] even if that particular place in our world is on the other side of the globe. Other times they must construct a vision of the past or future of our world that strains the limits of imagination (as with any number of historical epics or the *Star Trek* series), create alternative worlds that would parallel and exist within our own (as with Hogwarts and its environs in the *Harry Potter* films), or even take us to a world that stands in spatial and temporal relationships so remote as to be effectively unrelated to our own (as with the *Star Wars* films). Depending on the scriptural text treated, sermons must also do each and every one of these things. Consequently, preaching may benefit not only by entering into dialogue with films that have already done such work for us but also by adapting some cinematic techniques to its own oral medium.

Thinking about dialogue with film in preaching as "seeing a sermon" thus involves two key components: "showing" the films to our listeners so clearly that they can "see"—in the sense of understand—the vision created in the movie, and "showing" the sermon itself in such a way that the vision of Scripture and the theological tradition is as compelling and persuasive as a film. Seeing a sermon is ultimately about preaching that enables the congregation to see the world as God sees it and hopes it will be.

SEEING A FILM IN A SERMON

I argued in the preceding chapter that dialoguing with film in preaching requires interpreting movies by using the tools and approaches of film criticism, and I proposed that movie reviews and critical film analyses suggest models by which films can be translated into other modes of discourse (written and oral) and still have their "say." What must be emphasized at this point is that preaching is such a different context of communication as compared to these other venues for discussing movies that they can only "suggest models" for how preaching can dialogue with films. Just as movie reviews and more-formal film analyses differ as genres by how they construe their purposes and anticipated audiences, so likewise the differing purposes and audiences of preaching will determine the ways that a film can be "seen" through preaching.

Within the circle of film critics, a "review" is a specific genre that assumes "the reader has *not* seen the movie in question" and that serves two typical functions: "to *summarize* or *provide an overview* and *make an evaluation* of a movie."[2] Reviews differ from "analytical critiques" both in terms of their assumptions about the audience and their functions. An analytical critique "assumes that the reader is familiar with the subject in question" (both the film being considered and the methods of analysis) and has as its purpose an "in-depth development of [a] thesis and minor inferences with specific examples" offered in their support.[3] Both reviews and analytical critiques can be oriented in terms of genre, auteur, theme, or ideology in their methodological approach to interpreting the movie. Analytical critiques may also be focused on issues of cinematic technique, and reviews are often plot driven in structuring their film summary.

Reflecting on these generic characteristics, I would argue that a dialogue with film in preaching must share the assumptions about the audience of a review and the functions of an analytical critique. Preachers cannot assume that every member of their congregation will have seen the film (or has direct, personal knowledge of anything brought to the sermon as an illustration, for that matter). Their purposes are not to provide suggestions for leisure-time entertainments among the congregants, and so they are not evaluating movies by rating them either in terms of "thumbs up/thumbs down" or ranking them between one and four stars. Since the dialogue will function like an analytical critique, there will generally not be a need (nor will there usually be time) to retrace the plot of the entire film. Rather, preachers should offer their thesis about the film (the point at which the dialogue with Scripture and theological tradition will be engaged) and provide specific examples that would support that thesis. I would once more argue that to be most effective the thesis must originate *in the film* rather than from a point in the sermon; lifting a scene from its context in a movie because it can support a point of a sermon is proof-texting and subject to all the same weaknesses and abuses. Seeing a film in a sermon, then, requires a review's assumption about audience and general brevity, and a critique's analytical purpose.

The approach to analyzing the film may, as with both reviews and analytical critiques, focus on genre, auteur, theme, or ideology. In thinking about how the results of such analyses might be presented in preaching, it seems best to take the genre and thematic approaches together as emphasizing narrative aspects of the film. As mentioned in the previous chapter, auteur approaches will necessarily be comparative, drawing on several films by a director, actor, or even studio to support the thesis. And finally, cultural-criticism or ideological approaches will focus explicitly on the ways a film both reflects and shapes the society.

Genre and Thematic Approaches to Dialogue: Overviews and Key Scenes

Feature films are, at their most basic, stories, and they go about making their point (the theme) by the choice of the type of story they relate (genre) and the details of the depiction (the plot elements and the cinematic conventions employed).[4] The most direct means of bringing them into dialogue with Scripture in preaching, then, is for the preacher to tell their story. It is easy to say, but harder to do.

The chief problem for the preacher, as for the filmmaker, is deciding what to leave on the cutting-room floor. A delicate balance must be struck between providing enough detail to engage and persuade the listeners while at the same time reigning in how much of the sermon is taken up with the film. It is possible to summarize the plot of an entire film in a few or even a single sentence,[5] but doing so effectively requires invoking some of its generic conventions in the sermon itself. For example, it will not be possible to trace every plot complication of an action-adventure film within the summary, but using descriptive language like "twists and turns," "nailbiter," "swashbuckler," and so forth, can evoke the necessary response from cinemate listeners. Because those listening to the sermon have seen many movies (and heard even more discussed), simply identifying the film's genre may be enough to plant into their minds certain plot elements characteristic of that genre. To refer to a film as a "romantic comedy" is probably all that is needed to communicate that the plot includes a number of humorous obstacles that must be overcome before the lovers eventually come together. With that label as preamble, the sermon can give its attention to specific applications of and variations on those plot conventions through which the film's particular theme is developed. The preacher's criteria for selection are the same as for the filmmakers: whatever is not essential to move the story along and to develop the theme needs to be cut.

It is not necessary, however, for the preacher always to recreate the narrative process the filmmakers used to make their point. Films must make their points through relating their stories; preachers can state the result of a thematic analysis of the film and then support it with descriptions of one of more key scenes from the film. Unlike movie reviewers, however, preachers need not be concerned if the key scene required to demonstrate the theme (perhaps not surprisingly) gives away the ending of the movie. The reason for discussing the film in the sermon in the first place is not to steer people either toward or away from viewing it but to engage the movie in dialogue. That being said, if it is possible to support the analysis of the movie's theme without giving away the ending, then your listeners will almost certainly prefer that you structure the dialogue in that way. They are, after all, cinemate—accustomed not only to watching films but also to reading film reviews—and so will have a built-in resistance to discussions of films that give away too much narrative detail. After all, the sermon may develop a desire in them to test your interpretation of a movie by their own viewing of it.

The preacher does need to take care in describing aspects of a film to match the tone in that portion of the sermon's development with the tone of the film. If the film is a comedy, then a scene should not be related in the sermon for dramatic effect. If it is a dramatic film, then don't play it up for laughs within the sermon. If the scene is wrought with tension and uncertainty in the film, then relating the scene in the sermon must recreate these same emotional responses. The more closely you follow the details of the film, the easier it will be to recreate its effects. This very need to match the tone of the film can itself bring variety into the different segments of the sermon for preachers who may be too didactic or too prone to sound one emotional pitch throughout the entire sermon.

I attended a preaching conference where the leader had the participants spend an evening watching the movie *Big Fish*. Like many Tim Burton films, this one had a complicated story line filled with implausibilities as compared to everyday life (e.g., a giant, a catfish the size of a human adult, and conjoined Korean twins who are musical performers—to name just a few) and imagery that mixed the commonplace with the truly bizarre. The theme of the film deals with a son's struggle to come to grips with the realization that the truth about his father is to be found more in the stories he told than in disentangling the real from the imagined within them.

One question put to the preachers the next morning was whether they would use the film in a sermon. The general consensus was that the film was just too complex in its layering of fact with imagination (even the characters in the film are unable at the end to say where the one leaves off and the other begins) to be treated as a whole. It would take entirely too long to tell the story with all its many flashbacks. Nevertheless, several of the preachers said they might use in a sermon the powerful scene near the film's conclusion showing the son's reconciliation with his father at the moment of the father's death. In this scene, the son spins a tale about that death by drawing together the many threads of his father's stories.

My reaction as I listened to the discussion was that the consensus response had it almost exactly backwards. It is the details of the reconciliation scene that are hopelessly complex and ultimately confusing when stripped from their narrative context, as they would be if *only* that scene were related to people who had not seen the film. *Big Fish* is a film that can only truly be engaged in dialogue within a sermon when it is taken as a whole, but to do so requires the preacher to come right out and state the theme. The constraints of a sermon do not permit replicating the narrative process that gradually but inexorably leads to the film's conclusion: that we are all ultimately the stories we have lived into rather than the bare facts of our existence, or, as the son says in a narrative voice-over to the film's final scene, "A man tells his stories so many times that he becomes the stories."

What could be narrated within a sermon is the experience of watching the film. As viewers, we are driven at the beginning to try, along with the son, to disentangle the facts from the fictions in the father's tall tales; yet as we experience the story of the son's wrestling with his father's stories, we too finally have the same epiphany that he reached. Recreating the experience of the film would still demand the use of some of its bizarre images and unlikely narrative turns, but any slight disorientation among listeners who overzealously try to force it all to "make sense" would aid rather than detract from the effectiveness of the dialogue. Surrendering to story is the message of *Big Fish*; surrendering to God's story and living into it is one message of the gospel.

That the film *Big Fish* deviated in some substantial ways from the novel on which it was based[6] raises another important point. Since one method for analyzing a film's theme is to compare it with its sources, there will be occasions when the sermon can be strengthened by incorporating some of the similarities and differences between the film and the material on which it may be based. Such comparison and contrast will be particularly important when the congregation may know these literary or historical antecedents better than the film itself. Failing to make these differences explicit can lead to misunderstanding by listeners who impose their knowledge of the source materials on the film. But if the sermon is dialoguing with the film, the movie must be given precedence both in the amount of attention given and in the statement of the theme. If you prefer the treatment in the novel, then dialogue with the novel; presenting the film as a straw target to be dispensed with in favor of the original story only adds unnecessary complexity to the sermon.

Auteur Approaches to Dialogue:
A Filmmaker's View of the World

As discussed in the previous chapter, the notion of auteur[7] is one of the most contested in film studies and consequently more difficult to incorporate into a sermon. Both reviews and analytical critiques can be focused on the specific contributions to an individual film by the director, the lead actor or actors, the producer, or even the studio, but almost always they will require reference to other films by the selected auteur to show how that film is either consistent with or departs from the auteur's usual vision. Adopting the assumptions about the audience of a review, then, requires that the listeners be familiar with the auteur's broader body of work even if they may not have seen the particular film. And while a movie reviewer has the luxury of writing specifically for the auteur's fans (or critics), knowing that those who are uninterested in the subject can just skip that particular review, the preacher cannot afford to do so. If a sermon is to dialogue with a filmmaker's view of the world as constructed by the overall corpus of the auteur's work, then the preacher must be sure that director, filmmaker, producer, or studio has a well-established and widely known take on the world as exhibited in those films.

The genuine auteur approach to dialogue is to be distinguished, then, from the rhetorical strategy of simply naming the director, actors, and so on, as a way of identifying a film for the listeners and calling on certain general associations they might be expected to have about them. In discussing *Big Fish*, I identified Tim Burton as the director in order to call on certain generic and cinematic conventions widely associated with his films. But that discussion was not an example of an auteur approach to film analysis. I did not draw any particular conclusions about Burton's view of the world based on *Big Fish* as part of a corpus of work that also includes *Edward Scissorhands*, *Beetlejuice*, *Sleepy Hollow*, *The Nightmare Before Christmas*, *James and the Giant Peach*, and the first two films in the *Batman* series. Nor did I explore how his vision of the world was different from that of Daniel Wallace, the author of the underlying novel, based on the changes Burton made to the book in his film. Either of those latter two approaches would have been examples of auteur-focused dialogue.

Sometimes a filmmaker will make a very clear statement about her or his view of the world in a single film. Should the dialogue in such cases be conducted with the statement made by the film itself, or should it be carried on rhetorically with the filmmaker? The answer depends on what evidence the preacher plans to marshal in support of that way of viewing the world. If all the specific examples are drawn from within the film—specific scenes, the way the film is photographed, the mood evoked by the sound track—then the dialogue should probably be constructed using the genre and thematic approaches. If, on the other hand, the preacher intends to emphasize quotations from interviews with the filmmakers concerning what they hoped to communicate about their vision of the world, even while drawing further support from details about the film, then structuring the sermonic dialogue with the auteur would be more appropriate. The approach needs to be determined based on who is the true dialogue partner: the film itself or the film's auteur?

Recalling the correlation that can be drawn between auteur criticism in film studies and tradition criticism within biblical studies, preachers might wish from time to time to construct their dialogues with more institutional auteurs. How have movies generally, or the movies of a particular studio, changed the ways they present certain themes over time? Consider the changing role of the heroine in Disney animated films. Snow White, Cinderella, and Aurora (in *Sleeping Beauty*) all dominated the stories in their films yet exemplified a cultural attitude of passive femininity that awaited the male deliverer, as famously expressed by Snow White singing, "Some day my prince will come." With the renaissance of animated Disney features marked by the film *The Little Mermaid*, critics were quick to point out that despite her spunkiness Ariel still directed all her actions toward getting her prince, with whom she could literally sail off happily-ever-after into the sunset. Disney responded with continued efforts to reshape their heroines for a more-feminist age with Belle (*Beauty and the Beast*), Jasmine (*Aladdin*), Esmeralda (*The Hunchback of Notre Dame*), Pocahontas, and Mulan. All of these characters explicitly reject aspects of their culture's dominant view of the feminine, Mulan going so far as to take her father's place in the military, where she encounters a commander who—thinking she is a male conscript—ironically sings to her, "I'll make a man out of you!" Yet all of them eventually fall in love and prefigure marriage in their films—all except Pocahontas, that is, who under historical constraints must await marriage to someone other than John Smith in the direct-to-video sequel.

What does this changing portrayal of the heroine say about Disney's view of the world in response to the feminist movement? Is its attitude as ambiguous or even conflicted as that found in the Pauline tradition, which can assert that in Christ there is no longer "male nor female" (Gal. 3:28) yet restrict the functions of women within the church (1 Cor. 11:2–16; 14:33b–40)? The Disney studio seems to have learned better, but it can't completely escape an older cultural norm; the same appears to be true of the apostle.

As previously mentioned, auteur-based approaches to dialogue with film in preaching can be more difficult because of the demands of background knowledge they place on the congregation. Thus, the chances for homiletical success increase in direct correlation to how well-known is the auteur and how well-known are the films that make up the auteur's opus. The film chosen to provide an example of a sermon following this strategy in chapter 9, Mel Gibson's *The Passion of the Christ*, obviously was positioned for this type of treatment.

Cultural Criticism Approaches to Dialogue: The World in the Film and the Film in the World

The example of the changing portrayal of the Disney heroine brings us naturally into our final approach to dialogue with popular films in preaching, namely, those arising from ideological methods of analysis.[8] As I mentioned in the previous chapter, these approaches to film analysis are far and away the most diverse, both in their specific areas of concern and in their methods. Loosened somewhat from any specific ideological underpinning (for example, feminism or race theory), they also represent a primary reason for dialoguing with films in preaching. Films provide a point of engagement for analyzing the culture they both shape and reflect. But their very effectiveness in this regard requires that they be subject to careful and critical analysis.

While there may be occasions in preaching for engaging the "Hollywood film industry" or "broadcast television" in general terms because of widespread tendencies in stereotyping women, racial groups, or culturally despised ethnicities or because of the way they reinforce concepts of "innate privilege," the use of ideological criticism in supporting such analyses would lead to a different form of preaching than what I am advocating here. Such cultural analysis is essential to preaching that takes seriously the social dimensions of the gospel, but that preaching would dialogue more directly with either the general culture or particular ideological insights. The issue, then, is one of relative balance. Is the focus of the dialogue in the sermon on the film, or is it on an aspect of cultural criticism? Preaching that is dialoguing with movies rather than theories will keep the focus fixed on the particulars of the film. By showing *how* a specific film constructs the relationships between the genders, between races and ethnicities, or between the powerful and the oppressed, preaching can unmask the similar processes at work behind the scenes in society.

As an example, let us consider briefly Disney's *Pocahontas* from the ideological perspective of race relations—a central theme of the film as expressed in the song "Colors of the Wind."[9] Criticizing the chauvinism of European colonization, this film generally presents the members of the Virginia Company in a decidedly more negative fashion than it does the Native Americans. The opening song extols the values of "glory, God, and gold" that drive the colonization endeavor, and even the hero of the film responds to a remark by a ship's crewmember as he boards that "you can't fight Indians without John Smith" by saying, "I'm not about to let you boys have all the fun." In contrast, the Algonquins first appear in dugout canoes, gracefully navigating a river as they return to their village and accompanied by a song asking the "Great Spirit" to "help us keep the ancient ways . . . [and] walk in balance all our days." As Pocahontas (Irene Bedard; singing voice by Judy Kuhn) sings to John Smith (Mel Gibson) in the prelude to "Colors of the Wind," the colonists may believe the indigenous peoples are "ignorant savages," but, she asks, "If the savage one is me, how can there be so much that you don't know?"[10] And in a pointed visual cue, at the very moment she acknowledges his view of her as a savage, she thrusts his musket back into his hands. The colonists, sure of their superiority, feed their gluttonous appetites (literally embodied in the obesity of Governor Ratcliffe [David Ogden Stiers]) by force as necessary, whereas the native peoples seek only to maintain a balance with nature.

Many have criticized the way Disney plays fast and loose with the facts of history in this film and have argued that they "have merely traded one stereotype [of Native Americans] for a new polar opposite . . . [as] peace-loving, environmentally enlightened sages."[11] But the film is more nuanced in its portrayal than some of these criticisms would suggest. Those Algonquins in the canoes during the title sequence are returning from having defeated the Massawomecks.[12] Throughout the film both cultural groups refer to the other in harshly negative ways; what they share in common is their mutual mistrust and bigotry toward one another. The animators have skillfully shown how each group fails to see within itself the savagery it displaces onto the other in the song "Savages,"[13] which sets the stage for the climactic confrontation. As Ratcliffe declares that the Algonquins' "skins are hellish red," his own flesh tones and those of the other colonists are presented in red hues cast by the light of campfires. In the same way, as the shaman decries that beneath the colonists' "milky hide there's emptiness inside," his flesh tones and those of the Algonquin warriors are presented in pale, blue shades from the night's darkness and shadows. And both groups share the same chorus, alleging of the other, "They're savages, savages, barely even human." They insist they are different from each other and the other necessarily "evil" or unworthy of "trust," but the film underscores that their hatred of the other has made them the same.[14]

The film then incorporates aspects of the ideological critiques of colonialism and racism while using its artistic conventions to make clear that these sins are not unique to any one culture. To be sure, some of these artistic conventions (ugliness and obesity as signs of irredeemable evil in Ratcliffe, physical beauty and fitness as signs of heroism in Pocahontas and John Smith) simultaneously reinforce other cultural stereotypes and bigotries. But relying solely on ideological methods of analysis without also carefully studying the ways cinematic conventions are employed in this particular film would distort the dialogue that might emerge from it. Disney is calling here for a dialogue between people founded not on "anger" but on "courage and understanding" that may open a way to peace rather than war.[15] It is a dialogue worth engaging homiletically.

There is another strategy for dialoguing with a film homiletically from a cultural-analysis vantage point, namely, focusing on the cultural reception or impact of the film. Some films become cultural juggernauts at the time of their release. Sometimes that is a result of marketing or, in the case of sequels, the popularity of earlier films in the series. But neither marketing nor "brand" can create in themselves not only large box-office receipts but also cultural buzz.

What cultural forces are at play in a film's success (or failure)? As we saw in discussing this cultural-criticism approach to film in the previous chapter, this line of analysis will frequently divert attention away from the particular aspects of the film itself toward the film as a cultural object. The sources for developing these dialogues with films in current release would be articles about the film in newspapers and magazines, and not even particularly the reviews of the film per se. But while it is interests similar to these that prompt me to explore movies as dialogue partners in preaching, my concern here is with the films themselves. What is it that the films are saying, and how are they saying it? I typically use these other aspects of cultural criticism only as a means of bringing the film before my congregation in the sermon.

However, I have on occasion preached in dialogue with movies specifically using one of these cultural-criticism approaches, and I include examples of them in chapter 9. The sermon presented there in dialogue with Disney's *Atlantis: The Lost Empire* is an example of what might be considered dialogue with "the world in the film," while the sermon responding to the Academy Awards given to *Million Dollar Baby* and *The Sea Inside* illustrates the strategy of dialogue with "the film in the world."

"To Screen or Not to Screen?"

One seemingly obvious way to bring film into dialogue with preaching would be to show a key scene that encapsulates the movie's theme rather than trying to relate it orally. I will just come right out and say it that this is a fundamentally bad idea. Having stolen the suspense (it wouldn't have lasted long anyway), let me explain why I think showing clips as part of theological engagement with films in other settings works, but screening clips while preaching won't work.

To begin, I return to the opening sentences of this book: "Preaching is one of the great bastions of oral culture. It is in its very essence an oral form of communication." Preaching did not devolve into just *writing* sermons in response to the shift from oral to literate culture, nor did it adopt a device whereby it began passing out an excerpt from a novel or a clipping from the newspaper and asking the congregation to read over it at a designated point in the sermon, after which the preacher would regain their attention and provide some brief commentary about how it fit into the sermon. Such a device is exactly what happens in showing a clip while preaching, and if its application to a novel or newspaper strikes you as just downright silly, then you see my point.

Why doesn't this device work? It fails because it requires the preacher to cede control over the source material. Whether the sources of preaching are oral, literate, or multimedia, the preacher must maintain control over how they function within the sermon. We do this in relating illustrations from the news, literature, or stories we have heard by controlling which parts of the information from the illustrative material we present and how they are presented. We are careful in our editorial handling of the material because we know someone in our congregation will call us on it if we play too fast and loose with our stories. But we are bringing the material into the sermon to serve a particular purpose, and so we control the oral inflection, the mood, the authoritative or dismissive treatment of the source, and myriad other details in order to have some reasonable expectation of how the aural end of the communicative process will work. We draw the listeners' attention to the places we wish to focus on by the way we structure the oral communication. If preachers must use such care in bringing other forms of word-based communication to the oral medium of preaching, how much more will it be required in the case of multimedia sources? But showing a clip while preaching gives complete control of that portion of the sermon over to the filmmakers.

The reason, then, that I show clips in lectures, adult education classes, or other settings but not in preaching is two-fold. The first aspect is the issue of control within the constraints of the preaching event, not the least of which is time. Religious education settings usually provide at least 50–60 minutes. Most of us who preach to mainline congregations have somewhere between 12–15 minutes on the low end to 18–20 minutes on the high end for our sermons. There simply isn't time within such constraints to show 3–5 minutes of film and then spend probably an equal amount of time before and/or after the clip making explicit the aspects of the scene that led it to be included in the sermon. Considerable time and effort is required to divert the congregation's attention from my oral communication to the film's multimedia communication and back again. Half my time would be gone, and all I would have accomplished would be to bring the raw material to my congregation for the interpretation and dialogue that is the purpose of the sermon. Far better to take the time I would use setting up and explaining the clip to relate directly what I want to emphasize from the material and do the important work of engaging it theologically.

The differing purposes of sermons and more-explicitly educational settings are the second aspect for why clips work in the latter but not in the former. One purpose for engagement with films in religious-education settings is to help people become more theologically cinemate—that is, to assist them in analyzing the movies they see and in understanding how films communicate meanings so that they are not passive consumers of this powerful medium. These educational settings are usually less constrictive in terms of time, but more importantly they have this different purpose and goal. They are about film interpretation itself as well as the theological analysis of the particular movie's theme; sermons are only about the latter. To learn film interpretation requires watching movies. Dialoguing with their themes requires only that those who carry on the dialogue have seen them. For those who listen to the dialogue it may be beneficial, but it is not essential—and anyway the benefits are greatest when they have seen the whole film rather than just isolated clips.

These might be considered more theoretical objections to using film clips in sermons, but there are a number of pragmatic obstacles as well. Say, for example, the movie that is the talk of the town and you wish to engage in your sermon is still in theatrical release. Where are you going to get the clip to show? Do you have to wait for it to be released on video, when perhaps the moment has passed? Say you manage to have the clip available. How are you going to display it? Is the architecture of your sanctuary truly conducive to showing film clips, so that everyone—including those who may be seated on the chancel—has an unobstructed view? Can the space be darkened sufficiently, or is your media projector bright enough for the image to be seen clearly? Be forewarned: the range of light levels used in filming makes this a much more daunting task than simply handling PowerPoint slides. What about adequately integrating the audio into your sound system so that it is clear and the clip can be properly heard as well as seen? And just having the clip available doesn't necessarily mean you have the right to display it publicly. Anyone can rent a video at the local Blockbuster, but the film producers actually mean that little notice at the beginning about it being licensed for private, home viewing and public displays being prohibited. Do you have a copyright release that allows you to show the clip publicly?[16] Does it permit you to include the material in audio or video recordings of your service that may subsequently be broadcast or otherwise disseminated?[17]

All of these pragmatic issues must be addressed whether you are showing the clips in religious-education settings or in a sermon. Many of them are, however, easier to handle in the more flexible surroundings where classes are conducted as compared to the constraints in sanctuaries. Given the time and expense that might be involved in redressing these pragmatic obstacles, consider this warning from Detweiler and Taylor in their book on the church's need to engage popular culture: "We fear that people of faith used to playing constant catch-up will embrace technology at the very moment the dot-com generation rejects it."[18] And in light of that warning, be sure to talk with the members of the congregation's governing board who are ensconced in corporate culture about the changing attitudes toward even PowerPoint. True, part of that growing backlash is the result of poorly designed and technologically inhibited presentations. But if corporations with their budgets struggle to overcome the pragmatic obstacles, what does that say about your congregation's budget and its priorities?

In my view, then, a cost-benefit analysis, assessed both in terms of real dollars and cents and, more importantly, in terms of the strains imposed on the communications process, weighs against the use of film clips in preaching. You may disagree, and even I avoid saying I would "never" do it (I just can't anticipate the circumstances in which I would). But the obstacles, both theoretical and pragmatic, are real and not just the imaginings of a naysayer. If you do choose to use film clips in your preaching, you will have to address these obstacles for the clip to be effective.

SEEING THE SERMON ITSELF

To this point we have considered only the general approach (the assumptions of reviews and the concerns of analyses) and, depending on the type of analysis, the kinds of materials (key scenes, theme statements, citations from interviews with the filmmakers) that might be used when dialoguing with films in sermons. We have not talked about specific ways these materials might be shaped homiletically. The reason is that the form the dialogue will take will depend on the overall structure of the sermon itself. There isn't just one way to incorporate a movie into preaching. There is no single form of sermon that could be called a dialogue with a film.

In what follows I will suggest four different ways that a preacher could include a dialogue with a film in preaching. The first three approaches are based on different models of preaching that have gained wide discussion among homileticians, and the final approach builds on a cinematic technique. Beginning with the most conventional model, we will consider how the film can be treated homiletically simply as an illustration within a "move" of a sermon (using David Buttrick's terminology). Next, taking as our starting point film's role in our increasingly narrative culture, we will see how the very process of dialogue itself can serve as the underlying structure for a homiletic plot (drawing on the work of Eugene Lowry). The third model to be considered constructs a direct parallel between the ways a Bible passage and a film contrast "trouble" and "grace" within the Scriptures and our own world, respectively (borrowing Wilson's "four pages of the sermon" model). Finally, I will argue that the inter-cutting techniques of contemporary films suggest that the interplay among film, Scripture, and application can be multiplied beyond Wilson's "four pages" so that the details explicitly drawn out and emphasized guide the interpretation of the parallel stories from film and Scripture.

"Moving" from Film to Scripture

Ask most preachers how they might use a film in preaching and the first response you are likely to get is, "As a sermon illustration." It seems almost self-evident. But just how do you go about doing it? I have already talked about some of the issues from a film-critical perspective (not lifting scenes out of their contexts, for example), but what are the homiletic issues? To begin, we need to remind ourselves that the use of illustrations more generally within sermons has been rethought over the past few decades.

Most of us who are now preachers grew up listening to what became stereotyped as "three-points-and-a-poem" sermons. What seems to have been lost along the way is that the three-point structure was hardly coincidental. It apparently grew (either deliberately or quite unconsciously) out of a classical form of argumentation, the syllogism. A syllogistic argument at its simplest proceeds in three phases: the major premise, a minor premise, and a conclusion. To take the example most often found in philosophy textbooks, "Every animal is mortal; all human beings are animal[19]; therefore, all human beings are mortal." Sermons quite often adopted this overall structure for the sequencing of points in the sermon. The sermon's theme was the issue to be argued and proven, and the points of the sermon were the premises and conclusion that supported or proved the truthfulness of the theme. Perhaps the first point (the major premise) might be taken from the scriptural text; the second (the minor premise), from the theological or ecclesiastical tradition; and the third point (formulating the conclusion of the argument, not the rhetorical conclusion of the sermon itself), as application to contemporary life. Not infrequently the same pattern guided the development of the individual points. Illustrations served as "minor premises" that convinced or confirmed for the congregation the truth of the point within the sermon, depending on whether the preacher perceived the listeners as needing to be persuaded to accept it, despite initial resistance, or, conversely, as drawing out an inference of something the listeners already held to be true.

For many cultural reasons—not least the return to narrative as a primary form of discourse—public speech has moved away from syllogistic structures of persuasion. You can see it in political speeches, the ways newspaper stories are written, and even in the writings of homiletic theoreticians. In preaching, the theme has become *the* point of the sermon. We will see that there are differing ways that point can be worked out rhetorically (some closer to the more traditional forms of preaching, others adopting a much more overarching narrative quality), but what is true of all of them is that the illustration has become even more central to the persuasive force of a sermon. As David Buttrick has stated, "Examples and illustrations, as they function analogously, are the native tongue of faith. They are crucial to Christian preaching."[20]

While conceding that the two overlap in a practical sense, Buttrick draws a distinction between examples and illustrations. He distinguishes between material that is "at hand in the common consciousness [and experience] of a congregation"—what he terms "examples"—and material that the preacher has "imported into the sermon from outside the range of congregational consciousness . . . [and] shared experience"—namely, "illustrations."[21] With this distinction in mind (and recalling that dialogue with films in preaching will adopt the stance of film reviews—assuming the congregation has *not* seen the movie), this model of preaching would use cinema as a source of illustrations in developing sermon "moves."

I will not attempt here even an overview of all the elements of Buttrick's extensively developed homiletic. Suffice it to say that he replaces the customary language of sermon "points" with "moves" to underscore a concern with the progressive unfolding of the language event in preaching. Each "move" of the sermon—each stage in its progression—must work to form a single meaning within the consciousness of the listeners. Consequently, discussion of a film in and of itself would not constitute a proper move within this model. The move would be defined by the meaning the preacher wants to communicate; the film illustration would support and develop the move.

In order both to clarify this distinction and to show how it argues for a careful interpretation of films before they are used as illustrations in sermons, let me return once more to Tim Burton's film *Big Fish*. The theme of the film is that in the very process of repeatedly telling our stories over the course of our lives we in fact become our stories. That idea, quite apart from any of the details of the film, might contribute to the development of a sermon about the importance of biblical stories in forming us as Christians—perhaps in a sermon dealing with Paul's encouragement of the Thessalonians to be "imitators of us and of the Lord" and "an example to all the believers" (1 Thess. 1:2–10). The single meaning to be conveyed in this move of the sermon could be stated as follows: "In telling the gospel story we become gospel people." What guidance would Buttrick provide us for crafting an illustration from the film that would develop that move?

Well, Buttrick would begin by raising three questions about whether a dialogue with *Big Fish* could properly illustrate this move.[22] First, is there "a clear analogy between an idea in sermon content and some aspect of the illustration"? Second, is there "a parallel between the structure of content [in the move] and the shape of the illustration," or is it possible to shape the illustration in such a way so as not to distort it but nevertheless conform it to the structure of the move? And finally, is the illustration "appropriate," that is, does "the illustration's imagery . . . [have] much the same moral, aesthetic, or social *value* as the idea being illustrated"? Obviously I have concluded that each of these questions can be answered affirmatively, or I would have chosen another example to construct. But in choosing this example to develop I have taken these questions seriously. Notice, also, that unless I had carefully interpreted the film I could not answer these questions. Unless the film has been analyzed in a cinemate manner, I simply can't know whether the analogy is clear, whether the dialogue can be shaped so as not to distort the meaning of the film itself, or whether the move and the movie appropriately share a moral, aesthetic, or social value.

Having determined that *Big Fish* is an appropriate illustration of the idea that "in telling the gospel story we become gospel people," Buttrick would proceed to lay down five "ground rules" for developing the illustration within the move.[23] First, there can only be one illustration per move. Even if multiple aspects of the film interest me and might be relevant to the sermon as a whole, only one idea relative to the movie can be used to illustrate a move because the move expresses only a single idea.[24] Second, illustrations within moves must relate "strength to strength." The concern here is that the illustration not run away with the sermon. You cannot use an emotionally powerful film to develop a minor move in the progression of the sermon. The imagery from the film will dominate, and so ultimately skew, the listener's perception of what the sermon is about. Next, the "illustration must match the positive or negative character of the move statement." If the move is in support of the idea, the film must likewise support it. If the move is against the idea, the film must be against it. You cannot set up, say, a movie's endorsement of violence to solve problems as the antithesis of the gospel's call to be peacemakers within a single move. As Buttrick states, "The trouble with mixing negative and positive is that the illustration will be saying one thing and the move statement another." Confusion will be the result. Fourth, if the Scripture passage on which you are preaching develops a particular image, then the illustration must deal in related images, or you will "end with a jarring series of mixed metaphors." Finally, the illustration must be kept brief. Remember, it is a *part* of the development of a move in the sermon, not a move in itself. Buttrick's rule of thumb regarding illustration length is "no more than five, or at most, six sentences" so that they "will flash like metaphors in congregational consciousness, causing meaning to happen."

Keeping these issues in mind, how might we see the film *Big Fish* within this homiletic move? In order to place this particular move within the progressing structure of the sermon, let us suppose that it has been preceded by a move focusing on Paul's thankfulness for the lives of the Thessalonians, followed by a move speculating about doubts they might have concerning their own "work of faith and labor of love and steadfastness of hope in our Lord Jesus Christ" (1 Thess. 1:2–3). After all, they know the nitty-gritty facts about their lives better than the apostle. So we come to the move expressing the idea "in telling the gospel story we become gospel people":

> But we don't become people of faith, love and hope by focusing on every nitty-gritty detail of our lives; we become gospel people in telling the gospel story. That is why Paul stresses that his certainty about the Thessalonians is grounded on "our message of the gospel" that determined "what kind of persons we proved to be among you for your sake." Powerful stories have the power to shape our lives. In the film *Big Fish,* an adult son returns home to see his dying father. They have been alienated from each other because the son is convinced the father has hidden the truth about himself behind all the tall tales about his life he told his son since childhood—like confronting a giant, joining the circus, escaping from behind North Korean lines with the help of conjoined-twin singers, and struggling with a human-sized catfish on the day of his son's birth. One story the father never told was what he had learned from a witch about his own death, and it was that story he needed to recall to find peace on his deathbed. In quiet desperation the son wove together details from all the assorted tall tales into a grand send-off for his father who responded that the son's story was "exactly" how it happened, and slipped into the life to come. The son realizes a truth about his father that transcends the nitty-gritty details of his life: "A man tells his stories so many times that he becomes the stories." Paul had become the Apostle through the transforming power of the story of the Lord. The Thessalonians had become people of faith, love and hope as they had imitated Paul in reciting that same message themselves, and so become the message "to all the believers in Macedonia and in Achaia." We become gospel people in telling the gospel story.

In the compass of a brief illustration, this move has engaged in a dialogue with the film that is true both to the movie and to the theme of the sermon. It is the simplest form of hearing a film in a sermon. But there will be occasions when the preacher will want to engage in a much more extended dialogue than can be constructed in a single move. That is why preachers need in their homiletic repertoire other sermon models that can support more extensive engagement between Scripture and film.

Telling the Story of the Dialogue

Since a chief reason for dialoguing with film in preaching is the return to narrative forms of persuasion within our culture, another model that can be conceived is a thoroughgoing narrative homiletic. I have encountered preachers who have reduced the idea of narrative sermons to simply telling stories. The temptation then would be to simplify a narrative dialogue with a film to telling the story related in the movie. What I have in mind by a narrative sermon, however, is something more formally related to what may be called "narrative logic," the structuring of a story in order to persuade the hearers to adopt a particular view regarding the world.

In writing his *Poetics*, Aristotle described the classical structure of tragic narrative in terms of its plot. Although "tragedy" has come to refer popularly to stories with sad endings, that is not the way Aristotle understood the genre. Tragic narrative was intended to reestablish a belief in an order to the universe in the face of contrary evidence from life's experiences. As Charles Puskas has put it, "The religious soul of tragedy has been described as the affirmation of moral order, the assertion of transcendence, the mimesis of sacrifice, and faith in the overruling of justice."[25] Such stories affirmed people's experience of the hardships of life while at the same time persuading them that trouble and chaos were not the fundamental realities of life. Tragic narratives accomplished their persuasive work by progressing through five plot stages. At the core of the narrative and the heart of its work were the complication (the challenge to the world's order the characters must confront), the crisis (the point where the challenge has grown so great that it must be confronted or belief in the world's order will finally have to be abandoned), and the resolution (the overcoming of the challenge that reasserts the world's order). Framing these core plot elements were the prologue and epilogue that introduced the characters to the audience and showed how life continues following the resolution.

Aristotle's analysis of the plot structure of tragic narrative provided the basis for Eugene Lowry's work in narrative homiletics.[26] Although he has somewhat altered the identification of stages in the plot from Aristotle (and even varied the number between his earlier and more recent work),[27] the underlying logic clearly remains the same. Lowry presents the progression of plot elements in a narrative sermon as:

Conflict → Complication → Sudden Shift → Unfolding

To relate his plot elements to classical categories of analysis, we can note that Lowry's "conflict" corresponds to Aristotle's "complication"; his "complication," to the building toward "crisis"; the "sudden shift," to "resolution"; and, finally, the "unfolding," to the elaboration of the resolution moving toward the function of the "epilogue" (the movement back into the audience's own world from the story's world).

The critical role in this homiletic structure is played by the "sudden shift."

It provides the new view on reality that answers the problem raised in the "conflict" and relentlessly ratcheted up through the "complication." In Christian preaching (as potentially opposed to other types of narrative development) the "sudden shift" will be related to the announcement of the "good news" of the gospel. This announcement may precede and thus trigger the "sudden shift"; it may itself be the "sudden shift" in vantage point that resolves the complication; or it may follow on the analysis in the "sudden shift" and thus trigger the "unfolding."[28] But preaching is about bringing the congregation through a shift from how they have seen and experienced the world to seeing and experiencing it as God does.

For Lowry, it is the progression or "logic" of these plot elements that defines the narrative sermon. The sermon may not even be fabricated as a story at all. It may simply place before the congregation some conflict from life that is pressed in its complexity to a point where the tension must be resolved, a resolution accomplished through a shift in understanding related to the gospel that unfolds a new possibility for living. What makes a sermon "narrative" preaching is not the use of characterization, setting, or other conventions of storytelling (although such traditional story elements are not ruled out) but the use of a narrative logic founded on plot progression rather than a syllogistic logic founded on points or premises.

Such a sermon model provides the means for a much more protracted and engaged dialogue with a film in preaching, particularly when the message(s) communicated by the movie may be ones that the preacher wishes to challenge. What might such sermons look like? Preachers might begin by taking a film that has proven immensely popular. If the film is a drama, then most likely it will already have the elements of "conflict" and mounting "complication" already woven into its plot. Preachers could follow that story line, showing why it has such resonances with audiences because of how it relates to issues in their real lives. In the cases of films that preachers want to challenge, the homiletic complication (as opposed to the film's movement toward what Aristotle called the crisis) would expose the problems with the film's solution to the conflict. That is to say, the sermon would complicate the matter for the congregation by calling into question the means or even the ends the film presents as a resolution to the issues at stake in the conflict. For example, a sermon on *Thelma and Louise* (following Miles's interpretation of the film) would question just how liberating a strategy that ends in a suicidal plunge into a canyon really is for women. The sermon's "sudden shift" and "unfolding" would offer a new resolution to the cinematic and societal conflict grounded in the gospel.

A similar homiletic strategy can be used with many comedies. After all, much of comedy is based on conflicts the resolutions of which the audience sees as wildly inappropriate—that is what makes it funny in the first place. But the strategy can be modified with some comedic films so that the homiletic complication challenges the congregation's ready acceptance of the humor. The sermon might unmask the racism, sexism, classism, homophobia, and so forth, that the humor reinforces by what it considers inappropriate. The film *White Chicks*, starring Marlon and Shawn Wayans, was in the top ten films during the first four weeks of its release in the summer of 2004, grossing just over $65 million.[29] The movie is about two African American FBI agents who don latex masks to disguise themselves as young, white, high-society debutantes in order to foil a kidnapping plot. Their miscues as black males trying to pass as young white women provide the basis for the humor. But ask yourself this: Given our culture's long overdue reaction against the racist, black-face minstrel shows of the vaudeville era, would anyone think it funny in this day and age to reverse the racial identifications and have two white, male, FBI agents try to pass as black women? We laugh at black actors and a black director (Keenen Ivory Wayans) turning the tables on white society, but should we?

In both these instances we have considered films the preacher wants to challenge. What about films the preacher wishes to affirm? In such cases, the "sudden shift" can be taken from the film's plot, with the good news of the gospel coming after the shift and carrying forward the "unfolding" of the message from the cinematic and scriptural worlds into the world of the congregation's lives. But there is another model for sermons that is perhaps even better suited to dialogues with films whose messages parallel the message of the gospel in how they perceive both the conflict and the resolution.

The Four Pages of the Script

In the introduction I noted how Paul Scott Wilson used "filming" as a metaphor for "showing" things to those who listen to sermons. He employed that image in developing a homiletic structure that emphasizes four "pages" or major movements: trouble in the Bible, trouble in the world, grace in the Bible, and grace in the world. Wilson makes clear that he is not arguing that every sermon must include precisely these moves in precisely this order. Rather he is suggesting a "deep structure" that should be at work in preaching and is founded both on solid theological principles and current cultural analysis while assuring sermons remain "biblical: the Bible is our authority to preach and cannot be wisely bypassed."[30] By focusing in turn on both the Bible and our own world, the sermon draws the hearers' attention not only to what God did in the past but also concretely to what God is doing now.

This model can be used to bring a film into a sermon as an active dialogue partner that prevents the preacher from falling into the trap of preaching on the film rather than the scriptural text. The "trouble" and "grace in the world" could easily be developed through the conflict and resolution of a film. One might wonder whether a film can give a concrete-enough example of what God is doing now to fulfill the function of "grace in the world," but, as Wilson emphasizes, a key aspect of this portion of the sermon is to aid the congregation in developing the hermeneutical skills, if you will, to recognize God's activity in the world.[31] Precisely because some films do play up religious and spiritual themes in life, they can assist people in recognizing these dimensions in real life. The formal structure of the "four pages" suggests not only how a scriptural passage can be paired in dialogue with a film, as two windows for viewing a theme, but also how one can develop the sermonic treatment of the scriptural passage itself. How might one film a scene from Scripture to make explicit its definition of and/or resolution to a problem facing us? How does a film respond to the same problem, making explicit the filmmakers' and ultimately the culture's understanding of and answer to it?

To see how this model for sermon structure might be used to develop a more extended dialogue between Scripture and a film, let's return one final time to the movie *Big Fish*. This time, however, I will place it in dialogue not with 1 Thess. 1:2–10 but with Deut. 26:1–11, the liturgy for the presentation of the offering of "first fruits" and tithes. This passage may seem more naturally suited to autumn stewardship sermons, but the content of the worshipers' response and the setting of that act of worship generations after the exodus raises another possible theme. If God seemed to act so dramatically and in inescapably obvious ways in the past, then why don't we see God acting in such ways today?

Wilson's advice that sometimes we have to look for the trouble *behind* rather than explicitly *in* the biblical text[32] provides the entry point for the sermon. Note that even within the narrative context of Deuteronomy as Moses' final instructions to the Israelites, this liturgy is given for the future when they "come into the land . . . [and] possess it, and settle in it" (Deut. 26:1). Although even the wilderness generation might be expected to be close enough to the exodus to feel in their very bones the necessity of worshiping God with gifts of thanksgiving, there is already (that is, within the narrative setting) an expectation that future generations may be less certain of this need (an expectation long since fulfilled by the time that Deuteronomy was actually written). They would have known the land not as one "flowing with milk and honey" (Deut. 26:9; a justifiable hyperbole as compared to a life of slavery in Egypt), but more as a place where one often struggled to eke out even a subsistence standard of living. The facts of their hard-scrapple lives don't seem to square with the grand stories they have heard about being God's "chosen people."

The "second page" of the sermon then draws out this same sense of disconnect between story and reality that many people feel today, the same disparity played out in *Big Fish*. William Bloom (Billy Crudup) does not merely suspect but is absolutely convinced that his father Edward's (the older Edward played by Albert Finney; the younger, by Ewan McGregor) life wasn't really the "milk and honey" existence he heard about in all those tall tales. Why, several of those stories even bear striking resemblance to biblical stories: for example, confronting a giant that terrifies all the other inhabitants of the town—Edward Bloom as David; working for years in the circus where his only pay from the ringmaster is tiny bits of information that will enable him finally to marry the love of his life—Edward Bloom as Jacob. Just as William loses faith that he really knows anything at all of substance about his father, so many people today conclude that the Bible's stories cannot tell us anything about the reality of God.

But the liturgy of the offering of first fruits was a gift of grace to the Israelites. It opens by freely acknowledging the magnitude of God's acts in the past on behalf of others. " 'A wandering Aramean *was my ancestor;* he went down into Egypt and lived there as an alien, few in number, and there he became a great nation, mighty and populous' " (Deut. 26:5; emphasis added). In the middle sections it begins to transition to an identification of the worshiper with those in the past because they all belong to that nation. " 'The LORD *brought us* out of Egypt with a mighty hand and an outstretched arm, . . . *and gave us* this land, a land flowing with milk and honey' " (Deut. 26:8–9; emphasis added). Finally, the liturgy concludes with the focus on God's actions directly for the worshiper in the present. " 'So now I bring the first of the fruit of the ground that *you, O LORD, have given me'* " (Deut. 26:10; emphasis added). Through the act of telling the story, the worshiper has lived into that story, taking on the identity of those chosen by God. No longer is it a story locked in the past, shared only through a communal identity at best. The truths of the story beyond the mere facts, as it were, open the worshiper's eyes to see a truth about God that otherwise passes unseen. And the transforming power of that story only does its work when the worshipers make it their own.

So it is for William Bloom. The seeds for his reconciliation with his father may begin when Jennifer Hill (Helena Bonham Carter) and Dr. Bennett (Robert Guillaume) begin to fill in the facts about Edward Bloom's life that lie hidden behind his tall tales, but they both express the belief that it is the stories rather than the mere facts that reveal the truth about him. The reconciliation between son and father is only complete when William picks up Edward's tales and, not coincidentally, narrates himself into the story of his father's death. His own identity as his father's son is confirmed when he passes those same stories—confronting a giant and all—to his own son. It is then, in William's closing voice-over narration to the film's final scene, that he expresses its truth beyond the facts: "A man tells his stories so many times that he becomes the stories." That is the power of stories. They reveal truths beyond mere facts, about our fathers and about our Father.

Obviously a sermon developed along these lines would require going into much more detail about the film than the earlier use of it as a single illustration within a sermon. The preacher would have far more opportunity to draw the congregation into the story world of *Big Fish* while at the same time fleshing out the real world of the biblical story by making explicit those aspects of its narrative context that might otherwise go unnoticed. Both Scripture and film play important and genuinely interdependent roles as dialogue partners within the sermon.

This sermon differs from Wilson's basic assumption about "four page" sermons in that it draws all its material from only two sources—a single Scripture passage and a single film. The shifts back and forth between Bible and movie thus create two parallel tracks that the congregation is asked to follow, a "doublet" structure that Richard Eslinger identifies as one of the greatest "pitfalls in preaching."[33] The problem with such parallel stories, he argues, is that the congregation cannot follow both tracks at once.

> One of the two plots may be retained by the hearers, most likely the one that displays the strongest imagery and attention to character, setting, and immediacy of the issues (almost always the contemporary one). The other—usually the scriptural track—will fall out of communal awareness entirely. . . . [A] strategy of parallel alignment of the biblical text and the contemporary world does not serve to integrate; ironically, it functions more to split the two apart.[34]

In the case of a sermon relating a liturgy from Deuteronomy and a Tim Burton film story, there is little doubt as to which track would have the "strongest imagery and attention to character, setting, and immediacy of the issues" for Eslinger.

As a general rule I agree with Eslinger about the danger of doublets. Two illustrations within a single move of a sermon are too much for any preacher or congregation to handle and will almost certainly become muddled.[35] But is it true that in our narrative culture people cannot relate parallel stories in an integrative fashion where the details of one story line serve to draw attention to and indeed interpret the details of another? The "meanwhile back at the ranch" device is a time-honored tool in the narrative-logic toolbox. If it is to work, then, we need to pay attention to how filmmakers successfully employ this tool.

Sermon as Screenplay

Think about the way movies employ parallel story lines to create an integrated plot for the film as a whole. Before the story lines can diverge they must first be clearly established as intrinsically linked. If as viewers we don't *begin* with the certainty that there really is only *one* story, then all our attentive energies will be directed at trying desperately to create that unifying narrative from whatever common threads may be at hand. Only once the central theme has been established, then, can that theme be developed along parallel paths. Second, there must be unmistakable markers for the viewers when the film switches from one story line to another. The filmmaker must immediately establish not only that one line has been left but also precisely which story line has been once again taken up. Third, the divergent story lines need to parallel each other in how they proceed through the stages of narrative development. One story line cannot race ahead to its conclusion with the film then circling back to pick up the other. The time spent with each story line need not be the same, and one's sense of how fast or slow time is passing within the two paths may differ, but the viewer's attention generally must be directed through the stages of complication, crisis, and resolution in parallel between the stories. It is just as important that viewers know where they are in the narrative logic of the story as where they are in the settings of the story world's different story lines. The reason for this parallel unfolding of the elements of narrative arises from the final stage in integrating the overall plot: the story lines must reconnect into a single plotline that meaningfully draws the central theme to its conclusion.

When all these requirements are met, the viewer has the sense of a single, albeit complex, narrative; if any are missed, the viewers simply get lost. This narrative process can be easily seen in the example of the *Lord of the Rings* films. We don't trace the paths of all the characters to the Council of Elrond, but once the Fellowship is formed we are able to follow the divergent paths of its members in the overall quest to destroy Sauron's ring. Each time the film shifts from one story line to another, the filmmakers clearly mark the shift with shots that establish the presence of the characters whose story line we have entered, usually with care taken that the settings are likewise clearly differentiated. If we leave one story line inside a building, the next story line will probably be picked up in an outdoor setting. If our attention is directed away from characters in the forest, we may next find ourselves looking out on a vast plain or at high, rugged mountains. We know we have changed focus, and we know where our attention is now directed. Finally, all the story lines converge, and it is clear that the final resolution of the theme—the destruction of the one ring—could not have been accomplished without each story line having made its distinctive contribution to the quest.[36]

The intercutting techniques of contemporary films and television dramas suggest that the interplay between movies, Scripture, and application can be multiplied beyond Wilson's "four pages." To do so without falling into the "doublet pitfall" will require paying close attention to the narrative logic and tools for managing divergent story lines within an integrated plot. The sermon must open with an introduction crafted both to bring the Scripture and the film into dialogue with each other and also to establish clearly the theme around which that dialogue will be engaged. The transitions between scriptural text and movie must identify for the listeners not only which is the current focus of attention but also where they are in the unfolding of the dialogue through the narrative process. And the sermon must have a strong conclusion that flows from both sides of the dialogue and unites them in the single theme of the sermon.

COMING ATTRACTIONS

I have not included at this point any specific example of this final "sermon as screenplay" model because it will be amply illustrated by the sermons in the chapters that follow. What I hope will be evident, however, is that this final model draws on insights from the preceding three. It takes into consideration Buttrick's work on "moves" and "structures" in how it develops the sequential progression of the parts of the sermon. It understands Lowry's exposition of narrative logic (as opposed to syllogistic logic) so that the sermon seeks to lead the listeners to a discovery of the truth of its theme rather than to prove it. And it incorporates the deep theological structure of our "trouble" and God's "grace" that lies at the heart of Wilson's sermon structure.

If the sermons in these chapters do not seem, then, to be stereotypical examples of either Buttrick or Lowry or Wilson, it is because none were intentionally structured along one of these models. In each instance, they are sermons preached to congregations I pastored that sought to dialogue with our culture as it was expressed through films. They are not homiletic exercises in the abstract but pastoral work products. What has been added for the purposes of this book is the formal exegesis, if you will, that supports the interpretation of the film engaged in the sermonic dialogue. As with any exegesis exercise, I include research into what others have said about the movie that supports my interpretation and present arguments for why I favor my interpretation over others that may have been offered.

Each of the chapters begins with a "theological reading" of the film under consideration. In each instance I offer some guidance as to what aspects of the film interpretation I completed as part of the sermon preparation and what has been added for the purposes of this book. Again, I am working from an analogy with the ways in which preachers learn to interpret Scripture for their sermons. We study the exegetical work of others to develop habits of mind and an approach for ourselves. We engage the resources that are at hand in our week-in-and-week-out sermon interpretation but, if called on to substantiate that interpretation, would be more rigorous and expansive in our research. In the process, however, we would improve our interpretational skills more generally. Following the theological exegesis of the film, I provide some brief comments about what I hoped to accomplish in the sermon through the dialogue with the movie. The chapter concludes with the manuscript prepared for the sermon.

Having stressed in the introduction the distinction between "preaching" as an "oral/aural event" and "sermons" that can (and here will) be reduced to writing, allow me to say just a word about how I use manuscripts in my preaching. In my congregation, my sermon manuscripts are made available to hearing-impaired members as they enter the services where I will preach (and others pick them up as well). After the service, copies of the manuscript are available to others, mailed to shut-ins, and even posted on the church's Web site along with a streaming-audio recording of the sermon. Consequently, I put considerable work into *writing* my sermon manuscripts. But that writing work does not complete my preaching preparation. Although I deliberately work at writing in an oral language style, I practice delivering the sermon several times *out loud*—even from the pulpit—before I preach it to the congregation. There are extemporaneous additions, elaborations, and restatements to communicate through the oral rather than written medium, so that what is written is on average about 75–80 percent of what is preached. However, *reading* transcripts of preaching can be just as difficult to follow as *listening* to sermon manuscripts, so what are provided as examples here are the manuscripts of these sermons.

3

"Heaven's Light"

The Hunchback of Notre Dame

Disney's *The Hunchback of Notre Dame* raises the issue of Christian concern with theological anthropology by its major theme: What is it that makes a person genuinely human or a "monster"? (a question posed by the character Clopin [Paul Kandel] in both the film's introduction and conclusion).[1] The answer to that question provided by the film is that a person's actions toward other people will determine whether one is truly human or, instead, a "monster." Because the film is so steeped in Christian symbolism, not only by its setting in Paris's famous cathedral but in two extended depictions of prayer and many details of its mise-en-scène, it can leave the impression that this ethical answer to the nature of humanity is the church's answer as well.

That answer probably does reflect the general cultural attitude about Christian anthropology. God expects us to be good; if we are, there will be a happy ending, but if we aren't, a fiery destruction awaits us. Yet leaving aside this aspect of personal eschatology, is it really the case that Christian anthropology calls on us *to make ourselves* truly human through our actions? Isn't it more correct to say that God calls us to live in conformity with the true humanity that we were created to be as bearers of the divine image? Disney's film thus calls out to be engaged in dialogue regarding answers to the question, What makes us human?

A THEOLOGICAL READING OF *THE HUNCHBACK OF NOTRE DAME*

Although it should go without saying, any analysis of Disney's *The Hunchback of Notre Dame* must begin with the clear assertion that the story related in the

65

film is *not* the story related in Victor Hugo's *Notre-Dame de Paris*. That it should have even occurred to anyone to recast Hugo's tragic novel as a musical comedy is itself vivid testimony to how cinematic portrayals had already reshaped the story in primarily romantic terms.[2] While all the cinematic versions include the major characters and plot trajectory of Hugo's novel, Disney's decision to overlay the dramatic conventions of comedy on a literary tragedy fundamentally alters the shape of the story.[3] Only Frollo's (Tony Jay) death remains from the novel (although his fall from the cathedral bell tower is not directly caused by Quasimodo in the film). A marriage between Esmeralda (Demi Moore) and Phoebus (Kevin Kline) is prefigured by "Quasi"'s (as his gargoyle sidekicks have affectionately nicknamed him) symbolically joining their hands, while Quasimodo (Tom Hulce) becomes the hero of all Paris (rather than his literally embracing Esmeralda in death, as in the novel).

The purpose here is to deal with Disney's film and not to delve into a detailed source- or redaction-critical analysis comparing it with the original novel. Nevertheless, two further divergences should be noted. First, in the case of the most stereotypical of Disney devices incorporated into the film—the comic relief introduced by the gargoyle trio of Victor (Charles Kimbrough), Hugo (Jason Alexander), and Laverne (Mary Wickes)—Disney actually claims some warrant in the original novel's device of Quasimodo's talking with the gargoyles of the cathedral.[4] Second, and more important, Disney changes Frollo from Hugo's "archdeacon" to "Minister of Justice" in order to avoid offending religious sensibilities.[5] This change is one of several by which the film places the church in a more positive light than it stood in Hugo's novel. The character of the Archdeacon of Notre Dame (David Ogden Stiers) now becomes Quasimodo's protector, both successfully in the opening of the film, when Frollo would have drowned him in a well, and ineffectually near the film's conclusion, when he fails to stop Frollo from reaching the bell tower during the assault on the cathedral. He also becomes Esmeralda's spiritual advisor, suggesting, "Perhaps there is someone in here," that is, within Notre Dame, who can help to "right all the wrongs of this world" that so trouble her.

There is, however, a layering of meanings in this exchange between the archdeacon and Esmeralda. His advice leads Esmeralda to prayer in the song "God Help the Outcasts" (to which I will return). But as she sings, we watch Quasimodo up in the belltower, overhearing her prayer, being drawn down to her in the nave, and ultimately abetting her escape from the cathedral. No doubt he is also—along with God, the Virgin, and the Christ (as we shall see, the one to whom she addresses the prayer is ambiguous)—"someone in here" who will help her "right the wrongs" she and her people have experienced. I do not agree, however, with Ward in her conclusion that by having Quasimodo answer her prayer, Disney is "relegating the church, and more specifically God, to irrelevancy, . . . [and] refus[ing] to admit a serious role for religion."[6] It is, after all, "the very eyes of Notre Dame"[7] that condemn and stay Frollo's intention to murder Quasimodo in the prologue and the cathedral's gargoyle that casts him down into the flames near the conclusion. In this regard, then, Disney's film is more respectful of the church than Hugo's novel.

The central theme of the film, as I noted at the beginning of this chapter, is stated in "a riddle" both posed by Clopin at the end of the prologue and reprised in the film's finale—but importantly attributed by him in both instances to the "bells of Notre Dame."[8] Since the question is ultimately raised by the cathedral/church, it is thus an inherently theological one. Clopin states the riddle in slightly different form each time. In the prologue, the riddle asks the audience to consider two characters and decide: *who* is monstrous and "*who* is*" human? (emphasis added). Thus, the focus is "specific" to the story. By the reprise in the finale, however, the phrasing of the riddle has shifted to "*what makes*" one human or monstrous (again, emphasis added). The issue is, then, much broader than just the characters within the story; indeed, the whole story is transformed into a kind of parable. What is it that makes any of us properly human or, conversely, transforms us into monsters?

The impetus for the riddle in the story is given by Frollo's descriptions of the as-yet-unseen gypsy baby. Snatching a bundle from a fleeing gypsy woman (causing her death as her head falls on the steps of the cathedral), he asks, "A baby? A monster!" As he is about to drown the baby in a well, he tells the archdeacon, "This is an unholy demon. I'm sending it back to Hell, where it belongs." He goes on to describe the infant as "misshapen" and a "foul creature," and gives him (as Clopin explains) "a cruel name, a name that means, 'half-formed,' Quasimodo." Thus, all the explicit indications in the prologue are that Quasimodo is the monster.

Yet already the viewer has been given many subtle clues that one should not be too hasty in accepting Frollo's identification of Quasimodo as the monster. Every visual cue associated with Frollo ("black horse, black hat, black cape") is a cinematic convention for marking the villain.[9] Clopin describes him as a person with iron clutches. Far more subtle is the first of a number of Latin commentaries that are introduced by means of a choral sound track: as the dark figure of Frollo fills the screen, the background voices are singing, "*Kyrie Eleison*" ("Lord, have mercy") and continue, "*Dies irae, . . . Quando Judex est venturus*" ("Day of wrath . . . when the Judge is come").[10]

Throughout the sound track, elements of musical Latin masses are incorporated to provide such commentaries. One particular feature of Schwartz's adaptation of the Latin material is the shifting referent of "*Judex*" from Christ coming in judgment in the mass to the character of Frollo, the civil "judge," in Disney's film. In most instances the juxtaposition of image and sound track makes it clear that Frollo is the *Judex* and his arrival as such is to be feared. However, in the song "Sanctuary!"[11] the referent of *Judex* switches back and forth between Frollo and Christ. As Frollo brings Esmeralda to the stake, the chorus once again refers to him by the title *Judex*, as in the earlier instance from "The Bells of Notre Dame." But in the Latin choral sound track, following a plea to God to save God's people, we see the archdeacon emerge from the cathedral only to have his path blocked by guards as the choir sings in the background, "*Judex crederis*" ("In our Judge we believe"). This phrase, then, appears to be a plea to be judged by Christ (in whom "we believe") rather than by Frollo. The referent later shifts back to Frollo when the crowds rally against him, as the choir announces, in Latin, that once the *Judex* has taken the judgment seat every injustice will be punished—but here it is the evil judge's acts that stand condemned. Then, as the battle reaches its climax, the Latin sound track once again appeals for Christ to come as the righteous and merciful judge ("*Juste Judex ultionis . . . Kyrie Eleison*"). While one can marvel at the amount of effort involved in creating a level of meaning that is surely lost on the vast majority of viewers, the characterization of Frollo as a corrupt judge is nonetheless an important thematic element of the film.

Returning to Clopin's question, the very fact that he describes the query regarding what determines one's humanity as a "riddle" suggests to the audience that the correct answer is unlikely to be the one made explicit in Frollo's pronouncements in the prologue to the story. The whole film proceeds to lay out the proof that the "half-formed" Quasimodo is indeed more truly human than the monstrous Frollo. One clearly theological way in which the film seeks to answer its central question is by the contrast between Quasimodo and Frollo that is set up in the song "Heaven's Light/Hellfire"[12] that comes at the almost exact mid-point of the film.

Quasimodo sings the first movement of the song in response to the gargoyles' suggestion that Esmeralda is his "girl." He relates how he has watched from his high bell tower many loving couples walking the streets far below, basking in a "glow . . . like heaven's light." Yet he has always known that he could not hope to experience such warmth and love because his "hideous . . . face" was not intended to be seen in heaven's light. That is to say, he is a monster and has no right to share either human or divine love. But in Esmeralda's acceptance and insistence that neither he nor she is a monster, as Frollo had contended, he came to believe that even his life suddenly basked in heaven's light.

Quasimodo begins joyfully ringing the cathedral bells, calling the monks to evening prayer. As they process through Notre Dame, they chant the Latin prayer of confession. At the same moment, likewise no doubt called to prayer by the cathedral bells, Frollo also begins to offer his prayer to the Virgin Mary. Far from a prayer of confession, however, Frollo's prayer boasts of his righteousness and purity as compared to "the common, vulgar, weak, licentious crowd" (all characteristics that Frollo will soon demonstrate himself in the course of his song/prayer). Throughout his prayer, the confessional prayer of the monks continues in counterpoint so that as he insists on his purity, the monks are chanting, in Latin, admitting that they are sinners.

If, as seems likely, this scene deliberately borrows the structure of Jesus' parable of the Pharisee and the Tax Collector (Luke 18:9–14), then it is yet another indication that Disney has placed the church in a more favorable light than did Hugo. It is clearly Frollo who stands in the place of the hypocritical Pharisee of the parable, whereas the monks (representative of the church) offer genuine repentance, like the tax collector. Perhaps it is not going too far to also point out that the tax collector was an "outcast" in the Jewish culture of Jesus' day, and we will see that it is precisely the "outcast" that is privileged in Disney's film.

Whereas Quasimodo had sung about love and acceptance from Esmeralda, Frollo's song gives expression to his lust for Esmeralda, which blazes within him as he imagines her dancing before him in the form of a fire nymph in the flames of his fireplace. Quasimodo had described his love for Esmeralda as "heaven's light," yet even Frollo describes his lust for her as "Hellfire," leading him into sin. But Frollo insists he is not responsible for his adulterous thoughts (to which the monks rejoin, *"Mea culpa"* ["Through my fault"]); rather, it is both the fault of Esmeralda and ultimately God who created the devil with power to tempt far beyond humanity's ability to resist (which brings the response from the monks, *"Mea maxima culpa"* ["Through my most grievous fault"]). He pleads with Mary to destroy Esmeralda in Hellfire (his imagined fire nymph Esmeralda now screaming in pain as she is consumed by flames) if she cannot be his to possess (now imagining her as a wispy spirit advancing to accept his embrace). In his rage he casts a silk scarf that had belonged to her into the fire and for a brief moment draws back, praying for God's mercy on both their behalfs (the monks now chanting the *"Kyrie"*). But it is only for a moment, for his lust returns, and he ends the song, "But she will be mine / Or she will burn!"[13]

Clearly, then, in the view of this film, "monsters" are not to be identified by either their physical (in the case of Quasimodo) or their cultural (in the case of Esmeralda) characteristics. Indeed, the only physical characteristic the film allows (with tongue firmly in cheek) for "monsters" is a "monster line" that Esmeralda cannot find in reading Quasimodo's palm. She then offers her palm to Quasimodo saying, "Now you look at me. Do you think *I'm* evil?" (as Frollo had told Quasimodo all Gypsies were). He answers, "No! No, no. You are kind and good and—and . . ." at which she interjects, "And a Gypsy. And maybe Frollo's wrong about the both of us." Kindness and goodness are what make one truly human. Frollo may look like the proper man and declare his righteousness, but his murderous acts, his lust rather than love, and above all his total rejection of those unlike him (he calls both Quasimodo and Esmeralda "unholy demons" and declares his intention to send them "back to Hell where [they] belong") mark him, even more than his "black horse, black hat, black cape," as a monster.

Having answered its own riddle in this way, the film presses forward its parabolic function by encouraging its viewers not to treat society's "outcasts" as "monsters." Again, examples of this theme run throughout the film[14] (from the improper and short-lived acceptance of Quasimodo as the King of Fools in the opening sequence to his embrace and heralding as a hero in the conclusion). Attention here, as in the sermon, will be focused on the scene that incorporates the song "God Help the Outcasts."[15] That scene, as I noted earlier, is set up by an interchange between Esmeralda and the archdeacon inside the cathedral. In exasperation, she asks him, "What do they have against people who are different, anyway?" Rather than answer her question directly, he responds by telling her, "You can't right all the wrongs of this world by yourself," thus clearly identifying opposition to "people who are different" as one of the world's wrongs that should be righted. It is then that he suggests "perhaps there's someone in here who can" help.

As the archdeacon walks away, Esmeralda first glances at parishioners who have knelt in prayer in the cathedral, and then upon a statue in a niche of a crowned Madonna and Child. The parishioners are of course the same people who, when outside the cathedral, had joined in pillorying Quasimodo and had been unwilling to stand up with her against Frollo, so she turns to offer a prayer to the Madonna and Child. Her prayer is at first halting, the basis of her hesitancy grounded foremost in an uncertainty regarding whether God will shun her as she expects the parishioners would because she is a Gypsy.

To just whom this prayer is addressed is quite ambiguous. Is it Mary, crowned though she is, of whom Esmeralda wonders while gazing upon her face, "Were you once an outcast too?" Or is it to the Christ child Mary embraces that Esmeralda prays? Then again, the petitions explicitly call on "God [to] help the outcasts." There is a symbolic identification between Mary and Notre Dame in the film, seen most clearly in the prologue, where an almost identical statue of Madonna and Child on the exterior are the final and climactic eyes that open to cast judgment on Frollo's attempt to drown the infant Quasimodo. God is known and acts through the cathedral, foremost in the sanctuary that it provides outcasts like Quasimodo and Esmeralda—again a more positive view of the church than found in Hugo's novel. Thus, I would disagree with Ward's characterization of God in the film as "unknown" and "unknowable" and her contention that in particular this "song represents God as a whimsical Santa Claus without the joy."[16] That characterization of God does fit the attitude of the parishioners within the song, but the song itself is obviously critical of their attitudes as they contrast with Esmeralda's (see below).

Esmeralda is insightful enough, however, to recognize that the portrayal of the Madonna and Child as crowned and powerful disguises the basic truth about them that they were once outcasts as well. So she calls on God to help the outcasts because she has become convinced that no one else will. Like Frollo's soliloquy/song (that actually comes a bit later in the film's plot), Esmeralda's song employs an important counterpoint. In this instance, whether because it is provided by parishioners rather than monks or in order to make the contrast obvious to everyone in the audience, the counterpoint is not given in Latin. While she prays for the outcasts who are hungry and in need of mercy, the parishioners pray for their own "wealth," "fame," "glory," and—like Frollo—not for someone to love but for a love to be possessed. To further heighten the contrast, Esmeralda insists her prayers on behalf of outcasts do not include herself but rather only those even less fortunate—at which point the film cuts to Quasimodo as he follows her at a distance through the cathedral.

In a subtle but powerful visual cue to those familiar with the symbolism,[17] Esmeralda walks past a fresco portraying the "Slaughter of the Innocents" and "Flight into Egypt" as she prays for all those who, like the Gypsies, are poor and oppressed. The juxtaposition underscores both the continuing cruelty in the world and God's action both to spare the Christ child and, through Christ, to bring redemption for the world (the final panels of the fresco to come into view portray the "Presentation in the Temple," related of course to the redemption of the firstborn in Jewish tradition and the "Baptism of Jesus"). The song ends with Esmeralda singing, "God help the outcasts / Children of God" as she is bathed in the light streaming through the cathedral's famous rose window, prefiguring the "heaven's light" about which Quasimodo will later sing. Those who are outcasts in the eyes of the world are not "monsters" but "children of God."

Although it is not the case that the message of all Disney animated films is so consistent with the message of the gospel—and few secular films so deliberately Christian in their symbolism—Disney's *The Hunchback of Notre Dame* offers not only a message that, at one level, the church can endorse but also one that it needs to hear. Too many Christians, like the parishioners of Notre Dame in the film, are driven by a desire that God should protect and amply provide for them. But the purpose of the church is to provide sanctuary to the outcasts of the world and assurance that they are indeed "children of God" rather than "monsters." In a word, there is a lot in this film that will preach.

PREACHING *THE HUNCHBACK OF NOTRE DAME*

There is much to be appreciated and even admired in Disney's *The Hunchback of Notre Dame*. Its profound layering of meanings allows it to do its work on a wide range of people in the audience, from very young children to adults with the sophisticated linguistic and artistic abilities required to appreciate the use of Latin and religious art and symbolism. But at its core, its message is that we "make" ourselves either into proper human beings or into "monsters" by our actions toward others. God stands in judgment over our success or failure in this regard, but it is we who make ourselves.

In preaching on the film I wanted both to affirm its positive vision of inclusiveness as central to our humanity and to challenge its assertion that we make ourselves either human or monsters. God has made us human; our sinfulness makes us monstrous. And one sin that can transform us into monsters is self-righteousness, which can flow from an overassurance that we can solely by our own efforts realize the full potential of our humanity.

But with Disney, I also wanted to challenge my "audience" with the question of whether there are those whom they regard as "monsters" that God calls us to recognize as "children of God," worthy of love and "heaven's light." If our humanity is not at its core something we build through our own actions, then we should stand in relationship with all people based on the image of God created in them. Being in relationship demands more from us than simply performing ethical and charitable acts toward others. It is taking them within our embrace, no matter how unlovable they may appear within the view of society. That was Jesus' mission, and it is the one he has left us to continue.

Around the time I saw the film, I was preparing to preach on Matt. 11:16–19, 25–30 (the Gospel lesson appointed in the Revised Common Lectionary for the 14th Sunday in Ordinary Time, Year A). In order better to engage in the dialogue, I changed the Old Testament lesson from what was assigned in the lectionary in favor of a text in keeping with the sermon's theme, specifically Gen. 1:26–2:1. The only special research on the film that went into the sermon preparation was reviewing the sound track album to be sure I had the song lyrics correct (particularly the Latin) and a return trip to the theater to review certain details of the film in order to test my interpretation.

SERMON: "HEAVEN'S LIGHT"

(Matt. 11:16–19; 25–30; Gen. 1:26–2:1)

What is it that makes us genuinely human, and what is it that has the power to transform us into monsters? Those are the questions posed by one of the major forces in American popular culture this summer, Disney's *The Hunch-back of Notre Dame.* You cannot enter a discount store or get within one hundred yards of a Burger King without being innundated with images of Quasimodo, Esmeralda, and Phoebus. But given the alternative influences of *Eraser* and *Independence Day*, this summer's other blockbuster movies, one can only be thankful, for Disney has given us a moving and thoughtful tale in this animated feature film.

To be sure, Disney's *Hunchback of Notre Dame* is not Victor Hugo's *Notre-Dame de Paris.* Whereas the opening and closing songs of the Disney film call on us to recognize in the misshapen Quasimodo the true, heroic man and in the evil Frollo the genuine monster, Hugo presented both as monsters—albeit the former was pitiable and the latter loathsome. Disney answers the "riddle" by drawing out the moral that it is one's actions that make a monster and not one's physical attributes. Hugo, writing in the less "politically correct" 1830s, would grant only that Frollo's hypocrisy and murderous lust made him every bit the monster that the deformed Quasimodo was. But consideration of our Scripture readings for this morning might lead us to yet other answers to the riddle posed by the Disney film.

Reversing the elements of the riddle, what does make a human person according to the Scriptures? In the opening chapter of Genesis we have seen that what sets humanity apart from everything else within creation is that we have been made in God's "image." Yet what does that mean, to be the bearers of God's image? Theologians have long agreed that it does not mean that our physical appearance is like that of our spiritual God, but we still find ourselves in need of occasional reminders of this fact. God is not European, African, Asian, or of any other race. God even transcends the categories of gender that are so fundamental to our self-concepts, for it took the creation of "male and female" to form the divine image within humanity.

What then is this "image" of the divine that makes us human? Taking his lead from the need for maleness and femaleness to form the divine image within humanity, the Reformed theologian Karl Barth suggested that it was the ability to live in full, loving, and meaningful relationship that formed God's likeness in us. Just as the triune God—Father, Son, and Spirit—eternally exists in relationship, so God has given us this marvelous and mystical capacity.

What so intrigues me about this understanding of humanity as the bearers of God's image is that it suggests a powerful understanding of what sin is as well. Reformed theology has always insisted that humanity as it exists in the world now continues to bear the divine image, although it has been deformed by human sin. We are all now "Quasimodo," "half-formed" in terms of what God intended humanity to be. If the image of God is the ability to exist in relationship, then the sin that effaces it is most fundamentally a breaking of relationships. Our rebellion against God, like that of Adam and Eve, is a failure to trust the divine wisdom over our own. Our failures to act with love toward one another destroy the trust necessary for maintaining human relationships and efface the image of God in humanity.

Perhaps Disney's Quasimodo does have some sense of this ultimate purpose of human existence. In a touching song, he looks upon the "glow" that surrounds lovers as they walk together and likens it to "heaven's light." But he has concluded that his hideous face was never intended to see "heaven's light." As the story continues to unfold, however, Quasimodo begins to believe that perhaps he was made for "heaven's light"; and the glorious news of the gospel is that so were each of us. Physically deformed as Quasimodo was, spiritually and morally deformed as we are, God's light of love shines upon us, bringing us into relationship with the Divine and opening the possibility of genuine relationship with one another.

Yet like the mariner's maps of Quasimodo's fifteenth-century Europe, there is a warning here that "this way there be monsters." Our confidence in our restored relationship with God can, perhaps ironically, cause us to lose sight of the fact that God desires to recreate the fullness of the divine image in humanity as a whole, not in each of us as individuals. Our relationship with God, rooted in love and forgiveness, has yet to fully reverse the effects of sin upon the divine image that we bear. There is a real danger that our righteousness in Christ will be corrupted into self-righteousness.

Frollo's transformation into a monster in the film is complete only when he succumbs fully to self-righteousness. In his prayer he boasts, like a certain Pharisee in one of Jesus' parables, that he is not like all those sinners in the world. But despite his assertions that he is unlike the "weak licentious crowd," he still recognizes his lust for Esmeralda. Yet he protests he is not to blame; rather, it is Esmeralda's fault for bewitching him with her beauty and even God's fault for not giving him the strength to resist the devil's temptations. Frollo sees himself as righteous, and so his wicked thoughts must be blamed on someone else: a witch, the devil, even ultimately God.

Even as Frollo's self-righteousness transforms his sexual desire into lust for murder—crying out, "But she will be mine or she will burn!"—the monks in the cathedral can be heard chanting the traditional confession of sin: "I confess to God Almighty . . . that I have sinned in thought, in word and deed through my fault, through my most grievous fault" (but in Latin, of course). What God has hidden from "the wise and the intelligent" Frollos but revealed to infants is that God loves us even in our sinfulness. We cannot hide our sins from God, and we hide them from ourselves with monstrous results. But just as human parents love their children despite their faults, forgiving them and instructing them that they might mature, so the divine Spirit works in our lives, gently restoring God's image within us. The monks accepted this and their own continuing fault and need for forgiveness, but apparently Frollo could not.

Jesus continues to call "all [who] are weary and carrying heavy burdens" to come and receive the "rest" that he provides. We eagerly accept his "yoke" and seek to "learn from" him that we might "find rest for [our] souls." But are we willing to admit that even while we celebrate God's love for us we some-times begrudge the divine acceptance extended to others? Or perhaps we can allow that God accepts "those people" so long as we do not feel too much pressure to receive them into our immediate segment of God's extended family.

This is the sting of Jesus' proverb from our Gospel lesson this morning. Like petulant children, we become frustrated with God because the divine will does not conform to our desires: "We played the flute for you, and you did not dance; we wailed, and you did not mourn." "Come on, Jesus, get with the program!" John's calls to repentance and Jesus' association with social outcasts are not the rewards we are seeking as a consequence of having the divine image restored in us. We want "dominion," not only over fish, birds, and the land, but over other people as well. But God calls us to relationship, not dominance.

This point emerges in Disney's film as well. As the Gypsy Esmeralda strolls through the cathedral of Notre Dame praying, "God help the outcasts, chil-dren of God," there are other parishioners offering petitions for wealth, for fame, even "for glory to shine" not on God's name but their own. One woman prayed for love she could possess instead of an opportunity to love and care for another. Rather than asking that God's love be felt by all, they each asked for God's blessings only for themselves. The juxtaposition of their selfish petitions to Esmeralda's humble prayer recalled to my memory the Magnificat, Mary's glorious prayer in response to the announcement that she would give birth to the Messiah. She magnified God because the Divine "has scattered the proud in the thoughts of their hearts" and "brought down the powerful from their thrones." God has also "lifted up the lowly" and "filled the hungry with good things," granting mercy on those who reverence God in every generation. Esmeralda gazes upon a statue of the Madonna and Child, recognizing in their faces social outcasts like herself, despite the iconography of crowns, and pleads for "God [to] help the outcast, or nobody will." And we can hear Mary respond, "God has, and God does!"

But my question to each of us this morning is whom do we typically pat-tern our prayers after—Mary and Esmeralda, or the parishioners of Notre Dame? Are most of our prayers about ourselves, or do we with Esmeralda pray only for others? Would that the core of all our prayers were "God help the outcasts, children of God."

In our Gospel lesson for this morning Jesus says, "Wisdom is vindicated by her deeds," so let's press the question a bit further. We are a congregation that is concerned about the social responsibilities encumbent on those who accept the call of the gospel. Already this morning we have received a "hunger offering" that today is designated to help children in our own inner city. From these windows one can see a garden in which we grow fresh produce for the hungry of our community, and during the winter months we welcome the homeless to take shelter inside these very walls. We teach our children in the LOGOS ministry to respond to others by saying, "You are a child of God, and I will treat you that way."

Yet are there those whom we still treat as "outcasts"? Do we, like the Pharisee of Jesus' parable and Frollo in the Disney movie, ever thank God that we are not like those others whose lives are so ugly and deformed that they cannot possibly have been made for "heaven's light"? Who are the "sinners," with whom Jesus now celebrates the dawning of God's reign, who stir a desire in our hearts to take him aside and say to him, "But Jesus, associating with people *like that* will tarnish your reputation and hinder your mission"? I am certain that Jesus would respond, "Associating with people *like that* is my mission."

So we return to the riddle with which we began. Scripture has taught us that "what makes a truly human person" is that we have all been created "in the image of God." Our dignity and worthiness to be received into relationship with both the divine and human is not our outward appearance or even our actions; it is that God has made us all as "children of God" intended for the "heaven's light" of fellowship with the Divine in God's love. "What makes a monster" is a self-righteousness that leads people to view themselves as better than those they see as monsters. It is when we forget that we are all "Quasimodo," deformed by sin from what God intends us to be, that we become monsters.

Jesus calls to us to come to him, to be relieved of the burden of our sin and take upon ourselves the yoke of God's love. We hear his voice as Quasimodo received the accepting kiss of Esmeralda, basking in the warmth, love, and acceptance that is "heaven's light."

4

"Time to Get On with It"

Bruce Almighty

Since the previews of coming attractions before the feature presentation are meant to entice you to see a movie when it is released, I must confess that the trailer promoting the release of *Bruce Almighty* had exactly the opposite effect on me. Upon learning that he has "got the power" of God, Bruce Nolan (Jim Carrey) showers the street by blowing the caps off a fire hydrant, "enhances" the breasts of his girlfriend Grace Connelly (Jennifer Aniston), haltingly runs across Lake Erie, answers millions of prayer requests through a "Yahweh!" e-mail account, and enables his dog to use the toilet rather than a tree. I did not even bother to see the film during its theatrical release.[1]

All of us, however, have for one reason or another watched movies on home video that we would not have paid the theater price of admission to see. When I was compelled to watch the DVD of *Bruce Almighty* in advance of an adult fellowship meeting for which I had been asked to lead a discussion of the film, I found that this movie was worthy of serious reflection. To be sure, the trailer accurately reflected the juvenile ways that Bruce employed his divine powers; yet even as the movie has great fun with this device, it also clearly casts these acts as abuses of that power. Rather than portraying God as too much like humans (as in George Burns's cigar-smoking role in the *Oh, God!* films), the movie stresses the ways that humans should be more like God.

In their final face-to-face meeting, God (Morgan Freeman) tells Bruce that there was created within him a "divine spark." This "spark" did not make Bruce himself divine, but it should have made it possible for him to further God's grace in the world. With that gift—that "spark"—came the responsibility to use it not just for his personal benefit but also for the benefit of others. Bruce had wanted God to take just "five minutes" to make his life all he dreamed it could be. God wanted Bruce to "be the miracle" by using the gifts and abilities God had given him to make life better for both himself and others.

A THEOLOGICAL READING OF *BRUCE ALMIGHTY*

The plot of this film centers on the character Bruce Nolan, a features news reporter for a local television station in Buffalo, New York. He is denied a promotion to anchor that he was both certain he deserved and was going to get, and is ultimately fired as a consequence of his on-air meltdown when it is announced that his chief rival is receiving the position instead. Bruce launches into a tirade against God for the lousy job God is doing of taking care of his life, and he expresses complete confidence that he himself could do God's job better. The next day, he has a meeting with God, who bestows the full range of divine powers on Bruce and then leaves on vacation. Once Bruce realizes these powers are real, he immediately begins to use them for his personal enjoyment and enrichment, and even for revenge. But as the prayer requests of just a portion of the residents of Buffalo begin to pile up, God meets with Bruce once again to point out that doing God's job requires attending to far more than just one's personal desires. Being God comes with not only power but responsibilities.

Yet it is not only his responsibilities to the faceless masses who are filling his "Yahweh!" message board with millions of prayer requests that Bruce neglects. So self-centered is his view of life that he cannot comprehend why his happiness at receiving everything he ever wanted is not also reason for happiness for those who love him. Grace breaks off their relationship when she concludes she may be nothing more to Bruce than one of many things that together will make up his perfect life. The transformative moment of the film comes when Bruce finally recognizes that the only proper use of those divine powers is to meet the genuine needs of others rather than his own or even their personal desires.[2] Foremost among those needs is for one to know the love that God has for us, to have someone in our lives who, as Bruce expresses it to God, will love and see us through God's eyes.

Bruce Almighty simultaneously explores several dimensions of spirituality rather than simply running into the ground the single gag of playing with godlike powers. In fact, this film is literally chock-full of what Tom Shadyac, the director, referred to as "spiritual" rather than "religious" elements. His concern was that the film not be exclusively identified with a particular religion. For example, the prayer beads that Grace early on gives to Bruce and that show up at key moments throughout the story are made by the kids at her child-care center, so "they could be considered either Buddhist prayer beads or even a Catholic rosary."[3] Not surprisingly in a film for an American audience, however, most of the fleeting references can be traced to the biblical tradition. At a party, Bruce carries a clear-glass pitcher of water that nevertheless dispenses red wine into the revelers' glasses, and he briefly leans against a tabletop-sized golden statue of a bull. There is also a subtle Trinitarian reference when Bruce meets God. Initially he encounters the janitor cleaning the first floor of the Omni Presents warehouse. Having climbed a stairway (to heaven apparently, given that he goes to the seventh floor of a six-story building), Bruce meets the same person as an electrician, who then removes his work coveralls to reveal the "boss" dressed in a solid white suit. As Shadyac himself commented, "The janitor would be the Son, the one who came to serve, . . . the electrician . . . is the Holy Spirit, and then . . . in the white suit it's the Father."[4] Some deeper theological issues receive passing treatment as well. When Bruce asks God during one of their check-in sessions how he can make someone love him without violating her free will (one of the rules God sets down when endowing Bruce with divine powers), God responds, "Welcome to my world; let me know when you figure that one out."

Other spiritual or religious themes are developed more fully over the course of film. The desire for "signs" from God about how we should live our lives is one such leitmotif. Using the convention of a homeless man who holds up hand-painted cardboard signs, the filmmakers provide a running commentary on events in the film. Caught in a traffic jam on his way to work, Bruce stares straight ahead and screams, "This is my luck!" oblivious to the motor-vehicle crash victim being wheeled past his car window to an ambulance; once at work he reads the homeless man's sign: "R Ewe Blind." That evening, having been fired from his job, Bruce finds the man once more outside the TV station, being harassed by some gangbangers. When Bruce calls out at them, they assault him, leaving him bruised on the street. The homeless man holds up a sign reading, "Life is Just," to which Bruce replies, "Just? Just get a clue!" Driving around town that night, Bruce begins to pray to God, "Give me a sign," as he passes a flashing road signal displaying "Caution Ahead." Bruce continues, "Please send me a sign," and is cut-off by a truck loaded down with street signs reading, "Dead End," "Do Not Enter," "Wrong Way," "Yield," "Caution," and "Stop." Still Bruce is oblivious. Later in the film, once the ill-effects of his decision to answer everyone's prayer requests with a simple "Yes" leads to riots in the streets, the homeless man returns holding a sign reading, "Thy Kingdumb Come." In the movie's final shot, the man holds up the sign "Armagedon Outa Here" as his face morphs into God's face. As Shadyac observes, the point is that God is placing "messages in our lives all the time; we just don't pay attention to them."[5]

One of the most creative developments of a religious theme is the treatment of grace through the development of the romance between Bruce and his hardly coincidentally named love interest, Grace Connelly. As Shadyac phrased it in an interview, "She is literally grace in his life. And he doesn't see it."[6] Where Bruce is self-absorbed and selfishly desiring more from life, Grace is able to live in the moment, literally gives of her self in blood drives and through her work at a child-care center, and even focuses her prayers on Bruce rather than herself. The film's climax comes when, in hopes of winning her back, Bruce logs in to Grace's prayers on the "Yahweh! Insta-Prayer" message board he had created. At that moment she is praying that even though she still loves Bruce, she needs God to help her let him go because she can't stand to hurt anymore. Bruce gives up his desire to be God, and in heaven God asks Bruce to pray. Bruce offers a prayer for the hungry and for peace in the world that, God observes, would be fine if Bruce wanted to be Miss America. God presses Bruce, who then realizes that his greatest concern is for Grace (as God smiles knowingly). But God is taken aback when Bruce doesn't then pray for them to get back together. Instead, he prays only for her happiness, saying, "I want her to meet someone who will see her always as I do now, through your eyes." More than just the character Grace within the film, this story line traces the significance of grace itself in our lives. Grace is there in every moment of our lives, even when we are not "in the moment" and aware of its presence. What we care about more than anything else, when we are truly honest with ourselves, is grace. And grace, at its deepest level, is being able to see ourselves and the world through God's eyes.

Either of these two themes could be strong dialogue partners in a sermon, but it was another theme focused specifically in the character development of Bruce Nolan that I chose to engage homiletically: the need to use the gifts God has placed in our lives to "be the miracle." Although people outside the film haven't shared the experience of the character Bruce Nolan, Shadyac has been clear that in his understanding of the film God has given some power or "spark" to everyone that we consequently have a responsibility to use for others. In an interview at the time of the film, Shadyac isolated the theme of the source of "true power" as the "message of the film." God has placed "[t]he power . . . in you to make a difference." The problem that too many people have is that they misidentify their careers, their relationships, or something else as their sources of power and thus ultimately their personal identities, instead of "looking inside and up" and recognizing their "true power" resides in the person God has created them to be.

This need to "look inside and up" itself sparked something of a controversy among some of the film's more conservative Christian reviewers. In one key scene, God tells Bruce that his and everyone else's problem is that they "keep looking up" to God to resolve all the problems and crises within their lives rather than realizing that God has already placed power within them to address their needs (the dialogue from this scene is presented below in the sermon). These reviewers' criticism was that this scene was taken to suggest that people should stop praying and expecting God to intervene in their lives and instead just deal with things on their own. Shadyac responded, "The key word in that sentence is 'you *keep* looking up.'" He stressed that looking to God with humility and maintaining our relationship with the Divine are essential to what it means to be human. "However, to *keep* looking up means that we depend on God to do everything for us." Instead of such helplessness, people need to realize that God has created us with the ability not only to address needs in our own lives but also to be God's hands, feet, heart, and expression in the lives of others. "I hope people will look up, but don't just *keep* looking up."[7]

That everyone—and not just Bruce Almighty—already has this power is demonstrated in the film by the change in Bruce's activities following this interaction with God. He completes a photo scrapbook that he couldn't be bothered to help Grace with earlier in the film. Caught for a third time in a traffic tie-up (the second time he had parted a way for himself through the cars like Moses parted the Red Sea), he helps to push the overheated car onto a side street. Back at home, he pulls the plug on the "Yahweh! Insta-Prayer" message board. He turns down the promotion to anchor that he had eventually gained by turning his rival into a literal blithering idiot during a newscast. And finally he housebreaks his dog by teaching him to use a tree like all the other dogs. What is notable in all the vignettes in this montage is that Bruce never once uses his special divine powers even though he has yet to surrender those special powers back to God. All of these things are done by Bruce Nolan, not Bruce Almighty.

If the montage makes it clear that even those who have not been (even temporarily) endowed with all God's powers don't need to "*keep* looking up" to God to do everything for them, the conversation between Bruce and God that precedes it makes the point just as clearly that "looking up," engaging a personal relationship with God, is equally essential. It is because of this latest in a string of epiphanies that Bruce is able realize that indeed he not only "has got the power" to part his bowl of tomato soup but also has always had the power to be God's helping hands in cleaning up the mess that has been made of the world. It is that growing relationship with God that opens Bruce's eyes to see the world as God sees it and not simply in terms of how it can make his personal life all he might dream.

In keeping with the filmmakers' intentions, *Bruce Almighty* is more of a "spiritual" film than a "religious" or even specifically Christian one. The notion that a divine "spark" resides within people providing them with the power not only to actualize themselves as individuals but to benefit others is even older than Gnosticism and as current as New Age spiritualities that are warming over Gnosticism in such pop-culture phenomena as *The DaVinci Code*. Nevertheless, the idea that the Divine dwells within individuals through the Holy Spirit and empowers them to use their gifts and talents to aid others and even to work with God in the realization of justice and grace in the world is certainly consistent with Christian theology. Paired with appropriate scriptural texts to highlight this important distinction between Christian theology and pop spirituality, *Bruce Almighty* offers interesting possibilities for dialogues about such themes as the place of grace in our lives and the need for us to join with God's work in the world.

PREACHING *BRUCE ALMIGHTY*

Elsewhere I have explored the homiletical possibilities of engaging *Bruce Almighty* in a dialogue with two Scripture readings for the 13th Sunday in Ordinary time, year C, of the Revised Common Lectionary, which deal with Elisha's request for a "double share" of Elijah's spirit (2 Kgs. 2:1–2, 6–14) as well as Paul's discussion of the "fruit of the Spirit" (Gal. 5:1, 13–25).[8] Perhaps had Elisha really understood the "hard thing" that he had asked of Elijah— had he recognized that the "double share" of Elijah's spirit was to enable him to serve the prophets and the people as a "slave" rather than to lord power over them—perhaps then he would not have sought miraculous power to keep his own feet dry as the first proof that his wish had been fulfilled. "By contrast," as Paul wrote, "the fruit of the Spirit is love, joy, peace, patience, kindness, generosity, faithfulness, gentleness, and self-control" (Gal. 5:22). These qualities of life are directed toward the needs of others even as they unmistakably provide benefits for ourselves. We don't really need the ability to invoke miraculous power to deal with the mundane details or common problems we face in our daily lives. What we really need, like Bruce Nolan, is to be in relationships that sustain and nurture us. What we really need is freedom to find ourselves in service to others. God gives us the Spirit not for our own benefit but in order that we might benefit others as agents of divine grace.

The sermon I present here, however, focuses instead on the theme of Bruce's need to begin using the powers God has entrusted to him rather than continuing to "look up" to God to solve all his problems for him. The dialogue was suggested by the similar question raised by the "two men in white robes" who appeared among the apostles at the time of Jesus' ascension in the clouds: "Men of Galilee, why do you stand looking up toward heaven?" (Acts 1:1–11). The sermon acknowledges that the parallels are not perfect. Whereas the film stresses the gifts that God has already given to us, the apostles must wait in Jerusalem until they actually receive "the promise of the Father" as the "power" that will come upon them with the Holy Spirit's arrival. Nevertheless, even here in Acts the emphasis is not on the waiting but on the task that is set before the apostles until that time when Jesus will descend in the clouds. They are to continue and expand Jesus' ministry. Yes, the apostles need to "look up" until the Spirit comes, but they are not to "*keep* looking up" until Jesus himself returns to restore God's reign for them.

As the sermon makes explicit, this dialogue was occasioned not simply by the occurrence of the ascension story in the liturgical calendar. The timing coincided with an important stage in the life of the congregation when it needed to be challenged to move beyond the paralysis of analysis. Like many mainline congregations, it had struggled through years of declining membership and corresponding decline in impact on its community. Although the decline had been halted, there still was not a clear sense of vision regarding the future. From the scriptural text, this congregation needed to recognize that it was still in some ways waiting on the Spirit to bring an empowering vision to drive its work for God. But from the dialogue with the film, the congregation was also helped to recognize that even as the visioning process continued, two things were true: God had already given them gifts and abilities for ministry, and they needed to get on with "being the miracle" rather than sitting back and waiting for God to do all the work in revitalizing the congregation.

Earlier I emphasized the perils of trying to incorporate film clips into preaching, but let me note here that this is the only sermon in this collection (to my recollection, the only one I have ever preached) where I might have been tempted to show a scene if the technological obstacles could have been overcome. This sermon includes the most extensive bit of dialogue that I have ever included, and it might well have worked simply to let people watch the performances by Jim Carrey and Morgan Freeman rather than for me to reconstruct their interchange. However, if I had included the clip, I would have had to increase the proportion of the preaching event devoted to this bit of dialogue beyond the fifty-five seconds it would take to show it.

First, I would have had to expand the introduction of the clip to explain the visual aspects of the scene. Why is God dressed in work clothes and a ball cap? Why are they standing in the midst of a large empty room? Second, because the fifty-five seconds of dialogue is so quick, some people would have a difficult time simply latching on to the new focus of attention unless more of the scene were shown to transition them into it. But where should the clip start, then? The scene itself begins with Bruce's crying out to God and being transported into the warehouse building. Beginning the scene there would add only one-and-a-half minutes to the clip but would introduce many other elements that would need to be explained. Why the reference to the old "Clapper" commercials? What is the "mayhem out there," and why does God respond to Bruce's report of it by telling him he is "right on time" since it is "the seventh at seven"? Why do they both then begin mopping the floor as a solution to the "mayhem"? If you haven't seen the film or don't recall this particular scene and are having difficulty piecing together these brief references, then you are experiencing the same kind of confusion that those in the congregation who might be watching the clip would experience in the midst of the sermon. At this point the necessary setup of the clip introduces elements that are obvious and meaningful in the overall context of the film but nevertheless detract from the purpose for including the bit of dialogue in the sermon. It is tempting just to show the scene rather than orally present the dialogue—the scene is only two-and-a-half minutes long—but the loss of control over the pace of the sermon and the inability to control the points of emphasis may still make it a temptation best avoided.

SERMON: "TIME TO GET ON WITH IT"

(Acts 1:1–11; 1 Pet. 5:6–11)

I am generally not a fan of "divine comedies," even though I am certain God must have a sense of humor (the evidence, as is often said, is too overwhelming). Such films frequently go too far in making God too much like humans (as in George Burns's cigar-smoking portrayals in the *Oh, God!* films), or they are little more than a series of gags where humans play with omnipotence as if it where only a miracle-working toy. The trailers that promoted the film *Bruce Almighty* a couple of years ago seemed to place it firmly in this second camp.

The story is about Bruce Nolan (played by Jim Carrey), a local news reporter for a television station in Buffalo, New York. He is denied a promotion to anchor that he was both certain he deserved and was going to get. He launches into a tirade against God for the lousy job God is doing of taking care of his life and expresses complete confidence that he himself could do God's job better. The next day, he has a meeting with God (played by Morgan Freeman), who bestows the full range of divine powers upon Bruce and promptly leaves on vacation. Upon learning that he has "got the power" of God, Bruce immediately begins to use it in juvenile ways for his personal enjoyment and enrichment, and even for revenge. He parts his bowl of tomato soup in the same way Moses parted the Red Sea, "enhances" the breasts of his girlfriend Grace Connelly (Jennifer Aniston), haltingly runs across Lake Erie, and turns his news anchor rival into a blithering idiot on the air.

Yet even as the movie has great fun with this device, it raises a number of religious and theological issues in generally sensitive and constructive ways. (For instance, when Bruce asks God during one of their check-in sessions how to make someone love him without violating their free will, God responds, "Welcome to my world; let me know when you figure that one out.") Nevertheless, it will come as no surprise that the film did generate some controversy among some religiously conservative viewers, and precisely on this point of the proper uses of God's almighty power. The negative reaction was to a scene where God tells Bruce that the true miracles in the world are not tricks like parting a bowl of soup, but parents who juggle the competing demands of life to find time for their children, and adolescents who make good life choices rather than giving in to negative influences. Instead of expecting everything to be done for them miraculously by God, people need to use the power God has already placed in them.

> **God:**   You want to see a miracle, son? Be the miracle. (*God begins to climb a step ladder through a hole in the ceiling from which shines bright light.*)
>
> **Bruce:**   Wait, are you leaving?
>
> **God:**   Yeah, I see that you can handle things now.
>
> **Bruce:**   But what if I need you? What if I have questions?
>
> **God:**   (*chuckles*) That's your problem, Bruce; that's everybody's problem. You keep looking up.

Some viewers took this scene to mean that God was telling us to forget about prayer and solve our own problems. But the director, Tom Shadyac, pointed out that God began by saying that everyone—not just Bruce Almighty, everyone—has already received power from God. There comes a time when we need to stop just looking up and be the miracle. There comes a time to just get on with it.

It's a line that could have just as easily been delivered by those two men in their white robes standing atop the Mount of Olives. "That's your problem, Peter, James, John, and all the rest of you who have followed Jesus all the way from Galilee; that's everybody's problem. You keep looking up." The disciples and so many others had been following Jesus around for years, waiting for him to "restore the kingdom to Israel." Their hopes had been shattered by his passion and crucifixion far beyond what we from our vantage point looking back across two thousand years of Christian history can possibly imagine, and then—in ways just as beyond our comprehension—resurrected right along with Jesus on Easter morning. So still they looked to Jesus to restore the kingdom, even as he was taken away from their sight in clouds of glory rising to God's heavenly presence. Who knows what thoughts were passing through their minds? Amazement at the spectacle? Disbelief that all they had experienced over their years with Jesus was ending in this way? Disappointment that they would yet still have to wait? But there they stood, gazing up into heaven, until those two men in white reminded them, "That's your problem; that's everybody's problem. You keep looking up."

Just as God reminds Bruce in the film, these guys in white were not saying the disciples now had to sort things out on their own. Jesus himself had just promised them the "power of the Holy Spirit" to enable them. The guys in white had promised them that Jesus would someday return just as bathed in divine glory as they had seen him taken from them. But now was the time to stop just looking up. Now was the time to come down off that hilltop and just get on with it.

For much of the past two years, we here at Northwood Presbyterian Church have devoted much of our time and energy to "looking up." After years of fits-and-starts discussions between trustees, elders on the session, and members of the congregation-at-large about how to prepare our building for its second fifty years of ministry, we "looked up" to an architectural firm to tell us what might be possible given the constraints of engineering and county building codes. When we had received the architect's report, we continued to "look up" by commissioning a consulting firm to do a "financial feasibility study" to advise us on the likelihood of whether we could afford to pay for what was being recommended. When they reported back that there was not a shared vision of ministry, we "looked up" to yet another consultant with expertise in congregational re-visioning—not, mind you, to help us discern that vision, at least not right away, but to tell us what options there might be for going about that process. Now, mind you, there is nothing wrong with us "looking up" to people with special skills to help us with any and all of these things. But the time has come to ask ourselves in all seriousness, Is our problem one of buildings, or finances, or vision? Or is our problem that we just keep looking up? Are we gazing into heaven to avoid getting on with it?

Today, on this Sunday between Ascension Day and Pentecost, we as a church find ourselves in exactly the same place as those disciples on the Mount of Olives. We know it is time to stop just looking up, but we aren't quite in the place to get on with the work of the kingdom in our lives yet either. For those on the Mount of Olives, they still needed to receive the "power of the Holy Spirit," but that wasn't going to happen by standing around gazing into heaven. For us, we do need to find the empowering vision that will give focus to the gifts and callings of God to us as a community of faith, but that isn't going to happen by thinking about process instead of getting on with the process. Between now and Father's Day, we will be conducting a survey and small group meetings to make clear to ourselves as individuals and as a community how God is restoring the kingdom among us. We are going to shape a vision, and we are going to do the things necessary to make it a reality.

Our purpose in all this, in the words of our other Scripture lesson, is to humble ourselves so that God can exalt us (1 Pet. 5:6). We will recognize that we are not weak because the power of God is within us. We will lay aside our anxieties about the future in the faith that God cares for us (1 Pet. 5:7). Having looked up, we will now look ahead and get on with being the miracle.

5

"The Return of the King"

The Lord of the Rings: The Return of the King

I had waited three years to preach in dialogue with this movie. From the press reports about Peter Jackson's efforts to bring J. R. R. Tolkien's epic work to the screen, I knew at the time *The Lord of the Rings: The Fellowship of the Ring* came out in December 2001 that film adaptations of all three books were already in production and would be released in turn each of the following years. The appearance of these films in 2001 was certainly serendipitous, as I will discuss below, so I had made reference to their prominence in American culture in various venues. Nevertheless, I had decided early on not to preach in dialogue with the films until the release of *The Lord of the Rings: The Return of the King*, because I both wanted to treat the story as a whole and appreciated the coincidence of that final film debuting in the liturgical season of Advent.

From the beginning, Jackson's intention was to tell the whole story,[1] and in fact all three films were shot simultaneously. Although the breadth of Tolkien's novel and the length of its cinematic adaptation (over nine hours in the theatrical versions of the movies and just over twelve in the DVD extended editions) precluded a single film, in many ways everyone came to consider them a unified work. One indication of this can be seen in the way the films fared in the Academy Awards. While *Fellowship* received thirteen Oscar nominations and won in four categories,[2] *The Lord of the Rings: The Two Towers* won only two Oscars among its six nominations.[3] *The Return of the King*, however, won eleven Oscars (matching the record set by *Ben-Hur* and *Titanic*), including best picture, best director, and best screenplay adaptation, and it is the only film ever to receive more than ten nominations and sweep the awards in those categories. It doesn't stretch credulity to conclude that those eleven Oscars for *The Return of the King*—and especially the directing and writing awards—were for the film trilogy as a whole.[4]

Jackson's films launched a virtual Tolkien industry (to call it a "cottage industry" in keeping with the standard metaphor is to vastly understate its size). A search of "The Lord of the Rings" in only the book section of Amazon.com in mid-December 2003 when *The Return of the King* was released yielded 1,177 titles.[5] The interest in the films and in the books on which they were based grew consistently over the years as the films came out.[6] For roughly two-and-a-half years, as the films, their home video, and extended DVD special editions were being released, *The Lord of the Rings* was an inescapable presence in American popular culture.

A THEOLOGICAL READING OF *THE LORD OF THE RINGS: THE RETURN OF THE KING*

In part because of Tolkien's own devout Catholicism, a number of writers over the years have explored religious themes within his work. These books range from serious scholarly treatments to popular devotional guides to denunciations of the elements of wizardry and magic in the novels. A recurring debate within some of these books regards which character is the "Christ figure" of the saga. Is it Frodo (Elijah Wood), who carries the "one Ring" to its destruction at great personal cost and suffering? Is it Samwise Gamgee (Sean Astin), who embodies the ideal of servant ministry in his commitment and aid to Frodo during the quest? Or is it Aragorn (Viggo Mortensen)—perhaps the most common choice—who first appears as Strider, the ragged Ranger from the North, but who is revealed to be the long-awaited descendant of Isildur and rightful heir to the throne of Gondor and is crowned near the end of *The Return of the King*? Is it one of these, another, or none?

It is doubtful that Tolkien himself would have supported any of these identifications; indeed, for Tolkien the only real purpose of the novel was its telling:

> As for any inner meaning or "message," it has in the intention of the author none. It is neither allegorical nor topical. As the story grew it put down roots (into the past) and threw out unexpected branches: but its main theme was settled from the outset by the inevitable choice of the Ring as the link between it and *The Hobbit*. [Tolkien proceeds to show how, in his own view, the plot would have had to be quite different if it were, as had often been suggested, an allegory of the Second World War and particularly the threat of atomic and subsequently nuclear weapons.] . . . Other arrangements could be devised according to the tastes or views of those who like allegory or topical reference. But I cordially dislike allegory in all its manifestations, and

always have done so since I grew old and wary enough to detect its presence. I much prefer history, true or feigned, with its varied applicability to the thought and experience of readers. I think that many confuse "applicability" with "allegory"; but the one resides in the freedom of the reader, and the other in the purposed domination of the author.[7]

Out of deference for Tolkien's own "intention" then, what we will be looking for in the cinematic treatment of *The Lord of the Rings* is its theological applicability rather than something as potentially allegorical as deciding which of its characters might be the/a Christ figure.

Moreover, it will be the "cinematic treatment" that will be given precedence in my theological application rather than the novel. In part because Jackson and his collaborators were so intent on being faithful to Tolkien's work, it is possible to cite from the novel dialogue that more fully shows issues that are at work than might be possible drawing only on the more abbreviated dialogue in the films (and frankly, it is also simply easier to cite). But I will not rely on material that Jackson chose to pass over, or for that matter examples of the screenwriters' more extensive uses of artistic license.[8] Thus, as I discussed earlier in the chapter on film interpretation, while I will be applying a kind of redaction criticism in my analysis of *The Lord of the Rings* movies through comparison with the novel from which they were adapted, my purpose is to engage the films in dialogue. After all, while the popularity of the films sparked huge sales of the books, I am confident that many of those books were only partially read by their purchasers just as I am certain more people were exposed to the cultural ripples of the films than actually saw the movies either in theaters or on home video.

The central story of *The Lord of the Rings* both for Tolkien and for Jackson is Frodo's quest to return the "Ring of Power" to the volcanic cauldron from which it was formed in order to destroy it, or perhaps better, to unmake it. As I have already cited, Tolkien himself stated the "main theme was settled from the outset by the inevitable choice of the Ring as the link between it and *The Hobbit*." The "Ring of Power" was, as viewers of the films learn in the opening sequence of *Fellowship* and as the wizard Gandalf (Ian McKellen) explains to the hobbit Frodo Baggins in the same film, one of a number of rings made by Sauron and given to the rulers of men (inclusive language was not a value of Middle-earth), elves, and dwarves. What Sauron did not reveal, however, was that another secret ring had also been forged that was, in the words of its magical inscription that could be revealed only by fire,

One Ring to rule them all, One Ring to find them,
One Ring to bring them all and in the darkness bind them.[9]

The prologue to *Fellowship* states that the Dark Lord Sauron had poured "into this Ring . . . his cruelty, his malice, and his will to dominate all life." In an epic battle, however, Sauron had been defeated when the human prince Isildur cut the Ring from his hand. Isildur might have "destroyed evil forever" by destroying the Ring. Instead he sought to use it to increase his own power, but "the Ring of Power has a will of its own." It escaped Isildur and was lost for two-and-half-thousand years until it was discovered by two hobbits.

The story of the Ring's discovery is dramatized in the prologue to *The Return of the King*. Déagol (Thomas Robins) found it on a river bottom, and his cousin Sméagol (Andy Serkis) asked to receive it from him as a birthday present. When Déagol—already under the corrupting sway of the Ring—refused to give it to him, Sméagol murdered him in order to gain possession of it. But because he obtained it by such an act of violence, it would be more correct to say that the Ring possessed Sméagol. Over the span of another five hundred years, the Ring both extended Sméagol's mortality and sapped away his life and transformed him into the wasted creature Gollum. After all these millennia, the Ring sensed the stirrings of Sauron and abandoned Gollum only to be picked up by Bilbo Baggins (Ian Holm), as recounted in Tolkien's earlier children's novel *The Hobbit*. Although Bilbo had the opportunity to kill Gollum in an act of self-defense after finding the Ring, he instead took pity on the creature and used only the Ring's ability to make the wearer invisible to abet his own escape.

Although the films barely hint at it, Tolkien suggests explicitly in the novel that the difference in their means of acquiring the Ring and their initial actions with it determined Sméagol's and Bilbo's relative fates. Gandalf relates this history of the Ring to Frodo Baggins, Bilbo's nephew, after Bilbo has passed the Ring on to him. Frodo tells Gandalf, "What a pity that Bilbo did not stab that vile creature, when he had a chance!" Gandalf responds,

> Pity? It was Pity that stayed his hand. Pity, and Mercy: not to strike without need. And he has been well rewarded, Frodo. Be sure that he took so little hurt from the evil, and escaped in the end, because he began his ownership of the Ring so. With Pity.[10]

While the films leave aside the role of "pity" in sparing Bilbo some of the ill effects of the Ring, they do use the other aspect that "pity" plays in the continuing dialogue between Frodo and Gandalf.[11] The film version of *The Fellowship of the Ring* emphasizes Gandalf's response to Frodo's statement that Gollum deserves to die:

> Many that live deserve death. And some that die deserve life. Can you give it to them? Then do not be too eager to deal out death in judg-

ment. For even the very wise cannot see all ends. I have not much hope that Gollum can be cured before he dies, but there is a chance of it. . . . My heart tells me that Gollum has some part to play yet, for good or ill, before this is over. The pity of Bilbo may rule the fate of many—yours not least.[12]

As with all good literary foreshadowing, Gandalf speaks more truth than he knows.

Ralph Wood notes that the statement "the pity of Bilbo may rule the fate of many" is the only line to be repeated in all three volumes of *The Lord of the Rings* (it appears only in this scene among the films). More than a point of trivia, however, the declaration is in Wood's view "the leitmotiv of Tolkien's epic, its animating theme, its Christian epicenter as well as its circumference."[13] Inherent in the virtue of pity are also the virtues of mercy and forgiveness, and as Gandalf explains to Frodo, the need for them all is rooted in our own limitedness—both our inability to mete out true justice because of our lack of power and knowledge and our own needs for pity, mercy, and forgiveness from others. As Wood notes, the "pity" that Tolkien has in mind lacks the attitudes of self-superiority and condescension toward others that is a constant nuance of the word in modern English. For Tolkien, the meaning of "pity" is literally rooted in its Latin origins as *pietas* and thus "entails responsibility, duty, devotion, kindness, tenderness, even loyalty." Pity so understood is then at the core of what should bind the Fellowship to one another and at the same time calls on "Frodo to acknowledge his elemental kinship 'with that vile creature'" Gollum.[14]

The pity then that spares Bilbo and Frodo (if not finally Gollum, as we shall see) is the antithesis of the will to power and domination. The Ring is the very embodiment of that will to power, and *The Lord of the Rings* is a kind of epic demonstration of the dictum of the British historian Lord Acton: "Power tends to corrupt, and absolute power corrupts absolutely."[15] The first film of the trilogy is framed by Frodo's two attempts to free himself of the Ring's evil influence. Frodo offers the Ring first to Gandalf out of fear and second to Aragorn as something of a test.[16] Gandalf insistently responds to the offer of the Ring, "Don't tempt me, Frodo! I dare not take it. Not even to keep it safe. Understand Frodo, I would use this Ring from a desire to do good. But through me, it would wield a power too great and terrible to imagine." Good for others cannot be obtained by domination over them. When Bilbo later offers the Ring to Aragorn with the question "Would you destroy it?" he replies, "I would have gone with you to the end." Aragorn's responsibility is to the oath he has made to protect Frodo, and he will not use the Ring's power even to that end.

The reason for Frodo's question of Aragorn is that he had just been forced to flee from another member of the Fellowship, Boromir (Sean Bean), son of the steward of Gondor, who has raised the possibility of using the Ring against Sauron. Although the film dialogue is much more veiled than the extended discussion between Boromir and Frodo in the novel,[17] it nevertheless makes clear that Boromir has determined the Ring should at least first be used to defeat Sauron. Frodo, however, remains committed to the belief that the decision of the Council of Elrond to unmake the Ring is the only course of action. When Boromir then tries to take the Ring from Frodo, he is forced to use the Ring to make himself invisible in order to escape. Boromir's rejection of "pity" for even Sauron, his desire to turn Sauron's own destructive power in the Ring against him, shatters the Fellowship and forces Frodo to continue his quest with only Samwise Gamgee from among its members to accompany him. Boromir does come to recognize the terrible thing he has done and engages in a fierce defense against a cohort of Orcs in an effort to protect the hobbits Merry (Dominic Monaghan) and Pippin (Billy Boyd). As he lies mortally wounded, he asks Aragorn for forgiveness for his failure. Aragorn extends true pity, telling Boromir he has fought bravely and kept his honor. Aragorn asserts his commitment to the defense of Gondor and "our people," and with his dying breath Boromir gives allegiance to Aragorn as his king. Through mercy and forgiveness the solidarity of the Fellowship is restored.[18]

It may seem that Aragorn's role as a leader in the epic battle at Helm's Deep, his rallying of the Rohirrim to the defense of Minas Tirith, his leading the army of the Dead from Dwimorberg in the battle of the Pelennor Fields, and ultimately his attack on the Black Gate of Mordor itself, all indicate that Aragorn ultimately came to share Boromir's fateful conclusion that the only way to defeat Sauron was to destroy his Orc armies by the same violent means Sauron had turned against the Free Peoples of the West. Yet at least for Aragorn, the battles at Helm's Deep and Minas Tirith are defenses of cities under siege. As is clear from the debate at Minas Tirith following the battle of the Pelennor Fields in *The Return of the King*, Aragorn undertook the attack on the Black Gate not out of any hope of defeating Sauron there but only to provide a diversion of his attention that might yet allow Frodo and Samwise not only to complete their quest but to survive.[19] Aragorn's true commitments are demonstrated by his response to the dwarf Gimli's (John Rhys-Davies) statement that the Fellowship had failed in the wake of Boromir's actions at Parth Galen: "Not if we hold true to each other." They will not give up hope for Merry and Pippin but rather do all they can to rescue them from their captors. Pity, mercy, love—these are the virtues that bind together the Fellowship and properly determine its actions. To be sure, neither Tolkien's novel nor Jackson's films are pacifist manifestos (Aragorn's final line to Gimli in this scene is "Let us hunt some Orc"), but they are just as surely not defenses of "Might makes right."

It is through other acts of pity, however, that the "fate of many" is finally determined. Having early on wished that Bilbo had killed Gollum when he had the chance, Frodo's attitude toward Sméagol/Gollum is changed by his experience of bearing the Ring and of actually seeing the effects it has had on Sméagol. Gollum attacks Frodo and Samwise in an early scene from *The Two Towers*.[20] They manage to subdue him and lead him off on a leash of elven rope. But Samwise becomes concerned that his howls of protest will alert the Orcs to their presence and so suggests that they simply bind him and leave him to die. "Maybe he does deserve to die," Frodo says. "But now that I see him, I do pity him." Frodo binds Gollum with a promise sworn on the Ring itself ("the Precious" as Gollum refers to it) not only not to harm them but to assist them by leading the way to Mordor. Through much of *The Two Towers* Sméagol seems to be reemerging from the control of his Gollum side because of Frodo's mercy toward him. At one point Sméagol even banishes Gollum from him because "Master [as he calls Frodo because he bears the Ring] looks after us now." But by the opening of *The Return of the King*[21] the Gollum side has reasserted itself and persuaded Sméagol to assist in setting a trap for Frodo in an effort to regain possession of the Ring. Yet even as Samwise points out the mounting treachery to him, Frodo refuses to withdraw his mercy and pity from Gollum.

So it is that Gollum still survives to attack Frodo and Samwise once more on the very slopes of Mount Doom.[22] Samwise wounds Gollum with his sword and then follows Frodo into the volcano through a crack in its side. There Samwise pleads with Frodo to cast the Ring into the lava below, but Frodo's will to destroy the Ring has succumbed to its will to survive. He slips it onto his finger and disappears just as Gollum slips up behind Samwise and knocks him unconscious with a rock. Gollum locates Frodo through his tracks in the dust and leaps on him to wrestle the Ring away. He finally gains possession of it by biting off the finger on which Frodo was wearing it. Gollum begins to dance around in joy and delight. At this point the novel and films part company slightly. In the novel, Gollum loses his balance and falls into the abyss, where he and the Ring are consumed. In the end, the Ring is not destroyed by an act of will but simply unmade in the fires from which it was forged. Once more out on the slopes, Frodo says to Samwise, "But do you remember Gandalf's words: *Even Gollum may have something yet to do?* But for him, Sam, I could not have destroyed the Ring. The Quest would have been in vain, even at the bitter end. So let us forgive him! For the Quest is achieved, and now all is over."[23] Pity, mercy, and forgiveness in the end "rule the fate of many"—not power or violence.

Jackson felt that having Frodo stand almost passively by as Gollum accidentally falls to his death was too anticlimactic; he and his cowriters, however, realized that it went against the whole thrust of Tolkien's novel to have Frodo suddenly turn on Gollum and actively murder him in an effort finally to destroy the Ring. They wrote into the screenplay a renewed struggle between Gollum and Frodo for possession of the Ring that ends in both falling from the ledge. Frodo is able to catch himself on the rocks but must be persuaded by Samwise not to let go and follow Gollum into the abyss. For the filmmakers, it was important to show Frodo choosing hope, choosing mercy for himself after all that he had suffered from the Ring, by taking Samwise's hand and being pulled back from the brink.[24]

Both Tolkien and Jackson weave two important themes together around Frodo's quest to destroy the Ring of Power. The first of those themes is that good ends and intentions can never redeem evil means. Not even Gandalf or Aragorn could have harnessed the Ring's power so as to use it against Sauron, and it is Frodo's commitment not to use its power against others that makes it possible for him to bear it back to Mordor, where it was unmade. The second theme provides the basis for the first: pity, mercy, forgiveness—these are the powers that truly have the ability to remake the world.

Maybe it wasn't just a naïve desire for allegory that led some of Tolkien's first readers to find connections between the War of the Ring in Middle-earth and Earth's atomic war in the middle of the twentieth century. Maybe it was a genuine recognition of the need to forswear the use of ever-greater violence to bring an end to violent evil and instead remake the world through pity, mercy, and forgiveness of others. Maybe it was something more than just serendipity that Jackson's films debuted only months after the terrorist attacks of September 11, 2001. But as history has borne out—not in this instance feigned history but real history—since both these tellings of the story of the Ring, the literary and cinematic achievements of Tolkien and Jackson have been much appreciated even as these central themes of their work have yet to be applied.

PREACHING *THE LORD OF THE RINGS: THE RETURN OF THE KING*

Elsewhere I have explored the homiletical possibilities for bringing the story of the expectations regarding the return of the king of Gondor from the ancient line of Isildur into dialogue with the story of Jesus' arrival in Jerusalem, amid expectations for the return of a king of the Jews from the ancient line of David.[25] The scriptural partner to the dialogue was the Passion Sunday reading from the Gospel of Luke from Year C in the Revised Common Lectionary. One of the distinctive features of Luke's passion narrative among the Synoptic evangelists is its particular interest in the charge that Jesus was guilty of insurrection because of claims that he was "a king" (e.g., see Luke 23:2). Luke wants to show that Jesus is innocent of the charge of insurrection because even if he is in some sense "a king," he is not a king after the pattern of the Caesars, or even Herod for that matter.

What Luke seems to be particularly reacting against is a desire to see good triumph over evil by actively destroying it. This longing was an impulse rooted deep within both the Jewish people, who felt oppressed by Rome in the first century, and even by the Romans themselves, although obviously in opposing ways. For the Jewish nationalists in Roman Palestine, Caesar and his imperial legions were just as much the embodiment of evil as Sauron and his Orc armies were to the people of Middle-earth. Some longed for a king who would come backed by divine power, who would be able to defeat Rome on its own military terms and establish a just political realm. Although not seeing itself as evil, Rome nevertheless would have conceded that it enforced the *Pax Romana*, the "Roman Peace," at the tip of a sword. Any claimants to the throne that threatened that peace were to be crushed by overwhelming power. However each side identified evil, both agreed it had to be destroyed.

What makes Jesus the divine king is precisely his rejection of this destructive path to overcoming evil, and it is also what so confounds Pilate's ability to recognize any kingship within him. For Rome, power could be used to build, but, ultimately, power was the ability to destroy one's enemies. For Jesus, power resides in the ability to be a servant for others—even at the cost of personal suffering to the point of death—because it is by such acts that God is glorified and the world is redeemed. Evil is undone rather than destroyed when Jesus acts with mercy toward those corrupted by evil, even as they turn its destructive force against him. Aragorn is most like Christ the King not because of his success in the battles at Helm's Deep and the Pelennor Fields but because he is willing to risk almost certain death at the Black Gates of Mordor if it will provide opportunity for Frodo to complete his quest and free the peoples of Middle-earth from the evil shadow of Sauron that is cast over them.

The sermon I present here, however, is the one I preached just days before *The Lord of the Rings: The Return of the King* opened in December 2003. As I mention in the sermon's introduction, my son and I were fortunate to obtain tickets to the East Coast premiere of the movie at the American Film Institute's Silver Theater in Silver Spring, Maryland. The scriptural texts are the Old Testament and Gospel lessons appointed for the Third Sunday of Advent in Year C (Zeph. 3:14–20; Luke 3:7–18). The first lesson features prominently the imagery of the king's presence as dispelling fear and God's presence as "a warrior who gives victory." While the Gospel lesson lacks any specifically royal imagery, it does present some of the fiery rhetoric of judgment often associated with John the Baptizer's preaching and anticipates a coming Messiah who will "clear his threshing floor, . . . gather the wheat . . . , [and] the chaff he will burn with unquenchable fire" (Luke 3:17).

My concern in this sermon, preached just over two years after the September 11 attacks and not yet a year into the Iraq war, was that both culturally and within my congregation there had been a resignation (to put it most generously) to the notion that an increasingly violent world was calling for an ever-increasingly violent response. Even as we decried the violent rhetoric and acts of Islamic jihadis, we were far too often calling on the language of divine wrath and judgment from our own religious traditions to support our resorting to military responses to intractable problems. Even in the cultural appropriation of Jackson's film adaptation of *The Lord of the Rings*, there was far more attention being given to its epic battles cast as "good versus evil" than to those aspects of the story that warned against the real danger of being corrupted by the very evil you sought to destroy if you succumbed to using its own means.

By setting this film in dialogue with these scriptural texts, I hoped to be able to bring to the fore aspects of each of them that tended to be obscured by their most prominent and graphic images. I hoped to show that both in Middle-earth and our modern world what we really long for is the *end* of evil, and that that end might best be achieved by means other than engaging it in violent conflict to see which side is capable of destroying the other. The message of Jesus' first advent, which we recall even as we anticipate his second advent in each liturgical Advent season, is that God's means to ending evil and remaking the world is through a transformation set in motion by pity, mercy, and forgiveness. It may be that "judgment will be without mercy to anyone who has shown no mercy," but it is even more fundamentally true that "mercy triumphs over judgment" (Jas. 2:13).

SERMON: "THE RETURN OF THE KING"

(Zeph. 3:14–20; Luke 3:7–18)

The anticipation and excitement has been building for weeks, and with the increasing number of reminders in the culture all around us, it is reaching a fever pitch. Millions of people around the world simply can't wait to get a peek at what has been carefully wrapped up for them. And while for most people the unveiling is now just days away, for Eric and me Christmas came early. You see, thanks to a tip from a member of this congregation, we were able to see *The Lord of the Rings: The Return of the King* at its East Coast premiere on December 4. For millions of other dedicated fans of this trilogy, Christmas arrives this Wednesday.

If you loved the tremendous battle scenes of *The Two Towers,* then you will be totally awed by *The Return of the King.* If you preferred the more intimate battles within and among the members of "the Fellowship of the Ring" in the wonderful character treatments of the first film in the series, then you will be completely engrossed by this final installment. Director Peter Jackson has definitely saved the best for last in his stunning cinematic achievement. And if you concur with the view that Tolkien's purpose in writing the Middle-earth saga was to create a mythology for England to guide it through the Second World War and the Cold War that followed in its aftermath, then you will agree that Jackson has crafted the definitive version of that mythology for the global media cultures that now find themselves enmeshed in a "war against terrorism."

I doubt that Jackson was any more sufficiently clairvoyant to have had that as his purpose when he began work on the films years ago than Tolkien was able to foresee the dread horrors of a nuclear age, poised on the knife's-edge balance of a doctrine of "mutually assured destruction," when the seed of his novels germinated in the sentence he scribbled on an exam book in 1930 or 1931: "In a hole in the ground there lived a hobbit." But sometimes we achieve more than we intend. And therein lies both the promise and, frankly, the peril of the *Lord of the Rings* films at this cultural moment.

In adapting almost 1,200 pages of novels to more than twelve hours of film (as the extended versions will run on the special-edition DVDs), some things must necessarily be left aside. Jackson's films have remained very faithful to Tolkien's novels, but his selections of what to emphasize by what he omits have slightly shifted the center of gravity of the work. At the heart of this mythology, both on the page and on film, is the absolute conviction that one cannot destroy the destructive power of evil by turning its own destructive means against it. The evil power of the "one Ring" to destroy all others must literally be unmade in order to be undone. To do otherwise would be to fall under its corrupting power. Even the great wizard Gandalf knows that any attempts he might make to use the Ring's power against its evil maker, Sauron, would only serve to unleash more of its destructiveness on Middle-earth. That is why Frodo embarks on the quest to unmake the Ring by casting it back into the volcanic abyss in Mordor, where it was forged.

But this is no pacifist manifesto. The quest to bring the "one Ring" to Mount Doom in Mordor only succeeds because of the "return of the king" of Gondor, the unlikely Ranger Strider who is revealed to be Aragorn, the heir to the throne. Aragorn wages and wins battles against the forces of the Dark Lord Sauron to provide the time and cover that Frodo needs to bring the Ring to the place where it was made. It is these battles, and Frodo's own battles to reach his goal, that Jackson uses to provide the energy of the films. The desire to see good triumph over evil in precisely these ways is an impulse that lies deep within us.

It is the same impulse that we have seen in our Scripture lessons this morning. The prophet Zephaniah looked forward to a day when God would be "a warrior who gives victory" by destroying Judah's enemies. John the Baptizer spoke about the coming of God's wrath and warned, "Even now the ax is lying at the root of the trees" to cut down and destroy evil, to winnow the wheat from the chaff that the latter might be "burn[ed] with unquenchable fire." Those who have suffered from evil in every way imaginable—emotionally, socially, physically even to the point of death—delight in the prospects of the tables being turned, of exacting retribution in the form of vengeance, even the divine wrath that is God's vengeance.

But to celebrate such destruction of evil, to delight in the turning of its own destructive means against it, is to risk corruption by the very evil we seek to destroy. The most powerful symbol of this corrupting power in *The Lord of the Rings* is the character Gollum. In actions and monstrous appearance, he is the very embodiment of the duplicitous destructiveness of evil. But Gollum had begun life as Sméagol, a hobbit like Frodo himself, and had been brought to such wretchedness by centuries of possessing the "one Ring." Frodo's uncle, Bilbo Baggins, had had opportunity to kill Gollum in the prequel novel, *The Hobbit,* but had instead taken pity on him and allowed him to live. In an exchange key to the story, Frodo tells Gandalf near the beginning of the quest that he wished Bilbo had killed Gollum. But Gandalf replies, "The pity of Bilbo may rule the fate of many."[26]

As Ralph Wood in his fine book *The Gospel According to Tolkien* notes, " 'The pity of Bilbo may rule the fate of many' is the only declaration to be repeated in all three volumes of *The Lord of the Rings*. It is indeed the leitmotiv of Tolkien's epic" (150). And in a way that I will not reveal to those of you who have yet to read the novels or see the final film, it is the "pity of Bilbo"—the fact that Gollum still lives—that literally determines the fate of the quest. In the end, evil is vanquished not because the life of an evil one was taken by a heroic returning king but because an evil life was spared by an act of pity.

The hope for Middle-earth and for our Earth lies ultimately not in destroying evil but in undoing it by acts of mercy for those who have been evil's victims and corrupted by its powers. That is the lesson of Tolkien's novels when the stress isn't placed on the battles, and it is the lesson of our Scripture lessons when we do not likewise misplace the stress. Zephaniah's oracle says far more about God's grace and mercy for Judah than about God's wrath against her enemies. John's message was primarily a call to repentance that spoke of the surety of judgment to encourage that repentance rather than to delight in vengeance. Once again in the words of Ralph Wood, "While revenge curdles the soul and paralyzes the will, pity frees those who will receive it. Repentance does not produce forgiveness, Tolkien shows, but rather the other way around: mercy enables contrition" (153).

God's plan for the redemption of the world depends not on the divine ability to crush and destroy evil but on divine pity, mercy, and forgiveness for those who have been crushed and almost destroyed by evil. That is the message of the first advent of God in the birth of Jesus Christ two millennia ago in Bethlehem, and it is the hope of the world in anticipation of the second advent of God in the return of Christ the King. That is also the deep truth that we and all the world need to hear if we are to prevail in a "war against terrorism" rather than be corrupted by it.

6

Dialogues with Two Superheroes

Spider-Man and Superman Returns

The phenomenal box office success of *Spider-Man*[1] sparked a number of movies based on Marvel and DC Comics superhero characters. In some ways the trend was started by the 2000 release of *X-Men* (like *Spider-Man* it was based on Marvel Comics characters created by Stan Lee), but since the 2002 release of *Spider-Man* there have been nine other movies based on comic-book heroes—including the return from film retirement, as it were, of the DC Comics heroes Batman and Superman.[2] Additionally there have been several films about young superheroes in-the-making, including the highly successful Pixar film *The Incredibles* (2004) and *Sky High* (2005). One line in that last film underscored the cultural staying power of superheroes in American culture, even as it perhaps also shone the spotlight on generational differences. Lynda Carter played the role of Principal Powers in the movie about the high school children of super-heroes who were negotiating adolescence while waiting to see what, if any, superpowers they might have inherited. At one point Carter's character quips about the limits of what a school administrator might accomplish by saying, "I'm not Wonder Woman you know"; the parents in the audience of which I was a part all roared at the inside-reference to Carter's role on the 1970s television series, while our children gave us blank stares about what was so funny.

Superheroes are in many instances iconic figures in American popular cul-ture. Often they embody key societal values or aspirations, such as the associa-tion of Superman with "truth, justice, and the American way." But one very interesting aspect of many manifestations of superheroes in films at the turn of the twenty-first century has been their introspection and inner struggles. This self-analysis is particularly true of regular persons who gain superhero status or powers, such as Batman and Spider-Man, but is increasingly found among those who are themselves not human, like Superman. Although the desire to be more than we are—to be "supers" in the shorthand expression of *The Incredibles*—has always been part of the allure of these stories, there is also something of the postmodern deconstructionist turn evident in the exploration of the possible downsides to being so different. In what ways would even the abilities to do so much good for others still alienate one from one's community? Would it even be worth the effort to use these powers given the potential backlash?

Certainly this theme figures prominently in the character development of Peter Parker in the *Spider-Man* films. But it was reinforced for me when, at about the same time as I saw *Spider-Man*, I heard a song on the radio by John Ondrasik entitled "Superman (It's Not Easy)." The song lyrics mused about even the Man of Steel's struggles to meet the expectations of those on his adopted planet with regard to being a superhero.[3] Consequently I had already brought Spider-Man and Superman into dialogue with one another theologically when I appropriated *Spider-Man* homiletically back in 2002. Having dealt more directly with Superman after the release of *Superman Returns* in 2006, it seemed appropriate to continue that dialogue here.

A THEOLOGICAL READING OF *SPIDER-MAN* AND *SUPERMAN RETURNS*

The central theme of the movie *Spider-Man* is expressed in Peter Parker's (Tobey Maguire) final voice-over at the conclusion of the film:

> Whatever life holds in store for me I will never forget these words: "With great power comes great responsibility." This is my gift. My curse. Who am I? I'm Spider-Man.

The guiding words referenced in this conclusion had been spoken to Peter by his Uncle Ben Parker (Cliff Robertson), thinking that they were advice to guide his nephew in the normal passage from adolescence into adulthood. They are repeated at several points throughout the film as Peter is coming to terms with the changes that are happening to him. But of course those changes are hardly the usual physical and psychological developments of late adolescence, so the power for which Uncle Ben was asking Peter to assume responsibility is far greater than he realized.

During a high school field trip to a laboratory involved in research on spiders, Peter is bitten by a genetically manipulated superspider. By the time he reaches home that evening, he is not feeling well and so heads straight up to bed. He doesn't quite make it, and as he sleeps through the night on his floor, the DNA in the spider's venom begins to replace genetic sequences in his own

DNA. He awakes the next morning to find his eyesight has greatly improved; his muscular development is enhanced to the point that he has the same relative strength-to-size ratio as a spider; his reflexes are as quick as a spider's; and he has developed a spider's abilities to climb walls and spin webs.

Peter initially develops the persona of Spider-Man in order to enter an open-call wrestling match in hopes of winning $3,000 to buy a car that might impress his neighbor and classmate Mary Jane Watson (Kirsten Dunst). Because he knocks out his opponent in only two minutes rather than staying in the ring with him for three minutes as called for in the ad, he is paid only $100. He objects that he needs all the money promised, and the promoter responds, "I missed the part where that's my problem." As Peter leaves, another man passes him in the doorway to the office and proceeds to steal the gate receipts at gunpoint. The robber flees down the hallway and escapes via the elevator that has just opened before Peter. When the promoter asks Peter why he didn't stop the robber from getting away with the money, Peter throws his words back in his face: "I missed the part where that's my problem." He soon learns that it was indeed his problem. Outside he finds that his uncle has been fatally shot by the robber in a carjacking to obtain a getaway vehicle. Using his spider powers, Peter tracks down and confronts the robber, who dies in their ensuing altercation.

Recalling his uncle's words to him in their final conversation before his death, Peter decides to assume the responsibilities he believes are incumbent in his new powers. Spider-Man is transformed from wrestling persona to crime-fighting vigilante. Following graduation, he moves into a Manhattan loft with his closest friend from high school, Harry Osborn (James Franco). But the constant interruptions of dealing with common criminals make it impossible for him to keep his job as a lab assistant. He begins to rig his camera to take photos of Spider-Man in action that he then freelances to the *Daily Bugle*, not only to make some much-needed cash but perhaps to shape the public's perception of Spider-Man, which is decidedly mixed. To some he is a hero; others, like J. Jonah Jameson (J. K. Simmons), the editor of the *Bugle*, speculate that Spider-Man may be causing the crises to which he then comes to the rescue and wonder why he hides behind a mask.

Eventually Spider-Man's chief nemesis becomes the Green Goblin. Unbeknownst to Peter, the Goblin is actually Norman Osborn (Willem Dafoe), who has likewise been changed by an experiment gone horribly awry that gives him extraordinary strength but also creates this violent alternate personality. The Goblin tries to use the public's mixed attitudes toward its heroes to convince Spider-Man to join with him. The very public that cheers his exploits, the Goblin tells him, will eventually turn against him and cheer his demise. What is the point, then, in trying to help them? Yet even though the Goblin proves correct about the public's growing opposition to Spider-Man (the banner headlines on the *Bugle* the next morning read, "Spider-Man, Green Goblin Terrorize *Bugle*" and "Wanted! Citizens Call for Wall-Crawler's Arrest"), Peter remains committed to fulfilling the "great responsibility" to use his "great power" to aid others.

The particulars of the climactic conflict between Spider-Man and the Green Goblin do not need to be revealed here since they do not bear directly on the specific theme that concerns us. That theme is the way in which Peter's assuming the responsibilities that come with his new powers parallel in kind (while obviously differing in degree) those that everyone must face. The film makes this parallel explicit by the context in which Uncle Ben gave that pivotal advice to Peter:

> **Uncle Ben:** Pete, look, you're changing. I know. I went through exactly the same thing when I was your age.
>
> **Peter:** No. Not exactly.
>
> **Uncle Ben:** Peter, these are the years when a man changes into the man he's gonna become the rest of his life. Just be careful who you change into. . . . Remember, with great power comes great responsibility.

Peter's struggles to come of age not only as a man but as a superhero simply make more obvious the core struggles that everyone faces. In passing from adolescence into maturity, we are all Peter Parkers working out what it means to be Spider-Man.

In one of the great lines of the movie, Peter's Aunt May (Rosemary Harris), unaware that he is also Spider-Man, cautions him against spreading himself too thin between work, college, and family responsibilities, saying, "You're not Superman, you know." The line is not just comically ironic; it captures a core element of the Spider-Man myth. Unlike a superhero who hails from another planet whom we can never aspire to be, Spider-Man could potentially be anyone of us if we should happen to be bitten by that genetically manipulated spider. Being Superman, of course, is another story.

From its very beginnings, people have noted parallels between the Superman myth and Christian beliefs about Jesus.[4] Although in physical appearance Superman is entirely human, as with the incarnated Jesus, his humanity does not tell the whole story about who Kal-El (Superman's Kryptonian name) really is. In words resurrected from the first of the Superman movies[5] to promote *Superman Returns*[6]—words with clear echoes of John 3:16—his father, Jor-El (Marlon Brando), tells him that he is being sent as his "only son" so that he might provide humanity the one thing it lacks to be a great people: "the light to show the way." Kal-El's earthly parents, are named Jonathan and Martha Kent, their first initials matching those of Jesus' earthly parents,

Joseph and Mary. But perhaps no film version of the Superman story goes as far in drawing parallels with Jesus than *Superman Returns*, beginning with the clear allusion to Christ's Second Coming in the title. Imagery within both the film and its promotional materials evoke portrayals of both Jesus' crucifixion and his ascension into heaven in the Western artistic tradition. Superman is mortally wounded by a kryptonite shard thrust in his side, recalling one of the wounds of Jesus' passion. And not only is Superman resurrected following his death, but his suddenly empty hospital room is discovered by a female nurse in just the way that it was women who discovered Jesus' grave clothes left behind in an empty tomb. In the movie's closing shot, Superman is seen flying high above the Earth's atmosphere, looking down upon Earth and promising to be there always (compare Matt. 28:20b).

The premise of *Superman Returns* is that Superman (Brandon Routh) had left earth to confirm that his home planet of Krypton had actually been destroyed after he had been sent away by his parents. Five years later he returns to Earth and discovers that much has reverted back to the way it was before. Lex Luthor (Kevin Spacey) has been released from incarceration because Superman had not been available to testify against him at trial. In the first film Luthor tried to create new coastal real estate by separating California from the continental United States by triggering massive earthquakes along the San Andreas fault with nuclear weapons. Luthor this time wants to use kryptonite crystals to generate a whole new continent that in the process will inundate much of the eastern seaboard. (When Lois Lane [Kate Bosworth] is told of his plan, she exclaims, "But millions of people will die!" to which Luthor responds, "Billions! Once again, the press underestimates me").

Perhaps the biggest change that confronts Clark Kent back at work at the *Daily Planet* is that Lois Lane is now involved in a relationship with the son of its editor, and they are together raising her son, Jason (Tristan Lake Leabu). She has even written an award-winning article titled "Why the World Doesn't Need Superman." In an interview Superman grants to Lois after his return, they have the following exchange:

Superman: I read the article, Lois.

Lois Lane: Yeah, so did a lot of people. Tomorrow night, they're giving me the Pulitzer . . .

Superman: Why did you write it?

Lois Lane: How could you leave us like that? I moved on. So did the rest of us. That's why I wrote it. The world doesn't need a savior. And neither do I. . . .

Superman: Listen. What do you hear?

Lois Lane: Nothing.

Superman: I hear everything. You wrote that the world doesn't need a savior, but every day I hear people crying for one.

Yet even if the world is crying for a savior, the question remains, What kind of savior does it need?

Although viewers of the film are never provided more insight into the contents of Lois Lane's argument than what is revealed by this exchange, it would seem that her definition of the "savior" that the world does *not* need is one that cannot be counted on always to be present and to right every wrong. But it was just such a role that Jor-El had warned his son against in a scene from the extended version of the first movie. After his Superman persona had become public, Jor-El gave his son two reasons why he must continue to hide behind his Clark Kent identity:

Jor-El: First: You cannot serve humanity twenty-eight hours a day.

Superman: Twenty-four.

Jor-El: Or twenty-four, as it is in Earth time. Your help would be called for endlessly, even for those tasks that human beings could solve themselves. 'Tis their habit to abuse their resources in such a way.

Superman: And secondly?

Jor-El: Second: Your enemies would discover their only way to hurt you, by hurting the people you care for.[7]

What the world needs, then, is not *a* savior, *one* single person to solve all our problems. What the world needs are those who recognize the powers that they have as well as the limits of and the responsibilities inherent in those powers. In the end, not even Superman can be the Superman of our highest dreams and deepest desires. But he can always be there to embody our noblest ideals and to inspire us to work for truth and justice.

PREACHING *SPIDER-MAN*

By a coincidence of the calendar in 2002, it happened that the date designated in the bylaws for the election of church officers fell on Pentecost Sunday. For that reason I had decided to focus my preaching that particular year on the Old Testament lesson appointed for Pentecost in Year A that relates the story from

Num. 11:24–30 about God transferring "some of the spirit that was on" Moses to the seventy elders who were to assist him in overseeing the Israelites during their wilderness wanderings. Two aspects of the story stood out in my mind. First, while all the elders who were present began to prophesy when the spirit was transferred to them, the text emphatically states, "But they did not do so again" (Num. 11:25b). Second was the mention of the two elders who were elsewhere in the camp but nevertheless began to prophesy as well—and who continued to prophesy even after the other sixty-eight had stopped, prompting even Joshua to ask Moses to intervene to make them cease and desist (Num. 11:26–28). My interest was less with the internecine sniping that was apparently going on among the leadership (although what pastor isn't aware of that dynamic?), but rather with Moses' recognition that there were *only* two enthusiastic elders: "Would that all the LORD's people were prophets, and that the LORD would put his spirit on them!" (Num. 11:29b).

In the context of Pentecost Sunday and in light of the Gospel lesson from John 20:19–23, I wanted to point out that indeed Moses' wish had been fulfilled—or at least the second half had: God has put the divine Spirit within all God's people. The issue, then, wasn't just whether all those who would be elected that day would continue to draw on God's Spirit in fulfilling their tasks but whether all the people of the congregation would accept and fulfill their prophetic tasks with enthusiasm.

With that preparation mulling in the back of my mind, I took an evening to see *Spider-Man* with my family and quite unexpectedly found those same themes at play in the movie. Having received the Spirit in baptism, all of us within the church have "great power" and with it "great responsibilities." God doesn't expect any of us—not Moses, Joshua, the elders, or the people—to be Supermen or Superwomen, but we *are* expected to take responsibility to use what God has given us. We can't be looking to the pastors alone or even to the elected leadership with them to be our "saviors." We are all Spirit-Persons, empowered to be prophets.

SERMON ONE: "SPIRIT-PERSON"[8]

(Num. 11:24–30; John 20:19–23)

Who could have imagined that the biggest hit movie—not just of the still-young, summer movie season, but of all time—would be *Spider-Man*? In just nine days, this cinematic comic book generated more than $200 million in ticket sales, beating out last fall's mega-hit *Harry Potter and the Sorcerer's Stone* and setting such a blistering pace that not even this week's *Star Wars: Attack of the Clones* is likely to match it.

If you happen to be among the half-dozen or so Americans who have yet to see *Spider-Man,* then I should tell you that the story is about a geekish high school senior named Peter Parker. During a field trip to the arachnid study center at Columbia University, Peter is bitten by a genetically engineered superspider. He awakens the next morning to discover that his own DNA has been altered as a result. Suddenly he has the relative strength of a spider, the ability to climb walls like a spider, even the ability to spin webs and use them as a means to swing from place to place with incredible speed (after some practice, of course). It is not giving away too much of the story to tell you that he ultimately decides to use his new abilities to combat an evil villain. I can't resist, however, giving away the best line in the movie. Peter has kept his second identity secret from everyone, including the aunt he lives with. One day Aunt May is concerned that Peter is wearing himself out from all his mysterious running about, so she asks him to slow down, saying, "You're not Superman, you know."

The reason I can't resist giving away that line is not just because it is funny in a very ironic way. That Spider-Man is not Superman is in fact the whole point of the Spider-Man story. Superman was, as any comics afficionado can tell you, not really a "man" at all. He was an alien from the planet Krypton, whose parents sent him while still an infant to planet Earth to save him from the imminent destruction of his home world. As much as the stories of Superman's exploits might thrill us, even within their own narrative logic none of us could ever hope to be Superman. But Peter Parker, on the other hand, is the modern teenage "Everyman." Sure it is fantasy, and one shouldn't consider too closely its shaky scientific underpinnings. But within its narrative logic we can all long to be Spider-Man by virtue of an accidental bite from a genetically engineered superspider.

Who has never daydreamed about what it would be like to have superhuman powers? Probably all modern teenagers (and most of us who are adults!) have wished at one time or another for more powers or abilities to meet the challenges that confront us. If only I were Superman, or Spider-Man, or Wonder Woman, then all my problems would be solved. Yet I have been struck that at the very time *Spider-Man* has been dominating the box office, a song titled "Superman" has been climbing the charts. That song, however, takes a rather unconventional view of the "Man of Steel." In its words, we hear Superman himself admit that he hates flying and harbors no illusions about the limits of what superheroes can accomplish. We may all wish we had superpowers that could make all our problems go away, but Superman's refrain is, "It's not easy to be me."[9]

Surely one of the superheroes of faith was Moses. Yet in the background to our Old Testament lesson for this morning we find him on the verge of nervous breakdown. Early on in his leadership of the Israelites in the wilderness, his father-in-law Jethro had warned him that if he kept trying to do everything himself he would wear himself out (Exod. 18:13–27). Aunt May's words echo back across time: "Moses, you're not Superman." Somewhere in the wilderness he seems to have abandoned the assistants Jethro had encouraged upon him, so that here we find him saying to God, "It's not easy to be me." God responds by telling him to choose seventy elders, and then God's spirit descends upon them and gives them the power to prophesy—to look upon the world and see it as God sees it.

Somehow these elders seem to have concluded that this was to be a one-time experience, one amazing swing high above the mundane to change their perspective. Two of them, however, refused to relinquish their new-found powers of spiritual perception. Eldad and Medad had been transformed in their very being by the encounter with God's spirit, and they just kept right on prophesying, right on speaking God's word to the situation around them. Yet as Spider-Man learned, people can become uneasy and frightened even by those who do good with unusual power. So it was that even Joshua demands, "Moses, stop them!" Thankfully, Moses has by now learned his lesson. He is not Superman, and he needs all the Spider-Men—ordinary people transformed by extraordinary power—he can get to carry forward God's work. "Would that all the LORD's people were prophets, and that the LORD would put [the divine] spirit on them!"

The fulfillment of that hope is found in this morning's Gospel lesson. The resurrected Jesus stands in the midst of his rag-tag group of disciples. They are wracked with self-doubt and fear. They have locked themselves into a room, hiding from those they believe would do them harm. But Jesus appears in their midst, speaking "Peace" and breathing out on them the Holy Spirit of God. By that breath they receive into themselves the power to enable them to go back out into the world and continue the work that Jesus had begun. No promises that it will be easy, but by the Spirit and by the support that they will provide one another, it will be possible. They may not be Superman, but they are spirit-filled.

This morning we will be electing elders who will serve this congregation over the course of the coming twelve months. They won't be chosen because they are superheroes of faith. They will be chosen by the leading of God's Spirit and their willingness to respond to God's call through this congregation. What they will bring to their work are the gifts and talents God has given them and, most importantly, the enabling of the Spirit that has transformed and renewed them. As every year, I am eager to have their assistance. I am a pastor, not Superman, and sometimes it's not easy.

But like Moses, I am eager to have not only spirit-filled elders around me to help with the work God is doing in this place. It is more than what I and twelve elders, nine trustees, and all the committee members could accomplish. All of you who have gathered here have received God's Spirit into yourselves. "Would that all the LORD's people were prophets." Not Supermen, but spirit-filled prophets.

PREACHING *SUPERMAN RETURNS*

In preaching in dialogue specifically with the movie *Superman Returns*, what intrigued me most was the strange juxtaposition of two aspects of the film already apparent in the theatrical trailers. Here in what must be considered one of the most messianic portrayals of the Superman story yet, we find Lois Lane making the argument that the world doesn't need Superman precisely because it doesn't need a savior. It didn't take much to figure out that the movie would show Lois Lane coming around once again to her personal need (or at least longing) for Superman, but was the film actually also going to show that she was wrong about the world as well? Would the filmmakers make the case that the world itself needs a savior? It got me to wondering just what reasons Lois Lane would argue in her Pulitzer-winning article for "why the world doesn't need Superman."

Frankly, I was a bit disappointed that the film never directly treated the contents of her article. I realize there was, of course, no real article and that it served in the movie as a plot device to show how thoroughly Lois Lane has moved on with her life and thus how much she will have to move away from in order to move back toward Superman. But as I reflected on how Superman was actually portrayed in this film as contrasted with how we often think about the Superman myth, I began to wonder if perhaps she was right. Maybe we don't need a specific kind of Superman, a certain kind of Savior.

In the previous theological reading of the film, I explored one type of the Superman we don't need, the very kind that Jor-El had warned his son Kal-El not to become: a Superman at our beck and call to resolve all our problems. But there is another way that Superman is also often thought of in our culture: as one who participates in the myth of redemptive violence. Superman uses his superhuman strength to battle and destroy those who are enemies of "truth, justice, and the American way." Yet as I reflected on the movie at its conclusion, I was struck by how, relative to the film, this particular Superman myth was just that, in the sense of the popular use of the term "myth" to refer to something that is untrue. Certainly there is violence in the film, but in almost all cases it is directed toward Superman rather than performed by him, and in no case does he kill or destroy those who attack him. Superman works to prevent, restrain, and, if necessary, undo the effects of evil in the world; he does not destroy those who do the evil acts.[10]

Maybe one way to engage this film is to ask ourselves, What kind of savior does the world often long for, and how does that savior compare with the one it actually needs? These questions fit nicely with the lectionary texts for the 14th Sunday in Ordinary Time, Year B, that came around about twelve days after the release of the film. The Gospel lesson for that day is Mark 6:1–13, and it relates the differing receptions that Jesus found among the people of his own small hometown. What kind of Superman spends so much of his time as the bumbling Clark Kent? What kind of Messiah/Christ comes into the world as Jesus of Nazareth? The Epistle lesson from 2 Cor. 12:2–10 provided not only the catchy parallel between Paul's thorn in the flesh and the kryptonite shard thrust into Superman's side, but more importantly the apostle's observation that God's strength is perfected in weakness. God's salvation has yet to destroy every evil or even to undo all its effects on our lives, but it is salvation nevertheless.

SERMON TWO: "LOIS LANE WAS RIGHT—ALMOST"

(Mark 6:1–13; 2. Cor. 12:2–10)

"They could be a great people . . . ," the distinguished voice intones. "They only lack the light to show the way. For this reason above all—their capacity for good—I have sent them you, my only son." Sounds like a retelling of the Gospels, doesn't it? But actually it is the resurrection of a line from an almost thirty-year-old movie as part of a teaser for this summer's latest blockbuster. They aren't words put in God's mouth for Jesus, but words of another father to his son Kal-El, known in American culture as Superman.

A son, sent from a father in the heavens, to be a savior for humanity—these are only the most basic parallels that make Superman what is called in literary circles a Christ figure. There are his dual natures as the unassuming Clark Kent and the miraculously powerful Superman. Even his nemesis, Lex Luthor, has a name that suggests the Devil himself, Lucifer. But this new feature film takes the development of Superman as Christ figure to new heights. To begin with, there is the very title, *Superman Returns*, with its echoes of the Second Coming of the Christ. But in this film Superman literally dies as the result of a kryptonite shard thrust into his side, only to be subsequently resurrected and finally ascend into the heavens, from where he promises to "always be around" to assist those in need on earth. Superman as savior is hardly a subtle theme in this picture.

But amazingly, Lois Lane isn't buying it. During the five years Superman has been away trying to find the remnants of his home planet Krypton, we're told, she was awarded a Pulitzer Prize for an editorial titled "Why the World Doesn't Need Superman." The only hint we as viewers are given as to the content of her article comes in an exchange between Lois Lane and Superman upon his return. She tells him that during the time that he was away she has moved on with her life and the world has moved on as well. "The world doesn't need a savior," she tells Superman, "and neither do I." If Superman can't be counted on to destroy all their enemies, then they better get on with the struggle by themselves.

It is a sentiment not far removed from what we have read in our Gospel lesson for this morning. Mark tells us that at roughly the mid-point of his ministry Jesus returned to his hometown. On the sabbath he came to the synagogue where he had been known since he was a boy. Like any honored guest he was invited to expound on the Scriptures that were read that day. Mark states that "many who heard him were astounded." But apparently not everyone was so impressed.

The saying goes, "Familiarity breeds contempt." Perhaps some there in Nazareth were just too familiar with Jesus. "Is not this the carpenter, the son of Mary . . . and are not his [brothers and] sisters here with us?" "He thinks he is some great prophet or miracle worker, does he? Well, we knew him as a runny-nosed kid, covered in dirt, playing in the streets." These people were not simply unimpressed or unreceptive, they were "offended" that Jesus would claim such authority over them. Apparently this reaction to his teaching did not come as a surprise to Jesus. He quoted to them a proverb: "Prophets are not without honor, except in their hometown, and among their own kin, and in their own house." What did seem to amaze Jesus, however, was their "unbelief" in the face of what few healings he was able to perform there. Indeed, Mark seems to say that their "unbelief" limited Jesus' ability to perform "deed[s] of power" in Nazareth.

It is as if the inhabitants of Nazareth knew the truth that Clark Kent was Superman. They might eagerly have accepted Superman, but they couldn't accept the reality that Clark Kent was Superman. They may well have longed for one who would weald supernatural power to destroy disease, death, even those villainous Romans who were occupying their land. But they knew Jesus all to well. This meek and mild carpenter's son didn't have it in his nature to destroy their enemies even if there were indications that he might have the power to do so. They didn't need someone who combined the power of Superman with the restraint of a Clark Kent. Give them a Super-Savior, a Super-Christ, who used divine power to destroy evil. They didn't need a savior who combined power with weakness.

Like Jesus at Nazareth, Paul found himself in a situation at Corinth where his authority as an apostle was being challenged by a group that he derisively called the "super-apostles" (2 Cor. 11:5). These challengers basically had charged that the great apostle simply lacked the spiritual experiences and power that they had. Although convinced nothing good could come from it, Paul allowed himself to be dragged into a spiritual bragging contest, a *mano-a-mano* confrontation of macho-faith.

Dripping with irony, Paul said that he knew "a person in Christ" who had a spiritual experience so real and vivid that it was impossible to discern whether it had been merely visionary or was a literal physical transportation into the very heavenly dwelling place of God. This "person" was of course Paul himself. During this experience Paul saw things that he was not even permitted to speak about.

No one could top this experience, so why had they ever thought to challenge him in the first place? Well, Paul himself concedes that he was afflicted with some infirmity—"a thorn in the flesh" put there by Satan himself, Paul contends. Although it was obvious to the Corinthians who knew him personally just what this "thorn" was, no one since has been quite sure. What is known is that Paul had repeatedly prayed to be relieved from it, but to no avail. The only answer God offered was, "My grace is sufficient for you, for power is made perfect in weakness." Here again we find the combination of power and weakness. Once more we confront the apparent ability to destroy something that is bringing harm but an unwillingness to use that power to do so.

In one way it is as if Jesus in Nazareth and Paul in Corinth were saying to Lois Lane in Metropolis that she was right, or at least almost right. If she and the rest of the world were looking for a Superman who would destroy every evil, then they really didn't need such a savior. In a world of violent Lex Luthors, salvation cannot come through one who is simply strong enough to confront violence with even more powerful violence and so destroy it. It is time to move on from such fantasies. But just because we don't need that kind of savior doesn't mean that we don't need any savior at all. We need a savior who brings power to weakness, who turns back the effects of evil without destroying those who do evil. We need a savior who helps us to move on from disastrous belief in redemptive violence.

That the world might be ready for such a savior may be the most striking feature of *Superman Returns*. Superman doesn't destroy Lex Luthor, but rather undoes the evil effects Lex Luthor had let loose in the world—and does his most powerful exploit while weakened by a kryptonite thorn in his flesh. If even our superheroes renounce the myth of redemptive violence, then there may be hope for the rest of us. Lois Lane was right, almost. We don't need a man of steel to destroy evil; we need a Son of Man to unleash divine power in a world weakened by evil.

7

"Better Days Ahead"

Pleasantville

I first saw the movie *Pleasantville* with a group of clergy colleagues on a free evening during a preaching conference. It was a Tuesday night, so there were not a lot of other people in the theater. About two-thirds of the way through the movie and thus near the beginning of its "third act," where the plot elements are building to a level of tension that will demand a resolution, there was a scene that drew markedly different reactions from the various groups of viewers scattered about the auditorium. Margaret Henderson (Marley Shelton), a high school girl out on a first date to Lover's Lane with her new romantic interest, rushes over and picks a bright red apple from a tree. She comes back, sits down opposite her boyfriend, and extends her arm to offer the apple to him. The row of preachers burst into howls of laughter at this obvious allusion to the story about Eve, Adam, and the fruit from the tree of knowledge of good and evil.[1] But our laughter drew in turn the same blank stares from the audience members that I experienced years later from my children when the character played by Lynda Carter in *Sky High* plaintively explained, "I'm not Wonder Woman." The allusion was simply lost on them.

Afterwards we preachers talked about the lack of biblical literacy that had prevented the viewers from catching this and other allusions to the Bible—images such as a tree that bursts into flames without its wood being consumed; a rainbow that appears over Pleasantville, followed by references to a "deluge"; a fleeting glimpse of a painting of Adam and Eve's expulsion from Eden, followed later by one character telling another he no longer deserves such a paradise. What had happened to American culture that people could no longer immediately recognize the source of these images?[2]

It was only later that the irony of that discussion sunk in for me. Our longing for a previous time when things were different, when things were "as they should be," is precisely what the film *Pleasantville* is about. The movie makes it clear that it is pointless to long for such a paradise lost, not only because change is inevitable but, even more importantly, because there never was such a paradise in reality that might subsequently have become lost.

A THEOLOGICAL READING OF *PLEASANTVILLE*

The plot construction of *Pleasantville* invokes a complex layering of worlds.[3] The story is set in the late 1990s, contemporaneous with the film's production. The movie centers on David (Tobey Maguire) and Jennifer (Reese Wither-spoon), twin siblings who attend a California high school. Their different genders only begin to suggest the vast differences between them. Jennifer is a sexually experienced young woman, who will admit late in the film that she has played the slut. David is socially awkward—what his classmates would refer to as a geekish nerd—and obsessed with reruns of a 1950s television sitcom called "Pleasantville." For most of the movie, David and Jennifer have been magically transported into the television show where they assume the roles of "Bud" and "Mary Sue" Parker within the series.[4]

But there is one other discreet layer that is carefully constructed at the outset of the film. The usual title credits are displayed over a series of flashing colored lights that gradually resolve themselves into fuzzy pictures on a television screen, suffering, it appears, from poor reception, while we hear the rapid-fire change of sounds unmistakably associated with channel surfing. Quickly the surfing stops when it reaches the "TV Time" channel, a station that only shows programs from before the advent of color-broadcast technology. The network's own graphics intermix vibrant colors with the black-and-white title screens from genuine 1950s sitcoms. The network plug gives way to a promotional spot for a twenty-four-hour "Pleasantville" marathon that serves to introduce the setting and roles of what will be the sitcom within the movie. At the end of the promo, the screen gives the appearance of a television set being turned off and onto the now-blackened screen the words "Once Upon a Time . . ." fade in and then out. The opening accomplishes two important things. First, it explicitly reminds us as viewers that we are just that, a discrete layer outside the movie watching its characters as they see themselves drawn into a television show. Second, use of the phrase "once upon a time" establishes the genre as that of a fairy tale, signaling the need for the suspension of disbelief necessary for the magic about to happen and the expectation of some moral to the story at its end.

Just how unpleasant life for David and Jennifer may prove to be in the future is established by a montage of presentations they face in a typical school day. The guidance counselor drolly lectures them about the slim prospects of a tightening job market and diminishing salaries for what few entry-level positions that will remain by the time they graduate; a health teacher warns of the rapid rise in the risk of contracting AIDS for those involved in nonmonogamous sexual relationships; and the science teacher describes the prospects for environmental catastrophe brought on by global warming. But David and Jennifer don't need these reminders of broad cultural unpleasantries. Their parents are divorced, and their now-single mother is going through something of a crisis with her current lover. Little wonder, then, that they might try to escape their lives—we even see David trying to drown out his mother's phone argument with his absent father by repeatedly turning up the volume as he watches the idyllic family life of the Parker family in "Pleasantville."

The night of the "Pleasantville" marathon, David and Jennifer get involved in a tussle over control of the television (Jennifer wants to watch an MTV concert while engaged in a makeout session with a boy from school) that ends with the remote lying in pieces on the floor. At just that moment a TV repairman (Don Knotts) shows up unbidden at the door and inquires as to whether their television needs some work. After quizzing David about "Pleasantville" trivia in apparent polite conversation, he offers them a new remote with "a little more oomph," capable of putting "you right in the show." David tunes in "Pleasantville" just as Bud and Mary Sue are tussling over a transistor radio, and the tussle simultaneously resumes with Jennifer for control of the new television remote. She accidentally activates a button on the remote and they suddenly replace Bud and Mary Sue in the Parker's living room on "Pleasantville."

To be clear, they are not on the set where "Pleasantville" would have been filmed; they are subsumed into a world where the television show is reality. David and Jennifer appear in black-and-white not because we are watching them through circa 1950s technology but because they and everything around them are devoid of all colors except black and white and all hues other than shades of grey. As they will come to understand, the town of Pleasantville is something of a hermetically sealed universe where the only reality is the broadcast reality. Restrooms don't actually have toilets; the pages of books are blank; roads circle back on themselves in never-ending loops; and parents not only sleep in separate twin beds but don't even know what sex is.

When the TV repairman appears on the screen of the Parker's television set, David and Jennifer plead with him to bring them back home. He is dismayed by what he perceives as a lack of gratitude on their parts and decides to give them a couple of weeks to change their attitudes. David tries to convince Jennifer that their only hope of getting home is to play along as "Bud" and "Mary Sue," hewing as closely as possible to the actions already scripted for them so as not to disrupt this universe in which they find themselves. David looks for clues as to which episode they may be in and soon discovers that it is one in which "Mary Sue" is to go out on a date with Skip Martin (Paul Walker), the captain of the Pleasantville High School basketball team. He persuades Jennifer to meet Skip at the Soda Shop.

But Jennifer finds it impossible simply to play along as "Mary Sue." She convinces Skip to take her to Lover's Lane, where she goes far beyond the holding hands that Skip thought she would be reticent about on a first date. Jennifer brings sexual intercourse to Pleasantville, and when Skip arrives at home later that night he spots a *red* rose, or as citizens of Pleasantville would later come to phrase it when colors begin emerging into their black-and-white world, a "real red" rose.[5] Soon many of the teenagers are having sex in their cars down at Lover's Lane, and red begins to flash on inadvertently bumped brake lights and to show up on the tongues of some of the girls. A double bed even shows up in the display window of the local furniture store. At first it seems that emerging color is directly related to emerging sexuality. It is "Mary Sue" who tells her mother Betty Parker (Joan Allen) what sex is. At the end of this classically role-reversed conversation, "Mary Sue" even tells her mother how to pleasure herself if her husband is unwilling to join her in this new experience. Betty proceeds to go upstairs and draw herself a bath, and as she moans in sexual release, the colors in her bathroom and even of a bird outside her window begin to explode into view, until finally the tree in her front yard bursts into flames. So strong is the connection between color and sexuality that Jennifer eventually complains to David that she is vastly more sexually experienced (apparently both back home in California and in Pleasantville) than the other girls, and asks him, "How come I'm still in black-and-white?"

But Betty Parker's "burning bush experience" (and apart from vague hints of personal revelation, nothing would suggest a religious or even spiritual dimension to this imagery) ushers in the next phase of color explosion. As the tree burns, "Bud" rushes to the fire station to summon help and eventually has to show them how to use the hoses on their truck to douse the flames.[6] "Bud" receives an award for his "heroic" action, which leads the other teenagers to ask him how he knew what fire was and what to do about it. Those questions lead to questions about books, since when "Mary Sue" had told folks what she remembered about *The Adventures of Huckleberry Finn*, the first chapter (as far as she ever got in reading it in school back home in California) had magically filled itself in on the heretofore blank pages. When "Bud" tells them that the book is about the discovery that Huck and Jim make while going up the river, that the quest for freedom is a kind of freedom itself, the entire book fills itself in, and people begin to ask "Bud" about other books, about which their previous knowledge had been limited to what appeared on the cover of the blank books. Long lines soon form at the library, and colors continue to emerge everywhere. It is ultimately through books (and perhaps not surprisingly through D. H. Lawrence) that "Mary Sue" finally gets her colors.

"Bud" has learned that his boss at the Soda Shop, Bill Johnson (Jeff Daniels), loves painting the once-a-year holiday murals in the Soda Shop windows, so he brings him a book of paintings that sparks within Mr. Johnson a rush of creativity and, as might be expected, the emergence of his own colors. His is one of several breakthroughs among the characters of "Pleasantville": for example, Betty Parker decides to leave home because she will no longer cover up her colorful complexion with grey makeup (first applied to her by "Bud" in a touching scene while she was still ashamed of her new appearance); "Bud's" new girlfriend Margaret has an awakening after Pleasantville's first-ever rain storm (after which a colorful rainbow appears over the town, clearly an endorsement of what has been happening rather than a promise not to repeat an act of judgment); and Jennifer awakes through books. But when Mr. Johnson paints a nude mural of Betty Parker on the Soda Shop window, all the unpleasantries bottled up beneath the surface of Pleasantville erupt.

In scenes reminiscent of the Nazi *Kristallnacht* attacks on Jews, crowds vandalize the Soda Shop, throwing a park bench through the muraled window, and begin to burn the now-printed books in the library. Signs begin to emerge around town reading, "No Coloreds," unmistakably recalling for the audience another context in which many towns of 1950s America displayed such signs. The "Coloreds" begin to be targets of abuse, including sexually motivated taunts and assaults. It is when "Bud" steps in to defend his mother from such an assault that color comes to him, as well as to the young man he punches, from the corner of whose mouth red blood begins to flow.

The mayor of Pleasantville asks George Parker (William H. Macy) and another member of the Chamber of Commerce to draft a "Code of Conduct" to be voted on by the citizens as a set of ordinances to return things to the way they were. The first two points find acceptance with "Coloreds" and noncoloreds alike: all acts of violence and vandalism are to cease, and all citizens are to treat each other in a "courteous and pleasant manner." But other points of the code approved in a town meeting where no "Coloreds" were present took such actions as closing Lover's Lane and the library, narrowly restricting the kinds of music that could be played, limiting bed frames and mattresses to thirty-eight inches in width, and banning all paint colors other than black, white, or grey.

"Bud" and Mr. Johnson are arrested for an act of civil disobedience when they paint on a brick wall of the police station a large, colorful mural symbolically depicting many of the recent changes in Pleasantville. The staging of the trial is patterned after the famous trial scene of *To Kill a Mockingbird*, with the only "Coloreds" allowed on the main floor being the two accused while all the others are consigned to a balcony. When "Bud" asks where their lawyer is, the mayor, who is presiding as judge, responds that lawyers are unnecessary since the goal is to keep things pleasant. The trial comes to an end when "Bud" uses his defense to bring color to his father, a member of the jury, by evoking from him continuing feelings of love and affection for Betty even though she has left him. He then brings color to the mayor by provoking the expression of anger that has built up inside of him. With that, all of Pleasantville is awash in the colors of spring, and color televisions even appear in the storefront windows.

In the end it is only David who returns, via the remote with extra "oomph," through the television and back to California. Jennifer decides to remain as "Mary Sue" on "Pleasantville" and to attend college in the town of Springfield that now has bus service from Pleasantville.

So what is the moral of this fairy tale? Fittingly, it is delivered in two pieces—one in California and one in Pleasantville. Once back home, David discovers that only an hour has elapsed in California time, and he finds his real mother crying at the dining room table. He learns from her that she has turned back from her weekend rendezvous with her lover because she has become distraught about the direction her life has taken:

> **Mother:** When your father was here, I used to think this was it. This was the way it was always gonna be. I had the right house, I had the right car, I had the right life—
>
> **David:** There is no right house, there is no right car.

She becomes self-conscious about her disheveled appearance, caused by her crying. David begins to clean off makeup smeared by her tears in the same way he had tenderly applied makeup to Betty Parker, and he assures her that there is no certain way things ought to be that their lives have failed to realize. She now looks at her son in a new way:

> **Mother:** How'd you get so smart all of a sudden?
>
> **David:** I had a good day.

With that, the picture fades back to Pleasantville, where after several brief glimpses of life that is largely back to normal save for the ever-present colors, we arrive at a view of George and Betty Parker sitting on a park bench. George asks her what they can expect next. She admits, "I don't know," and then turns the question back on him. The camera shot changes to a closeup of just

George as he chuckles that he doesn't know either. Then the camera pans back toward Betty until George is completely out of the frame, and it shows Betty chuckling as well. Betty turns to look straight ahead into the camera, then turns her gaze back toward where George had been sitting. As the camera pans with her, it reveals that it is now Bill Johnson seated on the park bench with her, and he tells her, "I guess I don't either." The screen cuts to black, and the end credits roll.

There is no "supposed to be"; there is no knowing what will happen next. There is only change and the sure knowledge that, in the words of the tagline from the promotional materials of *Pleasantville*, "Nothing is as simple as black and white."

So what is one to do with these insights? How does one live in order to deal with change and the uncertainty of life? One answer is given by "Bud" in his defense while on trial. By asking George a series of questions about his feelings for Betty and by deliberately provoking the mayor, he is able to draw out what is buried inside them and thereby bring out their true colors. As Adele Reinhartz observed, this "message is no more than the trite and tired truism that we must be true to our inner selves." For her, the film is rescued from this sentimentality "by emphasizing that change, while threatening, is not only inevitable but enriching; and by exposing the perfection of the past as an illusion that covers a dark and oppressive core."[7]

But there is another way in which *Pleasantville* deepens its message about self-actualization: it takes work. True, the colors begin to emerge in Pleasantville with the pleasures of sexual exploration, but they only really begin to take hold when people work at things. Mr. Johnson must work at producing his paintings, and he and "Bud" literally fall asleep on the street after the long night spent producing the mural that gets them arrested. "Mary Sue" must do the work of studying and reading that Jennifer wouldn't do back home in California. The teenagers of Pleasantville must work to clean up the Soda Shop after it is trashed before they can discover that, yes, the jukebox with its 1950s rock and roll still works, despite the ban in the "Code of Conduct" on such music.

PREACHING *PLEASANTVILLE*

Both Reinhartz and George Aichele stress the deconstructive unveiling of the dystopia beneath the utopian surface of Pleasantville in their readings of the film alongside Scripture—she by focusing on the "new heavens and new earth" of Revelation, and he by returning to Eden.[8] For my homiletical dialogue with *Pleasantville*, I chose different scriptural partners: Hag. 1:15b–2:9 and

2 Thess. 2:13–17, the Old Testament and Epistle lessons appointed for the 32nd Sunday in Ordinary Time, Year C. These scriptural texts allowed me to emphasize the work that went on in Pleasantville that was as essential to bringing out its color as the recognition of the restrictiveness of its monochromatic palette, which concealed much unpleasantness beneath its blandly uniform façade. As Haggai offered the comfort not of past glory but of new glory to the returned exiles as they worked to build and not simply rebuild their community, and as Paul encouraged the Thessalonians to both "stand firm and hold fast to . . . [what] you were taught" even as they "strengthen [their hearts] in every good work and word" (2 Thess. 2:15–17), so we too must replace a nostalgic longing for a past that, in reality, never was for the hard and uncertain work of creating a vibrant future.

As is mentioned in the sermon, the occasion for this dialogue was the congregation's observance of its fortieth anniversary. In what could not have been more appropriate, it had been founded in the same 1950s America (mis)represented in the fictional sitcom "Pleasantville." Like Haggai and the returned exiles, there were those who carried with them memories of times when the congregation had been larger and seemingly more glorious. Without pouring cold water on the celebration, the sermon seeks to remind the congregation that nostalgic memories seldom square with what were the then-present realities of what is now the past. If the present is a time of uncertainty and challenge, so was the past. If God could bring glory to this church in the past, then God can bring glory to it in the present as we work to realize its future.

SERMON: "BETTER DAYS AHEAD"

(Hag. 1:15b–2:9; 2 Thess. 2:13–17)

Things weren't so pleasant in Pleasantville, after all. That, of course, is a central theme of the new movie named after the imaginary town that is the setting for an imaginary sitcom. Even if you haven't yet seen the film, you have probably seen the promotional trailers either on television, as a "coming attraction" at the theater, or on a video rental. The premise is simple enough. David is a teenager here in 1998 and an obsessive fan of the interminable reruns of a 1950s sitcom. In the midst of a tussle with his sister, Jennifer, over the television remote control, the brother-and-sister pair is drawn through the modern "looking-glass" of the television screen and into the world that is Pleasantville. Here they assume the roles of "Bud" and "Mary Sue," in all their black-and-white television blandness.

You might think David would believe he had found his way into a kind of heaven. After all, his devotion to the television show "Pleasantville" seems clearly to have arisen as an escape from his own daily life. "Bud" lived in an idyllic world with two loving and doting parents where everything was predictable and pleasant—a world where it never rains and all firefighters ever do is rescue cats stranded in treetops. David's world, on the other hand, was filled with all the uncertainties and stresses of a single-parent home, where his mother was going through yet another crisis with her most recent lover. Yet, living in the black-and-white world of Pleasantville quickly convinces David that his 1990s life, with all its problems, was much to be preferred. Even in a sitcom, the glories he had attributed to the "golden age" of the 1950s did not really exist.

In a similar way, the returned exiles to whom Haggai preaches were disillusioned by what they found in their new-again homeland. For almost seventy years, their families had lived in Babylon. There they had kept hope alive by telling the stories of Jerusalem's glory and splendor. The children had been raised on the stories of Judah's golden age. At least in their minds they had walked through the glories of Solomon's temple, and they had participated in the triumphs of Josiah, Judah's last great king. Over the course of those decades, the lines separating mythic grandeur and somber reality had become blurred. Jerusalem existed in their minds as Pleasantville.

So when they, too, were pulled through the "looking glass" of Cyrus's decree that transported them from exile in Babylon to life again in Jerusalem, they were confronted with a reality quite different from the glory that had existed in their heads. Now, instead of a king, they have a governor. Now, instead of the glory of Solomon's temple, they have little more than the foundation stones for a temple that will be only a fraction the size of its predecessor. So maybe they had exaggerated and embellished their memories of Solomon's temple, but surely it must have been better than this. The comparison was hard to accept. "Who is left among you that saw this house in its former glory?" Haggai asks. "How does it look to you now? Is it not in your sight as nothing?" They had expected the glory that lived in their imaginations; they found disillusionment and disappointment that exceeded the blandness of a black-and-white world.

"Yet now take courage," God proclaims through the prophet. There is something that is moving and stirring beneath the surface. The world around them seems bleak and increasingly harsh, but that external reality is not the full story. "My spirit abides among you," God declares; "do not fear." As if the assertion of the divine power is enough to drive back the gloom, God announces the divine self as "the LORD of hosts" six times within this short oracle, and with mounting frequency as it reaches its crescendo. "I will fill this house with splendor, says the LORD of hosts. . . . The splendor of this house shall be greater than the former, says the LORD of hosts; and in this place I will give prosperity, says the LORD of hosts." Take courage, for the awakening of God's spirit within the leaders and within the common folk will renew the splendor of Jerusalem. Somewhat like what happens in Pleasantville.

Gradually color begins to break through into Pleasantville. It starts out as a single red rose, but soon it is literally bursting into flame and spreading among many of the inhabitants of the city. The change is exhilarating, and at the same time frightening. When Betty Parker is transformed from black-and-white pastiness into color, she knows that her relationship with her husband George will not remain the same either. Initially David tries to work through his character "Bud" to stem the mounting tide of color, to preserve the existence that everyone has known in Pleasantville. He even helps his sitcom mother, Betty, to cover over the color that has emerged on her face by applying her old black-and-white-hued makeup. Such is the power of the familiar, the routine, even when it is bland and stifling. But something even more powerful is the stirring inside.

As you see the story of *Pleasantville* played out before your eyes, you may at first think the film buys into the idea that what is stirring inside us, yearning to be set free, is a sexuality and sensuality bound up by conventionality. That first red rose I mentioned emerges as two teenagers progress beyond simply holding hands at "Lovers' Lane." Jennifer, through her role as "Mary Sue," seems at first to be the prophetess of this message. She is the one who breaks through the innocence of "Lovers' Lane." She is the one who explains sex to her sitcom mother, Betty Parker, setting in motion her mother's transformation into color. But not even Jennifer will let you persist in this notion. As color breaks through all around her, she protests to David that she has had more sex than any of the other girls, and asks him, "How come I'm still in black-and-white?" The answer, as Jennifer and we all learn, is that the color and splendor come not from sexuality but from the opening up of the person inside. More than their adolescent sexuality, the teenagers' color comes from discovering books and ideas beyond Pleasantville. Indeed, reading books to one another becomes a common activity even at "Lovers' Lane." For Mr. Johnson, the owner of the soda shop, color comes after he is introduced to the vibrancy of the art of Van Gogh and Picasso and when he gives expression to the artistic muse within himself. For Jennifer, "living color" comes through a love for literature that draws out depths in her that she had tried to suppress by playing the slut. Even the most resistant inhabitants of Pleasantville burst into color when what is truly inside them breaks through the black-and-white façade.

"Take courage, all you people of the land, says the LORD; . . . The latter splendor of this house shall be greater than the former, says the LORD of hosts." It took courage for Mr. Johnson to give up the routines of running the soda shop, and it took work for him to produce his own paintings. It took courage for Zerubbabel, Joshua, and all the "people of the land" to dare to imagine a future as bright as their past, and it would take work empowered by God's spirit to bring it to reality. But better days were ahead if they would answer God's spirit stirring within them—days as full of splendor as the streets of Pleasantville were full of color by the time David traversed "through the looking-glass" of the television screen once again to return to his modern life.

Over the course of the next week, we will, as a congregation, take a nostalgic look back to the fifties as we celebrate Northwood's fortieth anniversary. There will be a temptation to think back on some of those times as a golden age, as periods when this church was new and filled with almost three times its current membership. It will be a "temptation" because it may also lead us to think that by comparison to that splendor, what we see now is "nothing." But God's promise to the returned exiles is God's promise to us: "The latter splendor of this house shall be greater than the former, says the LORD of hosts." To realize that splendor will require from us courage and work.

Where will we find the courage we need? We will find it in the words written to the Thessalonians but which come to us as God's word this morning: "God chose [us] as the first fruits for salvation . . . so that [we] may obtain the glory of our Lord Jesus Christ." We will find courage in the knowledge that God's Spirit is with us as surely as with the exiles who returned to their homeland in Judah. Faith and courage in this instance go hand in hand. We will have courage when we have the faith to believe that this is and will be a place where God's splendor shines. Don't underestimate the need for this courage. The transformation of even a bleak present into a glorious future is nevertheless threatening because it requires us to risk change. It was easy for the returned exiles to moan and complain that things were not as they had remembered; it was hard work for them to forge their hopes. It was easy for the good citizens of Pleasantville to allow unpleasantness to rise up in an effort to preserve the routine they knew so well; it was hard for them to risk difference and change even when they could see the splendid colors it brought to their lives. Yet God's Spirit is in us to give us this courage.

Just as all the inhabitants of Pleasantville, even those drawn into that imaginative place from the world in which we live, had to respond to the stirrings within them to find the colorful splendor of their future, so God is calling us to "stand firm and hold fast to . . . [what we] were taught" by the examples lived before us by other Christians and by God's word to us in the Scriptures. We must "comfort [our] hearts" by the experience of God's love and grace to us through Christ, "and strengthen [our hearts] in every good work and word." We must give ourselves to the work of this place, to answering the call of God's Spirit within us, if we are to see the splendor and the color of the better days ahead.

8

"In His Shoes"

In Her Shoes

Of all the films engaged in this book, *In Her Shoes* had the least commercial success,[1] and by that measure, the least cultural impact. Its performance at the box office is more a reflection of its association with the popularly used label "chick flick" than with the quality of the performances of the actors or filmmakers, as its generally positive reviews attest.[2] That label is usually applied derisively to movies in the romantic-comedy genre or primarily about relationships in which the leading characters are predominately women. While each of those characteristics applies with some justification to *In Her Shoes*, it is not a film worthy of derision.

The movie includes a genuine romance (and early on, more than a little sleeping around) and has some wonderful comedic moments, but it is a film primarily about relationships among three women, the sisters Rose (Toni Collette) and Maggie Feller (Cameron Diaz) and their grandmother Ella Hirsch (Shirley MacLaine). Carol Fenelon, one of the movie's producers, commented that it is "about connecting to those most important to us, our friends and our family." As the discussion that follows will demonstrate, the relationships presented in this film are complex, to say the least. But it is a subtheme related to this interest in relationships that will provide the focus of my reading of the film. The movie presents the view that the only way truly to be in relationship with others is to be authentically one's self. Again citing Fenelon, "So often we succumb to other people's perceptions of what we should be. . . . *In Her Shoes* explores the challenge of making the most of what we're capable of—about being comfortable in one's own shoes."[3]

The film ultimately, however, demands more of its characters than that they be "comfortable in [their] own shoes." All of them are indeed pressed to move outside their comfort zones by bringing out parts of themselves they have longed buried and using those things for the sake of others. In this way the film critiques the cultural notion that self-actualization is fundamentally about the *self*; human beings are relational beings, and we can never be all that we have within our potential unless we genuinely give of ourselves in relationship to others. By its conclusion, then, it has exposed precisely why all that sleeping around at the beginning proves to be not merely hollow but incredibly destructive. More importantly, it implicitly extends the challenge beyond its characters to encourage its audience as well to move outside their comfort zones and into another's shoes.

A THEOLOGICAL READING OF *IN HER SHOES*

The Feller family is something of a train wreck, and in precisely that way it is like many American families. Drawing on revelations scattered throughout the movie, we learn that the disarray stems directly and indirectly from the woman who is the now-missing connection between the three leading characters— Ella's daughter, Rose and Maggie's mother. Caroline Hirsch Feller appears only in a photograph within the movie,[4] but her absence has in many ways determined this family's relationships. Caroline had suffered from bipolar disorder. When Maggie was only six years old—too young to understand her mother's disease or its consequences—Caroline had intentionally driven her car into a tree, committing suicide rather than face being separated from her daughters by the hospitalization that her husband had determined was finally going to be necessary.

The reverberations of her disease can be felt in a key scene involving Ella and Maggie, which occurs in the film at a point when Maggie still has not learned the specific circumstances surrounding her mother's death. Ella asks Maggie about her memories of her mother. Because the two had earlier in the scene disagreed about whether Rose should be invited to Ella's Florida retirement-village bungalow so that Ella could be reunited with her other granddaughter, Maggie at first snidely suggests such a question would be better put to her sister. After Ella curtly replies that she needs to grow up, Maggie begins to recall ways that her mother had been unlike other moms. In wistfully relating an occasion when Caroline had placed a tiara in her school lunch box rather than her sandwich, Maggie reveals herself to be as unable now to recognize symptoms of mental illness in her mother's actions as she had been when only a six-year-old child. Maggie then asks her grandmother what it was like to have Caroline for a daughter:

Ella: I loved her so much. But loving her in the right way was difficult, for me, anyway.

Maggie: I didn't know there was a right way and a wrong way.

Ella: Neither did I.

Ella goes on to relate the differences between what she had felt was best for Caroline and what Caroline had wanted for herself. Her deepest regret was that she had been so certain of the rightness of her own opinions about managing Caroline's illness and the limitations it placed on her that she had never been able to hear what Caroline desired for herself.

Many of the film's central themes are at play in this scene—right and wrong ways to love, efforts at protection of others that only inhibit their maturation, challenges to take responsibility for one's actions and inactions, and recognition that we are in relationship for the sake of others at least as much as for ourselves. But to return to the film's backstory, Michael Feller (Ken Howard) had cut off all contact between Ella and his daughters following his wife's suicide because he felt she held him responsible for her death. Both he and Rose, the older of the sisters, had then spent the next roughly twenty years coddling and protecting Maggie until neither could do so any longer (in Michael's case, by the intervention of his second wife; in Rose's, from emotional exhaustion).

The trailers promoting the film emphasized how differently Rose and Maggie had turned out as adults. Rose had graduated from Princeton and gone on to become an associate at a large law firm with an apartment in an upscale Philadelphia neighborhood. She has defined herself by the responsibilities she has assumed, both professionally and within the family. At one point she explains that it was not a love of law or a drive to succeed that had pushed her into a workaholic lifestyle; rather, she was frightened that the only thing that was keeping her intact was the responsibility she felt to please others and to complete the tasks delegated to her. It was not that she saw herself as indispensable to the firm, but more that the firm was indispensable to her own sense of identity. Her insecurities were greatest about her appearance, particularly her weight. In what becomes the dominant metaphor of the film, Rose explains to her sister why it is that she has a closet full of very expensive designer shoes: "When I feel bad, I like to treat myself. Clothes never look any good. Food just makes me fatter. Shoes always fit."[5]

Maggie was Rose's opposite in every way. Having barely graduated from high school, she has never been able to hold a steady job. She had lost jobs because she couldn't do the basic math required for the retail transactions (though she blamed her firing on irrational demands of customers) and because of childish antics (like removing the "C" from the sign of the "Canal House" restaurant where she was a waitress). She floated back and forth between her father's house and sister's apartment or otherwise would have been homeless. She uses her beauty and flirtatiousness to allure and seduce men into buying her drinks and meals. Her personality is perfectly captured by the exchange between her and Rose that led to Rose's comment that shoes "always fit." As Maggie was admiring herself in a pair of Rose's shoes before a dressing mirror, she chastised her sister for keeping so many pairs of shoes stored away. Instead of languishing in a closet, such shoes deserved to be worn in illicit trysts with anonymous rich men, whose wives waited unsuspectingly in their chauffered cars in front of a bar. Rose begs to be reassured that such a scenario is a figment of Maggie's vivid imagination and not a recollection, to which Maggie only replies that Rose should either wear the shoes she buys or leave them for purchase by others who will get some use from them. Maggie's life in its own terms is exemplified by her attempt to get a job as an MTV vee-jay; she gets a call-back audition based on her looks but is unable to read well enough to keep pace with the teleprompter.

Despite these differences, the film actually opens with intercut scenes of both sisters engaged in one-night stands, suggesting that each is more like the other than either would choose to admit. Maggie's tryst takes place at her high school reunion—in a public restroom stall with a man whose name she is too drunk to remember even during the act itself, and it ends abruptly when her vomiting into the toilet leaves her partner no longer able to perform. Rose's liaison is with Jim Danvers (Richard Burgi), a partner from her law firm, and is so unexpected to her that she snaps a digital picture of him asleep next to her because, as she explains in a voice-over, "the lawyer in [her] wants proof." Her night is abruptly ended when she gets a call to pick up Maggie, who is passed out on a couch at the reunion. Rose is hopeful, however, that her relationship with Jim will be more lasting, particularly when it seems she will accompany him on a business trip to Chicago. When the car picks her up to go to the airport, however, she finds instead Simon Stein (Mark Feuerstein), another associate from the firm.

Jim stops by Rose's apartment with flowers and apparently an apology, but he finds only Maggie, who has been staying with Rose since that eventful night. When she lets Jim into the apartment, Maggie is wearing little more than a blouse closed by only two of its buttons and a pair of Rose's sexy, open-toed boots. Rose soon arrives home from the office to find Maggie and Jim engaged in sexual intercourse in her own bed, with Maggie still wearing Rose's shoes. She throws Maggie out of her apartment with a cry of "Get out of my life!"

While rifling through drawers in her father's house looking for cash several days earlier, Maggie had found some birthday cards sent to her when she was just a child by her grandmother. They had never been opened but were instead hidden away by her father when he had broken off contact with his mother-in-law after his wife's death. Using the small bills she had found in them and the $200 she had received from Jim when he dropped her off at the train station (an amount she flatly suggested to him is appropriate for such a sexual encounter), Maggie makes her way to her grandmother's residence at a retirement community in Florida. The first contact between them is when Maggie calls her on the phone and asks her grandmother to come pick her up at the beach. Ella is dismayed to learn that Maggie has only recently found the cards, although as she tells Maggie she had not "pulled away" from her granddaughters, she "was pushed." Nevertheless, Ella feels tremendous guilt about the loss of the relationship with her granddaughters because, as she reveals to her friend Mrs. Lefkowitz (Francine Beers), the only line of Caroline's suicide note was "Please take care of my girls."

While Maggie is in Florida, Rose's life is taking marked turns back in Philadelphia. Maggie had brought home a dog (that reminded her of a briefly owned childhood pet) from a pet salon where she worked just before Rose had thrown her out. While walking the dog, Rose had been stopped by someone who recognized the dog and knew where it was usually kenneled. Covering for her sister, Rose tells the woman that she makes her living by walking dogs and running errands for people. Both the woman and other well-heeled visitors in the park mention that they could use such services. So Rose leaves the law firm and begins actually living this hastily concocted cover story. She also eventually finds herself in a relationship with Simon, the associate from her old law firm. Over time they fall in love and become engaged.

Maggie's life is changing as well. Having caught her once again rifling through drawers looking for cash, Ella confronts her and demands to know just how much money Maggie hoped to milk out of her since it now seemed obvious that this visit was not really about renewing their relationship. Maggie at first falls into old habits of behavior, initially looking shocked that Ella should make such a suggestion and almost immediately becoming demure when Ella presses her for a specific dollar amount. Maggie asks for $3,000 to set herself up in New York in hopes of becoming an actress. Ella refuses to give her that much but does offer her a deal. If Maggie takes a job at the assisted living center in the community, Ella will match her salary so that Maggie can save up the money she will need. Maggie is genuinely surprised:

Maggie: You would do that? [*Ella nods yes.*] Why?

    Ella: Because I'm your grandmother.

The way to the future Maggie desires passes not through her past manipulative and deceitful practices, but rather through the relationship Ella had concluded she didn't really want and from meeting the responsibilities of work that she had avoided because of past failure.

Maggie gets the job. One of the residents at the center is a former professor who has now gone blind. He asks her several times to read for him, and she finally consents. As she haltingly reads aloud, he immediately perceives that she has dyslexia. She slowly reads the poem, and then he begins to quiz her about its interpretation. With leading questions, he walks her through her ideas about Elizabeth Bishop's poem "One Art." She concludes that it is about losing the love of a friend, and the professor announces, "A-plus. Smart girl." It is an epiphany for her; she realizes that her inability to read does not mean she isn't smart and that she has other abilities than her powers of seduction. She opens herself to the community and eventually begins a business as a personal shopper for the residents. With her grandmother's assistance with the numbers and her own empathic ability to pick what is just right for the individual and the occasion, the business endeavor thrives.

By this time, however, Rose's new life is coming unraveled—in part by an infidelity of her own of a nonsexual kind. Simon is growing uneasy about her closing off parts of her life from him. While at a friend's wedding, Rose encounters Jim, who offers an excuse-laden apology for having slept with Maggie. Rose cuts him off but in the process pours out her grief that Jim's fling with Maggie had cost her her sister. Simon finds her confiding with *Jim* what she would not share with him, and he breaks off their engagement. At this moment when her life is at a new low, an invitation and an airline ticket arrive from Ella.

Rose arrives in Florida and is shocked to be greeted at the bungalow's door by Maggie, who is equally shocked to see Rose, for she was unaware Ella had sent the invitation. Rose's verbal assault on Maggie picks up right where it had left off when she threw her out of the apartment, in hushed tones but with equal lethality. The reunion with her grandmother, however, is warm and immediate. Rapprochement with Maggie, however, is not long in coming. Rose begins to warm up to her sister on a tour of the retirement community when she sees how Maggie relates to the residents. The breakthrough comes back at the bungalow where Ella has brought out a scrapbook of old photos. The conversation quickly leads to a discussion of the events that had led Michael to determine Caroline needed to be hospitalized, and consequently to her suicide. Both Rose and Michael had kept Maggie so shielded from that harsh reality that she had forgotten that her mother's impulsive gift of the dog had come only two days before her death. Later that evening she realizes her mother's fatal car crash had not been an accident. The renewal of what can only now be a truly shared grief of their mother's death brings renewal to the shared bonds between Rose and Maggie.

Maggie and Rose's reconciliation is only possible, then, by their moving out from the carefully constructed façades behind which they have hidden and by their digging up and using what they have buried in the past. Curtis Hanson, the film's director, described how he used elements of mise-en-scène to express this theme. In the early parts of the film he had established Maggie's instability and reliance on such externals as her beauty by shooting her scenes with a handheld camera and incorporating mirrors or other reflective surfaces into the sets. By contrast, Rose's negative perception of her appearance leads her to avoid mirrors. The sisters' reconciliation, however, takes place as they are preparing for bed before the vanity mirror in Ella's home. As Hanson explains, "Near the end of the movie, when both sisters are seeing themselves and each other more clearly, it felt right to stage that critical bathroom scene between the two of them in front of a large mirror."[6]

Spurred on by many of the widows residing in the retirement community, Maggie engineers a reunion between Rose and Simon. She convinces him to come to Florida by falsely telling him that Rose is pregnant. Once together again, Simon asks Rose whether she is pregnant, and when she tells him she is not, he presses her about whether she had been pregnant (leaving open the possibility she may have terminated the pregnancy). Rose seems incredulous that Simon should even consider the possibility that she would have withheld such information from him, to which he reminds her that it was precisely her keeping things back from him that had ended their relationship. Rose insists that anything she had not told him was not about them but about her relationship with Maggie. She warns Simon that Maggie will make a wreck not only of her own life but also of Rose and Simon's life if they should get back together. He will plead with her once more to get Maggie out of her life, but she can never do that again because she now realizes how inseparably intertwined she is with her sister. Simon's only response is that he sees once more the woman with whom he had fallen in love. Finally able to be the person she truly is, Rose is able to be in relationship with Simon, and the wedding is back on. Maggie tells Rose not to buy a wedding dress because she wants it to be her gift to her. Rose resists, not wanting to be married "in some hootchie-mama monstrosity," but Maggie responds, "Look, I'm good at this. Trust me." Being in relationship requires drawing out of ourselves *and* trusting what others bring of themselves.

The wedding celebration at the end of the film ties together two major themes of the movie. In keeping with the tradition of "something old, something new, something borrowed, and something blue," Ella loans Rose the shoes she wore in her own wedding, and with Rose literally standing in her grandmother's shoes, the symbolism of restored relationships within the family is complete.[7] In a surprise, the prospects of which at first bring a look of mortification to Rose's face, the rabbi officiating the ceremony calls on Maggie to read a poem she has chosen. The poem is e.e. cumming's "i carry your heart with me," perfectly suited to the occasion by virtue of its applicability both to the couple being married and to the relationship between the sisters and flawlessly and movingly read by the dyslexic Maggie. The repetition of the poem in a voice-over in the film's final scene, in a subtle way, extends to those watching the movie (since voice-overs are by convention and by their very nature aimed directly at the audience) the challenge to do likewise: "i carry your heart (i carry it in my heart)." Recalling Maggie's comments early in movie about the life of shoes, such relationships are finally possible because the shoes have been dug out of the closet and are getting some use.

PREACHING *IN HER SHOES*

In preaching in dialogue with the film *In Her Shoes*, I chose to focus less on the relational dynamics and dysfunction per se and more on what was required to restore the broken relationships—namely, the willingness of each character to dig up those things that had been buried away and to put them to use for the sake of others. The sermon was part of a stewardship series, with this particular sermon focused on the stewardship of our "talents" rather than our finances. Like countless preachers before me, I chose for my text Jesus' parable of the Talents (Matt. 25:14–30) and raised the possibility of considering what it might have been like to be "in the shoes" of the slave who buried his master's talent rather than putting it to use.

Since the sermon was preached while the movie was in current release, I made a deliberate choice not to include many of the specific details that I have included in the preceding theological reading. There is no direct mention of Caroline's bipolar disorder or her suicide, only a reference to "another family crisis from when [Maggie] was too young to remember." I do not say that Maggie had a sexual liaison with Rose's boyfriend, Jim, only that "Maggie literally steps into Rose's shoes and walks them into an unbelievably scandalous act against her." The reason for this decision was to avoid introducing "spoilers" that would give away too much to folks in the congregation who might go to see the movie only after hearing the sermon. Sure, some will accurately surmise the general nature of Maggie's "unbelievably scandalous act," but while it was not necessary homiletically to give all the specifics, it was necessary to make it clear that this fight between sisters was not just "a girl thing" (as Rose herself had tried to diminish it in a remark to Simon before she was willing to open that part of her life to him). Again, a cinemate audience accustomed to movie reviews will generally not appreciate someone's unnecessarily revealing things from a film that might detract from a subsequent viewing.

SERMON: "IN HIS SHOES"

(Matt. 25:14–30)

Whether we are young or old, we often make naïve assumptions about things because what seems so obvious on the surface is not really at all what is going on behind the scenes. For example, I pointed out in my children's message earlier how it is hardly coincidental that the word Jesus uses in the parable we have read this morning refers in English both to an amount of money in his ancient culture and to innate personal abilities and gifts in ours. But the fact is that even on Jesus' own lips this parable was never just about money. Indeed at its very core it is about a failure to make use of things that have been entrusted to us—whether those things are financial or more personal assets. We may only have the word "talent" in English because the church long ago decided this parable was about things entrusted to us by God, but that hardly contorted the meaning of what the parable was about. Yes, the parable is about money on its surface, but at a deeper level it is about trust given and trust violated. It is about things far more essential to who we are than how we handle other people's money.

Of course, I had other naïve, simplistic understandings of this parable as well. As a kid, it was always obvious to me—maybe because it was obvious to two of three characters in the parable as well—that the natural thing for the slaves to do was to use what had been entrusted to them. After all, who wouldn't want to use their "talents"? Kids worry about not having talents; if they know they have even one talent, then they're eager to show it off. Besides, these characters in the parable were slaves. Slavery wasn't a reality of my childhood, but I did know enough about it to know that slaves had better do what their masters expected and that they had good reasons to be afraid if they didn't. It should have been only natural that all three slaves would have had something to show their master upon his return for what they had done with what he had entrusted to them.

Now that I'm older, I'm well aware that it is hardly "natural" that the majority of people will do what might obviously be expected of them. For myriad reasons—good, bad, and indifferent—many people choose not to use either their "talents" or any of the other things God has entrusted to them. Now that I'm older, I'm well aware that people are often more likely to be paralyzed by their fears than motivated by them. Whether we have what obviously seems like many talents or only a few, whether we feel God has entrusted us with much or only a little, fear can drive us to bury what we have and what we are rather than expose them to even minimal risk. Fear of failure and of success, fear of others and of ourselves—all are equally debilitating. It is easy to naïvely identify with the two good slaves of the parable, but far more of us are like the slave who buried his talent. As life goes by, we all have experiences of what it was like to have been in his shoes.

Rose Feller is one of two sisters in the recent film *In Her Shoes*. She is the good daughter who would make any father proud. A Princeton graduate, a rising associate at an important Philadelphia law firm, to all appearances she is the poster child of one who has made the most of everything entrusted to her—all the more so when compared to her sister Maggie. Maggie over the years has been unable to hold down even the simplest of jobs. She has no place of her own to live and relies on the certain knowledge that her older sister will take her in when her own life is coming apart at the seams. Maggie's only apparent asset is her beauty, and she uses it to allure and, yes, to seduce men into providing her the drinks at the bar, the dinner at the restaurant that she has no money to provide for herself.

But Maggie's very confidence in her beauty is nothing more than a façade behind which she has buried her true self, more fearful that her limitations will be exposed than that her body will be. Sexual intimacy hides her from the risk of personal intimacy. This fear of hers likewise stands out all the more clearly when compared to her sister, because Rose's professional success masks her fears and uncertainties about her personal life as well. In many respects, Rose has buried her personal life in a closet full of expensive shoes that, as Maggie points out, she never wears. Rose goes on shopping binges when she feels bad about herself and consoles herself with the knowledge that while clothes may not look good on her because she also tends to comfort herself with food binges, "shoes always fit."

Both sisters have only each other, and both sisters push and prod the other to risk the parts of themselves they have buried away. Rose uses her professional skills to push Maggie to write a resume to find work to support herself. Maggie taunts Rose that those stylish and, yes, sexy shoes stashed in her closet should be out in the world living a life of scandal. Yet neither sister can convince the other to lay aside her fears. And when Maggie literally steps into Rose's shoes and walks them into an unbelievably scandalous act against her, the trust they have placed in each other is utterly destroyed. There is weeping, and wailing, and gnashing of teeth; and they are cast out of each other's lives.

Yet it is in this moment of crisis that Maggie discovers another part of her life, hidden away for years. She finds a stash of birthday and other cards from a grandmother, buried in a drawer in the wake of another family crisis from when she was too young to remember. Maggie goes searching for this grandmother she has never known and finds a woman who likewise has buried parts of herself. Entrusted once more with a granddaughter long lost to her, the grandmother finds the courage to risk losing Maggie again by being lovingly harsh. She will help Maggie achieve a dream, but only if Maggie takes the first steps in achieving it for herself. As Maggie goes to work, she digs up the empathy and understanding of others long buried away under manipulation and passive control, and she finds a new understanding of herself and a corresponding new vision of her dream. Rose, too, finds someone to help her uncover her true self, and when the grandmother reaches out to her as well, the ground is laid for reconciliation even with Maggie. Three women, entrusted with each other, ultimately receive the blessing of freeing themselves from their fears as well.

All of us are stewards to whom God has entrusted many things—call them family, call them opportunities, call them resources, call them talents. True, some of us have been entrusted with demonstrably more than others, but as the parable makes clear, we all have been entrusted with what must be on the whole considered riches rather than chump change. And the parable makes something else clear as well: God will be lovingly harsh with each of us, holding us to account for what we do with what has been entrusted to us. That can be a terrifying thought. It can lead us to bury these things for what we hope will be safekeeping, to safeguard them and ourselves from risk. But Jesus is telling us that in fact there is no escaping risk. Yes, that truth can be terrifying, but it is not intended to be. When we see that even being held to account is an act of God's love for us, the prodding and pushing to risk the parts of ourselves we have buried away, to become the faithful stewards that God knows us to be, then as we are standing there in his shoes, we will be freed from our fears to act so as to hear God's "Well done!"

9

Hearing More than Just the Film

The Passion of the Christ, Atlantis, and *Million Dollar Baby / The Sea Inside*

The treatments of films in the preceding chapters have all been based primarily on genre and thematic approaches to film analysis. As I discussed in chapter 2, these approaches give primary attention to the overall plot of the movie and how the development of particular scenes express and create the overall meaning of the film. In that same chapter I also discussed other approaches to film analysis that take in factors beyond the film itself. Such factors may include how the movie is like or unlike other films by the same auteur, how the film relates to the world in which it was produced or that it purports to reflect, and how the world responds to the film as a cultural artifact.

This chapter presents examples of sermons developed using these particular strategies. In each instance, one specific factor beyond the film itself will play a primary role in constructing the dialogue. Just as these factors may have played subsidiary roles in the thematically oriented sermons in the previous chapters, so other factors external to the film or even thematic characteristics of the movies may play subsidiary roles in the development of these sermons. Because the focus here is on factors beyond the films themselves, the introductions to each sermon will not be formal analyses of the films. Rather, with each example I provide a brief discussion of why I chose to engage the particular film(s) in my preaching, and why I chose the particular dialogue strategy for each sermon.

PREACHING IN DIALOGUE WITH THE AUTEUR: MEL GIBSON'S *THE PASSION OF THE CHRIST*

Would Mel Gibson's *The Passion of the Christ*[1] have been the phenomenal box office success in America that it was apart from what might cynically be considered a carefully orchestrated and calibrated controversy about its alleged anti-Semitism?[2] Consider a comparison. The theatrical run of *The Lord of the Rings: The Return of the King* was winding down at the time of the release of *The Passion of the Christ*, but both eventually grossed just over $370 million in American box office receipts. Yet, worldwide, *The Return of the King* had almost double the box office receipts of *The Passion*.[3] Why is it that the only cinematic version of the life of Jesus to be in the top one hundred films in adjusted gross box office is *The Passion of the Christ*?[4]

While it was the controversy about the film's anti-Semitism and its claims to historical accuracy that led me to see the film in preparation for teaching an adult education class at my church, it was not that aspect of the film's reception by the culture that persuaded me to dialogue with it in a sermon. Much was being made in the controversy about how the movie fit into the overall corpus of Mel Gibson's work, particularly other violent films like *Braveheart* and *The Patriot*. These aspects of Gibson the auteur paired well with Gibson the armchair theologian, for his understanding of the atonement both as portrayed in the film and in the many interviews he gave at the time was that the violence inflicted on Jesus was the vicarious-substitutionary (not, I believe, words he used but certainly the classical theological language for the view he espoused) punishment for human sin. The violence is so great because the offense against a holy God is so great.

It was the theology proper, that is, what it says about the nature of God, inherent in this theory of atonement that I wanted to address in my Holy Week sermon. Certainly this understanding of the atonement is longstanding and has had many important proponents. It is not, however, the only way to understand the role of violence in Jesus' passion with respect to the work of atonement.[5] My concern was that the attitudes about violence in our culture generally, and as reflected in many of Mel Gibson's films specifically, are related to the prevalence of the logic of vicarious-substitutionary atonement for so many American Christians. It is not clear to me whether such attitudes toward violence predispose us to accept a certain view of atonement, or whether the attitude toward violence arises from a certain view of divine justice intrinsic to a particular atonement theory. What is clear is that the choice one makes between atonement theories has real effects in the world.

SERMON: "WHY SUCH A PASSION?"

(Isa. 53:1–12; Luke 22:33–37, 44–49)

Why did he do it? To answer that question in hindsight, one would be tempted to say that Mel Gibson made *The Passion of the Christ* for the money.

After all, that is why most big-budget movies get made, and this film has been a phenomenal box office success. If its Holy Week numbers should match its opening week figures (and of what other film in history could that have been held out as a possibility?), then it is set to move past $375 million dollars in U.S. ticket sales—ahead of even *The Lord of the Rings: The Return of the King.* But Gibson has always insisted that this is one film that he did not make for the money. That claim would seem to be borne out both by the fact that he financed the film himself and by the extreme difficulty he had in finding a distributor for it.

Then again, the "why?" question is not really about why Gibson made a film about Jesus. Many others had done so in the past, and no doubt many will do so in the future. No, the question really is why he made his cinematic interpretation of Jesus' passion one of the most relentlessly violent films ever produced. More than a few reviewers have commented that had this film been about anyone other than Jesus of Nazareth its violence would have earned an NC-17 rather than an R rating from the Motion Picture Association of America.

But as with the financial-motivation answers to the "why?" question, most of the answers to the question "Why such a violent film?" have been overly simplistic as well. To say that Gibson has always had an almost sadistic obsession with violence, from *Mad Max* to *Braveheart,* may be true enough, but he has insisted that the violence on the screen during *The Passion* is because of the violence on the ancient streets of Jerusalem. To his mind at least, if perhaps not to the pope's mind to whom this quote was originally attributed, "It is as it was." A historian of the first-century Mediterranean world might quibble with that assertion relative to many details of the film; but for a historian of the depiction of this story in the Western artistic tradition, there can be no serious doubt. Almost frame by frame, Gibson has created on film the images of Caravaggio, Bosch, the Isenheim altar, and others.

The reason for the violence in the film *The Passion of the Christ* is because of the brutally violent death experienced by Jesus of Nazareth. Within the long tradition of Western Christianity, stretching from the New Testament evangelists themselves through the medieval and Counter-Reformation painters right up to Gibson's film, the consistent assertion has been "that the Son of Man *must* undergo great suffering, and be rejected by the elders, the chief priests, and the scribes, and be killed, and after three days rise again" (Mark 8:31, emphasis added). Jesus' suffering—his passion—has been considered the greatest sign of God's love for humanity. As Gibson has asserted in interview after interview, understanding the depth and reality of God's love for us demands confronting the brutality and reality of Christ's death.

But how can that be? How can such unremitting violence be a demonstration of God's love? Gibson provides his answer to that question at the very outset of his film. The movie opens without so much as a title, much less the usual credits. It begins with a citation from our first Scripture lesson for today:

> He was wounded for our transgressions,
>   crushed for our iniquities;
> upon him was the punishment that made us whole,
>   and by his bruises we are healed. (Isa. 53:5)

It was to those words from a Jewish prophet that some of the first Christians turned to make sense of the horror of Jesus' death. It was the punishment for our evil. What we should have experienced as God's wrath against us, Jesus instead took on in our place. Why so violent? Because our evil is so great it demands such violent punishment.

And to underscore that he has made this explanation his own, Gibson drew a scene from the visions of a nineteenth-century mystic set in the Garden of Gethsemane. As he anguishes in prayer, we watch Jesus being challenged by Satan to give up. No one man, Satan insists, can bear the punishment for the sins of the whole world. But Jesus won't give up in Gethsemane. Beaten and bloody, he won't give up in Pilate's judgment hall. Nailed to a cross on Golgotha, Jesus still won't give up his mission, only his life for our sins. So great is Jesus' love for all of humanity that he will die such a horrible death. That is why Gibson briefly cuts away from the crucifixion to show a flashback to Jesus' final meal with his disciples, where Jesus tells them, "There is no greater love than for a man to lay down his life for his friends."

Theologians call this understanding of Jesus' passion "vicarious-substitutionary atonement." It is a fancy way of saying Jesus was sacrificed in our place to appease the just wrath of an angry God. As I have said, it is an ancient and well-established answer to the question "Why did he have to die, and how did his death accomplish our salvation?" But it is, when you really start to think about it, a deeply troubling answer. While it demonstrates the tremendous love of Jesus, it turns God into something of a blood-thirsty monster. God's creation has been violated by our evil, so someone must pay with his or her life—indeed pay through a torturous and agonizing death—in order to satisfy God's angry demand for vengeance. How can such a God be, as Christian Scriptures assert, love itself (1 John 4:16b)?

There is another answer to the question "Why such a passion?" It too has a long history in Christian religious tradition, and it too sees Jesus' death as a kind of sacrifice. But rather than seeing Jesus as a sacrifice offered to God in order to appease the divine wrath, it sees God incarnated in Jesus as sacrificing the divine self to the depth of human evil and depravity. Yes, the horror of death by crucifixion is key to how Jesus' death redeems us. But it displays not the magnitude of God's anger but the depth of our depravity. So great is our evil that humanity has done this not only to Jesus of Nazareth, but to multiple thousands of others who were crucified by the Romans and multiplied millions who have been killed in equally monstrous ways in the centuries before and since, right up until today. But God refuses to allow such evil to have the last word; so God overcomes our murderous evil by raising Christ from the dead. The brutal and violent nature of Jesus' death reveals the true evil of humanity; the resurrection reveals the power of divine love to overcome that evil, refusing to let it be the final reality.

What difference does it make which of these answers we, as Christians, should choose to the question "Why such a passion?" Maybe in the abstract it makes no difference at all. But in the reality of a world still awaiting the final triumph of God's loving justice, it does matter. As we seek to align ourselves with what God is doing in the world, will we see God as demanding and exacting punishment and retribution upon those doing evil? If so, then we may be quick to exact punishment and retribution ourselves from those we see as evil. Or are we willing to see that we more often than not align ourselves *against* rather than *with* God? Our very means of punishment often continue the relentless cycle of violence rather than break it. Are we willing to align ourselves with a Jesus who absorbs in himself the evils of our world, trusting in God's loving power to resurrect life from such a passion?

PREACHING IN DIALOGUE WITH THE WORLD IN THE FILM: *ATLANTIS: THE LOST EMPIRE*

Mark Pinsky, in concluding his treatment of *Atlantis*[6] in *The Gospel according to Disney*, observed, "It is hard to believe that Michael Eisner, a notorious micromanager, planned the film as a devastating, unrelenting attack on capitalism and American imperialism. Yet it is impossible to read the movie, at least the last third of the film, any other way."[7] What was going on in the world at the turn of the millennium when this film was in production that may have had as one of its results the making of this film?

Perhaps it was a fusion of ideas associated with postcolonialism and multiculturalism. As in *Pocahontas*, its sympathies clearly lie with the culture that is being disturbed by discovery rather than the one engaging in exploration in hopes of exploitation, even if here that culture is a completely imagined one conjured from ancient myths. It is certainly the case that the characters in this film (including a biracial medical doctor, with an African American father and Native American mother, and a Latina mechanic) are much more in keeping with values of inclusiveness found in 2001 when the film was released than in 1914 when it was set—regardless of whether they were the "best of the best" in their areas of responsibility. Whatever its sources, Pinsky is correct that the film indicts both the colonial enterprise and those who seek profit from militarization.

Looking back, I find it not a little ironic that this film and sermon preceded September 11, 2001, by only two months. *Atlantis* is set on the eve of the "Great War to End All Wars" and was released on the eve of the "War on Terrorism." The film invites the audience to see the American characters' execution of their mission as a series of acts that terrorize another civilization and threaten it with extinction. *Atlantis* challenges the audience to choose to stand with Milo Thatch (Michael J. Fox) and the members of the team who ultimately join him in opposing his own culture—or perhaps better, in opposing those who have corrupted its values, since Milo and his values are also a part of that culture—in order to protect the foreign one. The years since have seen many who have issued similar calls for people to reconsider America's response to 9/11 as both citizens and Christians.[8]

The scriptural partner to the dialogue in the sermon is taken primarily from Col. 1:15–28, the Epistle lesson appointed for the 16th Sunday in Ordinary Time, Year C. It allows the film's critique of imperialism and militarism to stand on its own and then explores the ways that the church may—like Milo Thatch and those of the expedition who ultimately decide to stand with him—have been co-opted by the powers of empire. Just as the writer of Colossians uses the language of "thrones," "dominions," and "powers" to exalt the work of Christ, we may have been too quick to buy into the means and even the aspirations of empire rather than the way of Christ in identification with suffering alongside the oppressed. Yet the way out of this danger lies in reclaiming a proper understanding of our traditions, not in abandoning them. When we see the ways that "power tends to corrupt," then we can reject for ourselves the desire for "absolute power [that] corrupts absolutely" (to return once again to Lord Acton's dictum).

SERMON: "LOST EMPIRE OR EMPIRE LOST?"

(Ps. 52; Col. 1:15–28)

> In a single day and night of misfortune, the island of Atlantis disappeared into the depths of the sea.—Plato, 360 B.C.

With those words emblazoned across the screen, Disney's latest animated adventure begins. The text gives way to a scene of many men fleeing a tremendous explosion, desperately trying to reach the city of Atlantis before the cataclysm strikes. Once there, we see a mother taken up into a beam of light as her terrified, toddler daughter cowers in her father's embrace. Suddenly from the source of the bright light there emanates a kind of protective force field that encloses the city just as giant tsunamis rush over it and immerse it in the waters of the sea.

Now we are standing here in our own city, just outside the Smithsonian Castle, but the year is 1914. An aspiring linguist and archaeologist, Milo Thatch, is rehearsing his speech regarding his theory for finding the ancient "Shepherd's Journal" that holds the key to locating the Lost Empire of Atlantis. Ridiculed and rejected by the museum's directors, Milo is drawn into an expedition being organized by a wealthy eccentric, Mr. Preston Whitmore (John Mahoney). We learn that the "Shepherd's Journal" had in fact already been discovered by Milo's beloved grandfather, Thadeus Thatch. Now Milo is being asked to translate and interpret the journal so that the expedition under the direction of Commander Rourke (James Garner) can reach the fabled sunken continent.

Once they do reach Atlantis, they meet the toddler—now grown to young womanhood—and her aged father, apparently blinded by the brightness of the light that had taken his wife, Kida's (Cree Summer) mother, on the day of the cataclysm. They have survived for literally thousands of years because of the symbiotic relationship the Atlanteans have with a crystal that provides them with energy and health while drawing strength from their emotions. We also learn that the cataclysm that had led to Atlantis being swallowed by the sea had been triggered by the king's attempt to harness and use the crystal's power as an ultimate weapon.

This revelation also unmasks Commander Rourke's true intention. You see, they had removed the page from the "Shepherd's Journal" that had described this mysterious, powerful crystal known as the "Heart of Atlantis." Rather than the grand and glorious archaeological expedition that Milo had envisioned, Rourke's purpose had always been to retrieve the crystal and sell it to whichever of the warring parties in Europe would offer the highest price— even the Kaiser himself, as Milo exclaims. Milo enlists his friends from the expedition and the Atlanteans themselves in an effort to stop Rourke, and they save the crystal, Kida, and all of Atlantis. The message is clear: the Lost Empire of Atlantis (and even our own modern civilizations) can only survive if the notion of empire is lost to them. Power is for nurture and sustenance, not for empire building.

Power. Empire. If you want to see the images of imperial power, then look at how Paul describes Christ here in the opening chapter of Colossians: "He is the image of the invisible God, the firstborn of all creation." Nothing visible or invisible in creation exists apart from him, not even the "thrones or dominions or rulers or powers" that falsely lay claim to being the genuine empires in control over our world. Christ "is before all things, and in him all things hold together." And if Christ is Lord over all creation, then there can be no doubt about who is in charge of the church: "He is the head of the body, the church; he is . . . the firstborn from the dead, so that he might come to have first place in everything." Paul sums up all that it means for Christ to be Lord by saying, "In him all the fullness of God was pleased to dwell." Now, here at last, is the one before whom the psalmist promised all those self-proclaimed "mighty ones" would be broken. This is *Christus Victor,* Christ the Conqueror who establishes the empire of God.

From at least the time of Constantine, through the Crusades, the Holy Roman Empire, and up to the modern age, *Christus Victor* was the dominant image of Christ in the church. The progress of European civilization and the expansion of Western cultural influence around the globe were considered of a piece with the spread of Christendom. Christ was Lord of all, and that dominion would be recognized by individuals and whole cultures alike—at the tip of a sword if necessary. Christ held the ultimate power of divinity itself, and the purpose of the church was to harness that power—as a weapon if need be—to build the empire of Christendom.

But the church's very desire to use its power to build an empire has unleashed a cultural backlash that, if not a cataclysm, was at least strong enough to swamp the church. We are now living in a time that is, as Stanley Hauerwas has described it, "after Christendom."[9] The European nations from which Christendom launched its spread around the world are now full of empty churches. Our own nation, whose motto "In God We Trust" is still struck on our coins, wrestles with not only the question of how but even whether religion has a function in the public square. And like Disney's Atlanteans, our very struggle to survive has severed us from our own traditions.

There are those who would say that the answer is for Christians to reassert the image of *Christus Victor,* to once again wage war against evil cultures and break their "mighty ones" with divine power. There are those who say such things, but they are wrong. They are wrong because they didn't read all of Paul's description of Christ there in Colossians 1. Right after announcing that the fullness of deity dwells in Christ, Paul describes the use to which that divine power was put: "Through him God was pleased to reconcile to [the divine] self all things, whether on earth or in heaven, by making peace through the blood of his cross." The Lord Christ was not building an empire but reconciling creation with God. The church was not to be on a crusade to force submission to Christ's lordship but was rather to join with the apostle in "rejoicing in . . . sufferings . . . completing what is lacking in Christ's afflictions for the sake of his body, that is, the church." It is a "mystery that has been hidden throughout the ages and generations but has now been revealed to [God's] saints" that the Messiah came not to restore a lost empire to the people of God but rather to urge the loss of empire as the goal.

Why are we here as a church? To rebuild a lost empire of the former glory of Christendom? We can only survive as the people of God if the notion of empire is lost to us. Christ's divine power is for nurture and sustenance, not for empire building.

PREACHING IN DIALOGUE WITH THE FILM IN THE WORLD: *MILLION DOLLAR BABY* AND *THE SEA INSIDE*

In 2005 the Academy-Award-winning films in both the "best picture" and "best foreign language film" dealt with the theme of assisted suicide. Such a coincidence of subject matter in these award categories is rare, to say the least, if not genuinely unique. That alone might have been enough to draw considerable attention among columnists, commentators, and the general public, but these films were also in release at the same time as the Terri Schiavo case was at its peak—with interventions in the courts, the Florida state legislature, and even the United States Congress over whether her husband had the legal authority to terminate her life-support care against her parents' wishes.[10] Although the films had obviously been in production long before the Schiavo case gained wide prominence, it is fair to ask what influence the public debate stirred by that case had on the reception of the films and the votes of Academy members.

Because the Schiavo case was at its peak at the time I preached the sermon (life support was removed on March 18, 2005, five days after the sermon was preached, and she died roughly two weeks later, on March 31), I determined that direct mention of her case was potentially too polarizing and would tend toward an illustration that would run away with the sermon. The awarding of the Oscars to *Million Dollar Baby* and *The Sea Inside*[11] just two weeks before the sermon provided an opportunity to engage broader cultural attitudes about death and disease without being drawn into partisan policy debates specifically about Terri Schiavo. The scriptural texts used in the sermon are the Revised Common Lectionary lessons from the Old Testament (Ezek. 37:1–14) and the Gospels (John 11:1–45) assigned for the Fifth Sunday in Lent, Year A.

SERMON: "SEEING LIFE IN THE MIDST OF DEATH"

(Ezek. 37:1–14; John 11:1–45)

What are we to make of the fact that this year's Academy-Award-winning films in both the "best picture" and "best foreign language film" categories end with the assisted suicide of a quadriplegic? And what about the fact that *Million Dollar Baby* won not only "best picture" but also "best director," "best actress in a leading role," and "best actor in a supporting role" Oscars for Clint Eastwood, Hillary Swank, and Morgan Freeman, respectively? Are we to conclude that "Hollywood"—as we call the entertainment and cultural juggernaut that is the mainline American film industry—is actively promoting euthanasia? Certainly there has been no shortage of critics who have tried to make that case.

The Sea Inside, the Spanish-language film that presents a fictionalized account of the final months of the real person Ramon Sampedro, has generally been reviewed as the more nuanced of the two movies in its portrayal of the ethical and moral issues surrounding the so-called "right to die." Sampedro was a sailor who had traveled around the world until a diving accident left him unable to move below the neck. For more than a quarter century he lived on, refusing to leave his room or even his bed. He was lovingly cared for by family and friends, but he himself lobbied the whole time to gain the right from the Spanish government to have his life ended.

Million Dollar Baby is based on characters from a pair of short stories, and so is completely a work of fiction. But in a world that once more argues its causes in stories rather than logic, it makes no less a statement about the truth that some people find in the world. It is the story of Maggie Fitzgerald, a young woman who convinces an old boxing trainer to develop her into a champion fighter. At the very moment of her—of their—success, she likewise is struck down and becomes a quadriplegic. She pleads with her trainer to help her end her life, and in the end he does. Yet despite assertions by some commentators, the portrayal of this story by Swank and Eastwood does not glamorize or heroize her decision or his actions. One character may be dead at the end of the film, but there are two lives that have been utterly and completely destroyed.

That both these particular films end in assisted suicide and that the members of the Academy of Motion Picture Arts and Sciences selected them as the best films of the past year does not indicate that either the filmmakers or film industry is promoting the euthanasia of quadriplegics. Nor do they represent the view that the decision to end one's own life with a "good death"— the root meaning of "euthanasia"—should be a universally recognized human right. No, what these two honored films illustrate is our cultural ability to see death in the midst of life. Both the real-life Ramon Sampedro and the fictional Maggie Fitzgerald embody the view that unless life is everything, then it is nothing. And though our society hopes never to be faced with that choice in such tragic form, its sympathies for Ramon and Maggie demonstrate a tendency to see the world in the same way.

Both our Scripture lessons for this morning argue a contrary view. They argue for looking out upon our world and lives and instead seeing life in the midst of death. They do not present the contrast between "seeing death in the midst of life" or "life in the midst of death" as simplistic as a "glass half empty" or "half full" choice. There is nothing Pollyannish about seeing "life in the midst of death"; it is neither a denial nor diminishment of death or its effects in the world. It is simply the hope, the faith, that the always-present God of life is there as well. Our Scripture lessons are in an ultimate sense the source of the priest's counsel to the trainer in *Million Dollar Baby*: even in the midst of such tragedy God is present, and to act in such a way as to deny that reality is to lose one's self forever.

The challenge to see "life in the midst of death" was at the heart of God's question to Ezekiel, "Can these bones live?" For the prophet, the question came as part of a vision, but the circumstances that gave rise to the vision were all too real. Judah, his homeland, had been dealt a deathblow by its adversaries. It was nothing more than a valley of dry bones, bereft of any future life so far as anyone could see, and scattered across the world as the bones were scattered across the valley floor. The only reasonable answer to God's question would be "No; more than even death has befallen us, and these bones cannot live." But as Ezekiel looked out upon bones in the valley, he found hope if not optimism in the one who stood beside him. "O Lord GOD, you know." If God stood with him there, then he could yet see life in the midst of death.

Again and again in our Gospel lesson, we encounter people who see "death in the midst of life." Even as Lazarus still lies ill, his sisters and even the disciples focus their attention on death. Once Lazarus has died and Jesus announces his intention to return to Bethany in Judea, his disciples continue to only see death—Lazarus's death, the threat of death for Jesus, the possibility of death for themselves—rather than the continuing promise of life. When Jesus arrives, Martha can only see the death of her brother. At Jesus' prodding, she confesses that there will one day, far in the future, be resurrection life for her brother. But not that day. On that day there is only death, only the tomb. Then Jesus challenges her to believe that life is indeed present: "I am the resurrection and the life. . . . Do you believe this?" Can you see that life is indeed present even in the midst of death? And Martha answers, "Yes, Lord, I believe that you are the Messiah, the Son of God, the one coming into the world." She believes many things, but she can't quite bring herself to say, "I believe that you are the resurrection and the life." But in her belief that he was "the Son of God," she could find in Jesus God's presence with her; she could see something of life in the midst of death.

This morning we will share together in a service for healing and wholeness. The very naming of our needs in the title of this rite is a concession of our suffering and brokenness, an admission of the power of death at work in our world. But it is also a declaration of our hope apparently against all hope. It is our answering with the prophet that only God knows whether life can be restored to the places of dry bones in our lives. It is our declaration of belief with Martha that Jesus is the Son of God who brings the divine presence to us even as we stand at the tombs. It is our affirmation of faith that if God is here, then it is possible for the voice that called all things into existence to call forth life from the grave. It is our commitment to see life in the midst of death because we know that God is with us—the God of life is with us even in the midst of death.

Conclusion

Opening the Preacher's Eyes and Ears

Throughout this book I have tried to argue for and to demonstrate what I believe are the benefits of dialoguing with popular films in preaching, as well as some of the problems that need to be avoided. As I prepare to send you off to your own theological engagement with movies and the expression of those insights in your sermons, I want to leave you with some words of caution about the terrain you are about to enter and a clear sense of why it remains worth the risk. These bits of closing advice are taken from two handbooks for preachers—one modern and directly responding to our cinemate culture; the other ancient enough to stand in the gap between preliterate and fully literate culture but speaking directly to preachers of any culture.

SEEING POTENTIAL "PITFALLS"

Richard Eslinger has written a fine book on "pitfalls" to be avoided in all aspects of the preaching task. In his chapter on the (mis)uses of illustrations he has a short section on "going to the movies."[1] He begins by identifying several of the reasons I have already discussed that movies could be of such potential benefit as illustrative material in sermons, such as "the increasingly visual orientation of our culture" and the way films both inform us about emerging cultural trends and also shape "the values, virtues, and character of church and society." But he identifies three particular "pitfalls" concerning which preachers must be aware so their sermons don't get lost in them.

First, there is what he calls "the Personalities Agenda." Eslinger notes that Americans' interest in movies goes far beyond simply what happens on the screens of the cineplex or the family television. Whole industries have grown up to satisfy people's interest in the lives of the stars who appear in movies and on television. All of this information lurks behind the preacher's intention in introducing the material from the film. Sometimes, as was the case with Mel Gibson and *The Passion of the Christ*, the headlines about the actor and the film are inextricably bound up in one another; other times the associations (whether positive or negative) will be far more individualized among members of the congregation. What is the risk that mention of a film starring Tom Cruise will send your listeners off into their own ruminations about Scientology rather than about the gospel? It is doubtful this potential problem can be avoided simply by using only the character names rather than the actors' names, for in a cinemate culture folks are aware of which movies the stars are in, or at least the (in)famous ones. If an actor is currently making headlines off-screen, it may not be a good time to engage a film in which that actor plays a leading character on-screen.

Eslinger next talks about the problems inherent with "the Generational Thing." Look at the demographics of who is attending a film, and you will see that it is the rare film indeed that draws an audience from a broad spectrum of society. Although his label focuses attention on age-related differences, the differences can be just as strongly correlated to gender (recall the "chick flick" label attached to *In Her Shoes*); race (Spike Lee films typically draw higher percentages of African American viewers than other racial groups); or even class (Merchant Ivory films and Woody Allen pictures don't tend to draw a lot of folks from lower socioeconomic groups). His advice is for preachers to ask whether it may be necessary "to devote more attention to providing a context for a film" if it is one the congregation is less likely to have seen or even have heard about. This concern is also one of the reasons I have suggested looking first to popular rather than niche films. Their box office success often leads to exposure in other places, particularly newspapers and magazines, which may provide some context for folks who either haven't or simply won't ever see the movie.

Finally, Eslinger identifies the pitfall of "the Cultural Myths of American Films." At this point he is of course dealing with an issue at the core of this book. He acknowledges that there can be both myths that run contrary to Christian theology as well as those that parallel or support Christian ideas. Whether the myth is to be affirmed or critiqued, I have tried to suggest that making these unstated myths explicit should be a primary goal of dialoguing with films in preaching. The chief value of Eslinger's warning at this point is in making explicit how much might be brought in unintentionally. The specific example he provides is with regard to the *Star Wars* movies. While their sharp distinctions between goodness and "the dark side" may be useful in helping people to grasp the dualism of light and darkness in the Johannine litera-ture, they bring along with "the force" a lot of ideas that might be associated with what he calls "pop Buddhism" that would need to be countered.

Eslinger ends where he began by endorsing the value of using movies in our preaching because of their great potential benefit. But he is correct that while the benefit may outweigh the risk, that does not mean the risks can simply be ignored.

HEARING AGAIN THE PURPOSE

I began this book by offering a pragmatic definition of "preaching" as oral communication intended to shape a person's religious understanding of the world and to motivate behavior in accord with that religious understanding. In formulating that definition, I explicitly avoided more technical or tradi-tional approaches to defining preaching and its purposes. But here at the end I want to consider the grandparent of all statements of the purposes of Chris-tian preaching.

Writing to the ministers under his care, Augustine argued that the three fundamental purposes of preaching were to teach (convey information), to delight (gain and hold the audience's attention), and to persuade (call forth a moral response).[2] In Augustine's view, only teaching was a "necessity." Only if people know the truth can they be held accountable for it. He describes per-suasion as a "triumph" because by it the audience grants their consent and then acts in accord with the truth they have been taught. It is not a necessity—something that must be explicitly present on every occasion of preaching—because sometimes simply learning the truth is enough to convince people to accept and abide by it. In a similar way, delight is also not a necessity because, in Augustine's mind, learning what is true and learning to distinguish it from what is false should be pleasure and delight enough. It might seem then that delight is of lesser importance than the other two purposes of preaching. But look again at the role delight plays among the purposes of preaching: it is what gains and holds the attention of the audience. Apart from their attention, it will not matter how clear the teaching is because no one will hear it. No mat-ter how persuasive the call to response, it will elicit no change in behavior or in the world if the audience, to use a modern metaphor, has already tuned out. Delight alone (what we might now call "entertainment") can never be the pur-pose of preaching, but if not for the attention gained by delight, there would be no one to learn the truth and transform their lives and the world by it.

What Augustine referred to as teaching corresponds in our pragmatic def-inition of preaching to shaping a person's religious understanding of the world, and what he called persuasion fits with our pragmatic definition of motivating behavior. Though Augustine's purpose of delight was not covered by the pragmatic definition with which we began, in a way this whole book has been about delight, about creating sermons that will both in their content and in their structure grab and hold the attention of folks in our cinemate culture. With Augustine I would stress that preaching can never be only about delight. Movies can be strictly about entertainment; genuine preaching cannot. Movies can and often are about much more than merely entertainment, and when they are, they may be able to bring an element of delight to our preaching that will grab and hold the attention of our congregations so that they can come to know the truth that will set them free (see John 8:32).

Notes

Introduction

1. One might say that Paul's letters are in some instances "sermons delivered at a distance" at a time when the technological means for delivering them orally was unavailable. The adoption of literate means of delivery, however, places them outside our definition of preaching as "oral communication." Again, "sermons" may be the content of what is preached, but they are not "preaching" outside oral performance.

2. Reading the literature in the field of "film studies," one becomes aware of the connotations of the terms *cinema*, *film*, and *movies*, associating them with points along a continuum from high culture to low, or even profane culture, respectively. Other technical distinctions are also occasionally introduced (such as using "cinema" to designate the full range of the film industry from production to distribution). I will use these words simply as synonyms, specifically trying to avoid distinctions between "high" and "low" culture, between "art films" and "popular movies" (for reasons I will discuss shortly). On the distinctions in denotation and connotation of these terms in film study, see James Monaco, *How to Read a Film: Multimedia Edition* (DVD-ROM; New York: Harbor Electronic Publishing and UNET 2 Corporation, 2000), 4.1 (i.e., "page 1" of the Adobe Acrobat file of ch. 4 in the book *How to Read a Film*, which provides a primary base for navigating the multimedia disc; I will use this convention throughout for citations from this work). For precedent in not getting drawn into distinctions between "film," "movies," etc., see Robert K. Johnston, *Reel Spirituality: Theology and Film in Dialogue* (Engaging Culture; Grand Rapids: Baker Academic, 2000), 16 and n. 7 on 197.

3. Monaco, *How to Read a Film*, 3.1.

4. See Johnston, *Reel Spirituality*, 24; Clive Marsh and Gaye Ortiz, eds., *Explorations in Theology and Film* (Oxford: Blackwell, 1997), 2; and, regarding movies as part of pop culture more generally, Craig Detweiler and Barry Taylor, *A Matrix of Meanings: Finding God in Pop Culture* (Engaging Culture; Grand Rapids: Baker Academic, 2003), 21.

5. Cf. Johnston, *Reel Spirituality*, 13–14. On issues raised by other forms of media and multimedia, see Monaco, *How to Read a Film*, chaps. 6 ("Media: In the Middle of Things") and 7 ("Multimedia: The Digital Revolution"), and his anthology (coedited with Curtis Church) *Reading about New Media*, included on the DVD-ROM.

6. Brian Godawa, *Hollywood Worldviews: Watching Films with Wisdom and Discernment* (Downers Grove, IL: InterVarsity Press, 2002), 17–18.

7. See Michael Medved, *Hollywood Versus America: Popular Culture and the War on Traditional Values* (New York: HarperCollins, 1992).

8. Clive Marsh, "Film and Theologies of Culture," in Marsh and Ortiz, eds., *Explorations in Theology and Film*, 32.

9. See David Browne, "Film, Movies, Meanings," in Marsh and Ortiz, eds., *Explorations in Theology and Film*, 10–12; Graeme Turner, "Cultural Studies and Film," in John Hill and Pamela Church Gibson, et al., eds., *The Oxford Guide to Film Studies* (New York: Oxford University Press, 1998), 195–201; and Douglas Kellner, "Hollywood Film and Society," in Hill and Church Gibson et al., eds., *Oxford Guide to Film Studies*, 354–62.

10. Obviously the United States' entry into World War II also impacted the hunting business, but the 1942 baseline in the comparison takes that into account.

11. Johnston, *Reel Spirituality*, 22.

12. See Marsh, "Film and Theologies of Culture," 21–34; David John Graham, "The Uses of Film in Theology," in Marsh and Ortiz, eds., *Explorations in Theology and Film*, 35–43; and Johnston, *Reel Spirituality*, 63–86.

13. Johnston, *Reel Spirituality*, 78–86; Godawa, *Hollywood Worldviews*, 25–41.

14. Marsh, "Films and Theologies of Culture," 32.

15. Ibid., 32–33; Johnston, *Reel Spirituality*, 65–74; and Detweiler and Taylor, *Matrix of Meanings*, 15–17.

16. Marsh, "Film and Theologies of Culture," 33; Johnston, *Reel Spirituality*, 74–78.

17. The "medium of preaching" would include a host of variables. Is the preacher addressing a congregation physically present for the preaching event, an audience tuned to a broadcast medium (radio, television, or video-conference link), or both? Beyond the oral-aural aspects of the medium, there is what is communicated by such nonverbal means as the preacher's body language; his or her presence in a pulpit or standing on chancel steps; the choice of wearing religious vestments or clothing from the broader culture (and, even then, whether "professional" or "casual" attire); the architecture of the space where the preacher speaks, etc. All of these things and more shape what is communicated in preaching.

18. As with most popular attributions of invention, the details are more complicated. Edison assigned the task of creating motion-picture-capture and -viewing devices to an employee, William K. L. Dickson, whose work led to the kinetoscope. Auguste and Louis Lumière subsequently invented the cinématographe, the basic technology on which the movie industry was launched.

19. The literature in this field is extensive and rapidly growing; see the annotated bibliographies in Marsh and Ortiz, eds., *Explorations in Theology and Film*, 257–76, and Johnston, *Reel Spirituality*, 209–21.

20. So also Robert Jewett, *Saint Paul at the Movies: The Apostle's Dialogue with American Culture* (Louisville, KY: Westminster/John Knox Press, 1993), 10.

21. Johnston, *Reel Spirituality*, 125.

22. Such as Hill and Church Gibson et al., eds., *Oxford Guide to Film Studies* and Monaco, *How to Read a Film*; other possibilities are Louis D. Gianneti, *Understanding Movies*, 9th ed. (New York: Prentice Hall, 2002); and Leo Braudy and Marshall Cohen, eds., *Film Theory and Criticism: Introductory Readings*, 5th ed. (Oxford: Oxford University Press, 1998).

23. Paul Scott Wilson, *The Four Pages of the Sermon: A Guide to Biblical Preaching* (Nashville: Abingdon Press, 1999). See especially his introductory chapter, "Movies, Pages, and God," 9–29.

24. See Thomas H. Troeger, *Ten Strategies for Preaching in a Multi Media Culture* (Nashville: Abingdon Press, 1996), 48–57.

25. The obvious exception is *The Sea Inside*, but it is paired with the much more popular *Million Dollar Baby* in a sermon that looks more at the reaction to the films and their awards than at the specific details of the films themselves.

26. See Clive Marsh, "Did You Say 'Grace'?: Eating in Community in *Babette's Feast*," in Marsh and Ortiz, eds., *Explorations in Theology and Film*, 207–18; Robert Jewett, "*Babette's Feast* and the Shaming of the Poor in Corinth," in *Saint Paul Returns to the Movies: Triumph Over Shame* (Grand Rapids: Wm. B. Eerdmans Publishing Co., 1999), 38–51; Andrew Greeley, "Babette's Feast of Love: Symbols Subtle but Patent," in Albert J. Bergesen and Andrew M. Greeley, *God in the Movies* (New Brunswick, NJ: Transaction Publishers, 2000), 49–53; and Bryan P. Stone, "The Communion of the Saints: *Babette's Feast*" in *Faith and Film: Theological Themes at the Cinema* (St. Louis: Chalice Press, 2000), 156–66.

27. Jewett, *Saint Paul at the Movies*, 10.

28. Of 354 films to gross more than $100 million in U.S. box office receipts through August 2006, twenty-two are Disney animated films (including the eight Disney/Pixar computer-animated films; http://www.the-movie-times .com/thrsdir/alltime.mv?/domestic+ByDG+All). Adjusted for inflation, such Disney animated movies accounted for seventeen of the top 130 films in all-time U.S. box office receipts (http://www.the-movie-times.com/thrsdir/ alltime.mv?adjusted+ByAG+All) and sixteen of the top 125 films in worldwide box office receipts (http://www.the-movie-times.com/thrsdir/alltime.mv?world +ByWG+All). Web pages and rankings reported on them accessed August 31, 2006.

Chapter 1: Hearing a Film

1. Herbert A. Jump, "The Religious Possibilities of the Motion Picture," quoted in Terry Lindvall, *The Silents of God: Selected Issues and Documents in Silent American Film and Religion, 1908–1925* (London: Scarecrow Press, 2001), 71 (cited from Craig Detweiler and Barry Taylor, *A Matrix of Meanings: Finding God in Pop Culture* [Engaging Culture; Grand Rapids: Baker Academic, 2000], 156–57).

2. K. S. Hover, "Motography as an Arm of the Church," in Lindvall, *Silents of God*, 48 (cited from Detweiler and Taylor, *Matrix of Meanings*, 157).

3. *Jesus*, dir. John Heyman, 1979, The JESUS Film Project, Campus Crusade for Christ. For a discussion of this film, see W. Barnes Tatum, *Jesus at the Movies: A Guide to the First Hundred Years* (Santa Rosa, CA: Polebridge Press, 1997), 147–57.

4. Brian Godawa, *Hollywood Worldviews: Watching Films with Wisdom and Discernment* (Downers Grove, IL: InterVarsity Press, 2002), 14. Godawa even offers a

defense for viewing explicitly violent or sexual films when such explicit material is "exhortative" rather than merely "exploitative" by noting the explicitness
of the Bible itself in these regards (*Hollywood Worldviews*, 187–208).

5. Rehearsing this history is beyond the scope of this book. For summaries of
church involvement with and criticism of the American film industry, see
Robert K. Johnston, *Reel Spirituality: Theology and Film in Dialogue* (Engaging
Culture; Grand Rapids: Baker Academic, 2000), 31–39; Richard A. Blake,
Screening America: Reflections on Five Classic Films (New York: Paulist Press,
1991), 17–90; and Frank Walsh, *Sin and Censorship: The Catholic Church and the
Motion Picture Industry* (New Haven, CT: Yale University Press, 1996).

6. H. Richard Niebuhr, *Christ and Culture* (New York: Harper & Brothers, 1951);
for discussions of this model applied to film, see Clive Marsh, "Film and Theologies of Culture," in Clive Marsh and Gaye Ortiz, eds., *Explorations in Theology and Film* (Oxford: Blackwell, 1972), 24–28; and Johnston, *Reel Spirituality*,
59.

7. Niebuhr divided this approach into three distinct views: "Christ above culture"; "Christ and culture in paradox"; and "Christ, the transformer of culture."

8. Godawa, *Hollywood Worldviews*, 177–82.

9. Margaret R. Miles, *Seeing and Believing: Religion and Values in the Movies*
(Boston: Beacon Press, 1996), 21–25. I will discuss cultural studies as an interpretative model later in this chapter.

10. Cf. Johnston's comments regarding the effects of her "hermeneutics of suspi-
cion" (*Reel Spirituality*, 48–49). John R. May raises concerns specifically about
her implementation of the cultural-studies model ("Religion and Film: Recent
Contributions to the Continuing Dialogue," *Critical Review of Books in Religion*
9 [1996]: 113–16). He is critical of a method that prioritizes "the context of a
film's production and release" over a careful analysis of "the film as text"
through its "screenplay, camera-work, narrative, and soundtrack" (114).

11. See, for example, Andrew M. Greeley, "God in the Movies," in Albert J. Bergesen and Andrew M. Greeley, *God in the Movies* (New Brunswick, NJ: Transaction Publishers, 2000), 5–13; and Thomas M. Martin, *Images and the Imageless:
A Study in Religious Consciousness and Film*, 2nd ed. (Lewisburg, PA: Bucknell
University Press, 1991).

12. Cited in David John Graham, "The Uses of Film in Theology," in Clive Marsh
and Gaye Ortiz, eds., *Explorations in Theology and Film* (Oxford: Blackwell,
1997), 37. See also the discussion of Tillich as the "preeminent 'theologian of
culture'" in Marsh, "Film and Theologies of Culture," 30–32.

13. Johnston, *Reel Spirituality*, 57.

14. So Johnston, *Reel Spirituality*, 55, who cites the work of Joel W. Martin and
Conrad E. Ostwalt, Jr. (*Screening the Sacred: Religion, Myth, and Ideology in Popular American Film* [Boulder, CO: Westview Press, 1995]) as raising the same
issue.

15. Bernard Brandon Scott, *Hollywood Dreams and Biblical Stories* (Minneapolis:
Augsburg Fortress Press, 1994), 14.

16. David Tracy, *Plurality and Ambiguity: Hermeneutics, Religion, Hope* (San Fran-
cisco, CA: Harper & Row, 1987), 18. Notice, by the way, how Tracy plays out
his metaphor in terms of unlike ("is not") and like ("is").

17. Robert Jewett, *Saint Paul at the Movies: The Apostle's Dialogue with American
Culture* (Louisville, KY: Westminster/John Knox Press, 1993), 7.

18. Herein lies a major difficulty with many preachers' reliance on collections of sermon illustrations. Too often they are relying on the reading of the novel, viewing of the play or movie, description of the painting, etc., by the illustration compiler rather than their own. By the time it filters out to the congregation in preaching, it is now at third hand (at least!). How effective can that be?

19. Johnston, *Reel Spirituality*, 49. Cf. Graham, "Uses of Film in Theology," 38.

20. Marsh, "Film and Theologies of Culture," 27.

21. Cf. Jewett, *Saint Paul at the Movies*, 7–12, and his musing in *Saint Paul Returns to the Movies: Triumph over Shame* (Grand Rapids: Eerdmans, 1999), 20: "Could it be that certain movies afford deeper access to the hidden heart of Paul's theology than mainstream theologians . . . have been able to penetrate? . . . Conversely, could Pauline theology help us to understand the deeper dimensions of *The Prince of Tides, Forrest Gump, Babe,* and *Shawshank Redemption?*" Such questions express the core of genuine dialogue.

22. Johnston, *Reel Spirituality*, 54.

23. Ibid., 42.

24. Ibid., 56.

25. Graham, "Uses of Film in Theology," 35. As he later remarked, "The science of interpreting texts, the technical term for which is hermeneutics, applies not just to the written word, and certainly not only to ancient texts such as the Bible, but also to other text forms such as film" (37).

26. Pierre Boulle, *The Planet of the Apes* (New York: Vanguard Press, 1963).

27. "What others will accept as fair" raises the issue of shared conventions of communication that I will take up in the next section.

28. May, "Religion and Film," 118; see further, John R. May, "Visual Story and the Religious Interpretation of Film," in John R. May and Michael Bird, eds., *Religion in Film* (Knoxville: University of Tennessee Press, 1982), 23–43.

29. If you object that my description along the way of "a realistic setting where the surroundings look normal in terms of color, size proportionality, appropriateness, and so on" is inconsistent with a singing lion cub, then you have failed to assume the attitude of "willful suspension of disbelief" that is essential to film viewing. But in this particular case, that suspension of disbelief is no different from what is required for understanding any fable (a genre category equally important to *The Lion King*) that uses the convention of personification of animal characters.

30. The cub Simba, who protests Zazu's announcement that his marriage to Nala has been arranged by asserting he could not possibly marry his friend, is like the five-year-old viewer still naively oblivious to the sexual nuances that adults see.

31. Monaco (*How to Read a Film*) devotes a full chapter of fifty-three pages to the "technological" means of film (chap. 2, "Technology: Image and Sound") and another chapter of forty-one pages to the meaning-creating conventions for relating the products of those technological means (chap. 3, "The Language of Film: Signs and Syntax"). Louis D. Giannetti (*Understanding Movies*, 9th ed. [New York: Prentice Hall, 2002]) devotes nine chapters and 409 pages to covering the same ground.

32. See Monaco's discussion of "Film, Recording, and the Other Arts" in chap. 1, "Film as Art," of *How to Read a Film* (1.19–38 [i.e., p. 19 of Adobe Acrobat file of ch. 1; see n. 2 to "Introduction: Preaching to a 'Cinemate' Culture," p. 157]).

33. Monaco, *How to Read a Film*, 3.14–16.

34. Consequently, it is not surprising that film-studies theorists are considering the changes brought to the film experience when movie viewing is moved from the cinema to the home theater. Just as technological advances in DVD players, "surround sound" systems for home audio, and widescreen-format video monitors are bringing some aspects of the cinema experience to the home, they are accompanied by developments such as movie chapterization, still and frame-by-frame advance, etc., that diminish the film's control over time. Filmmakers also are experimenting with new controls on a film's meaning absent to them in the multiplex by the addition of running commentaries and "making of" features on DVDs. Thus, new conventions are marking out differences between "film" and "video."
35. Giannetti, *Understanding Movies*, 45.
36. Ibid., 87–91. Thus, those fifteen points of analysis relate only to the final two formal elements of mise-en-scène (framing and photography) and not to the first two (action and setting).
37. See Monaco, *How to Read a Film*, 3.34.
38. Ibid., 3.37–41.
39. Johnston, *Reel Spirituality*, 126.
40. In addition to the discussion in Johnston (*Reel Spirituality*, 126–32), see also Giannetti's discussion of "story" (*Understanding Movies*, 333–72), and Tom Ryall, "Genre and Hollywood," in ed. John Hill and Pamela Church Gibson, *The Oxford Guide to Film Studies* (New York: Oxford University Press, 1998), 327–38.
41. In addition to the discussion in Johnston (*Reel Spirituality*, 132–39), see also Giannetti, *Understanding Movies*, 470–77; and Stephen Crofts, "Authorship and Hollywood," in Hill and Church Gibson, *Oxford Guide to Film Studies*, 310–24.
42. See Crofts, "Authorship," 322.
43. Johnston, *Reel Spirituality*, 134.
44. Ibid., 139–46.
45. Jon Boorstin, *Making Movies Work: Thinking Like a Filmmaker* (Los Angeles: Silman-James, 1995), 162 (cited from Johnston, *Reel Spirituality*, 139).
46. Johnston, *Reel Spirituality*, 141.
47. Dr. Sarah Harding (Julianne Moore), a paleontologist sent to study the dinosaurs, has a brief few lines suggesting how they overcame the enzyme deficiency, but they serve to overcome a plot-hurdle leftover from the first movie rather than to develop the novel's theme of evolutionary change in response to mass extinction.
48. *Jurassic Park III* suffers even more in the comparison with its predecessor films. It is an example of Boorstin's remark concerning "movies . . . made without themes," a film driven completely by plot and special effects (and the studio's desire to rake in millions at the box office).
49. See the discussions in Johnston, *Reel Spirituality*, 146–50; Giannetti, *Understanding Movies*, 411–54; and the essays in the sections on "gender, ideology and identities" and "culture, history, and reception" in Hill and Church Gibson et al., *Oxford Guide to Film Studies*, 102–223.
50. Johnston, *Reel Spirituality*, 147.
51. Miles, *Seeing and Believing*, 141; although she places this description within quotation marks as a repeated claim by critics, she does not provide a footnote citing a particular critic from whom she has drawn the claim. For her discussion of *Thelma and Louise* and feminist film criticism, see 136–49.

52. Khouri's quotes are taken from Janice C. Simpson, "Moving into the Driver's Seat," *Time*, June 24, 1991, 55; cited in Miles, *Seeing and Believing*, 141 and 143.
53. Miles, *Seeing and Believing*, 144–46.
54. Ibid., 146–48.
55. Ibid., 149.
56. May, "Religion and Film," 116.
57. Khouri, quoted in Simpson, "Driver's Seat," 55; cited in Miles, *Seeing and Believing*, 141.
58. For what follows here and in parts of the next chapter, I will be drawing at points on practical suggestions from John E. Moscowitz, *Critical Approaches to Writing About Film* (Upper Saddle River, NJ: Prentice Hall, 2000).
59. Ibid., 7 (and see his fuller discussion on 3–9).
60. Ibid., 8.

Chapter 2: Seeing a Sermon

1. Although the imagery of the film or television screen as a "window on the world" is widely invoked, in my view not even documentary films of the most minimalist form in their production are just windows. The selective and focusing control of the filmmaker far exceeds the architectural limits imposed by the location and frame of a window.
2. John E. Moscowitz, *Critical Approaches to Writing About Film* (Upper Saddle River, NJ: Prentice Hall, 2000), 51, emphases his.
3. Ibid, 103–4.
4. See the suggestions for and examples of genre and thematic approaches in Moscowitz, *Writing About Film*, 76–83, and 125–48. Here and throughout this chapter, my examples will primarily be general in nature; specific application of these techniques will be found in the analyses of films and the sermons dialoguing with them in the chapters that follow.
5. Moscowitz provides a plot-driven review of a film that also incorporates all the necessary "boilerplate" about director, actors, etc., into just 117 words (*Writing About Film*, 91–92).
6. Daniel Wallace, *Big Fish: A Novel of Mythic Proportions* (Chapel Hill, NC: Algonquin Books, 1998).
7. For reviews and analytical critiques adopting this approach, see Moscowitz, *Writing About Film*, 85–90, and 115–24.
8. Once more, examples of reviews and critical analyses with this focus may be found in Moscowitz, *Writing About Film*, 83–85, and 111–15.
9. Disney's press kit for the film stated that this song "best sums up the entire spirit and essence of the film" and in fact defined the core of the film. Cited in Annalee R. Ward, *Mouse Morality: The Rhetoric of Disney Animated Film* (Austin: University of Texas Press, 2002), 44. Ward's treatment of this film in chapter 3 of that book ("*Pocahontas*: The Symbolic Boundaries of Moral Order") is generally very good, but it suffers from one recurring weakness. She has relied on a related book published by Disney (Gina Ingoglia, *Disney's Pocahontas*, Illustrated Classic [New York: Disney Press, 1995]) for quotes key to her analysis. However, several of these quotes are not included in the movie itself (see as examples the final sentence Ward attributed to Powhatan on 43, and the conversations between Nakoma and Pocahontas recounted on 43 and 50). Certainly as a Disney publication the book reflects that corporation's vision for telling this story, but an analysis of Disney animated *film* should at

least note when quotes are taken from corollary materials rather than the movie itself.

10. "Colors of the Wind," music by Alan Menken, lyrics by Stephen Schwartz (©1995 Wonderland Music Company, Inc. [BMI]/Walt Disney Music Company [ASCAP]).

11. See the discussion in Ward, *Mouse Morality*, 35–38.

12. Although Powhatan (Russell Means) implies the battle was defensive in announcing "our villages are safe again," the historical likelihood would have been somewhat different. Powhatan subjugated some twenty other tribal groups (Ward, *Mouse Morality*, 37).

13. Music by Alan Menken, lyrics by Stephen Schwartz (©1995 Wonderland Music Company, Inc. [BMI]/Walt Disney Music Company [ASCAP]).

14. Mark I. Pinsky (*The Gospel according to Disney: Faith, Trust, and Pixie Dust* [Louisville, KY: Westminster John Knox Press, 2004] 163) likewise notes that both groups use the same words, but contends that "by this time in *Pocahontas*, even a child can see this is a false, belated symmetry. There is no moral equivalence in this battle." While the film as a whole may argue against a "moral equivalence," this scene at least warns that even the oppressed are not immune to the dangers of racism and intolerance.

15. As Powhatan says in his words to both his own people and the colonists when he responds to Pocahontas's plea not to execute John Smith and engage the battle. Ward correctly points out that in a film whose theme places such emphasis on communication across cultures, Disney has used its "magic" to gloss over the fundamental difficulty posed by the incommensurability of the English and Algonquin languages (*Mouse Morality*, 50–51). The resolution to this problem that she cites from the book (see n. 9 above)—that Pocahontas tells her friend Nakoma (Michelle St. John) that she and Smith communicate by "speak[ing] with our hearts"—is not found in the film, where the magic is even more pronounced. They first speak to the other in their own languages, and Smith admits, "You don't understand a word I'm saying, do you?" But then, in a recurring convention in this film that marks guidance from the spirits, the wind blows leaves (and, here, shining symbols intended to have a Native American quality) around their clasping hands as Grandmother Willow's (Linda Hunt's) voice on the sound track reprises a musical phrase from earlier in the movie advising Pocahontas to "listen with your heart; you will understand." Pocahontas does now understand and can speak English. Lest the magic be missed, we see John Smith and even Meeko the raccoon and Flit the hummingbird (her two animal sidekicks) react with amazement that she is not speaking her own language. Indeed, language itself never again is hinted at as a barrier to communication between the colonists and Algonquins. Prejudices and bigoted hatred, yes; but language, no.

16. The Motion Picture Licensing Corporation offers an "umbrella license" covering many (but not all) major film companies. They have a program specifically for churches through their related company, Christian Video Licensing International. Like the corresponding program regarding music copyright licensing for churches, the license fees are generally based on a congregation's average Sunday worship attendance and range from $180 to $600 per year. For full information, see their Web site at www.mplc.com.

17. I cannot stress enough how important these issues of licensing and permissions are. Movie studios diligently and strictly defend their intellectual property rights in their copyrighted films, and preachers who indiscriminately use such copyrighted material in preaching, and especially in sermons that are published

either in print or electronic media such as the Internet, put both themselves and their congregations at risk (since, under copyright law, a sermon written by a pastor is a "work-for-hire" that ultimately belongs to the congregation she or he serves). How stringent can studios be? Whole sections of this book had to be rewritten to comply with generally recognized "fair use" standards that do not require specific permissions when some studios would not grant a license or permission to use as little as 130 words of dialogue from a film (even for a fee). What about the "work-for-hire" issue? Since I publish homiletical works in a variety of settings, I have negotiated as part of my terms of call an agreement with my church that grants me the copyright to the *written* manuscript of my sermons with the provision that the church can make printed copies available and post the text on its Web site for a limited period of time; the church retains all rights to any audio or video *recordings* of my preaching in their services. Preachers need to make themselves aware of the current state of copyright law and to take special care that they don't infringe on others' intellectual property rights, especially if any version of their sermons are posted to the Internet.

18. Craig Detweiler and Barry Taylor, *Matrix of Meanings: Finding God in Pop Culture* (Engaging Culture: Grand Rapids: Baker Academic, 2003), 40.

19. That is, in the class "animal" as opposed to "mineral" or "vegetable" (as the classes are usually described in the game "Twenty Questions").

20. Buttrick lists the functions of illustrations beyond the traditional roles of "explain[ing] the obscure or convinc[ing] the dubious" as serving to "bridge time," to "build models in consciousness," to "gather huge sprawling meaning into a coherent system," to "join concept and precept," to "communicate on many levels at the same time," and to "bring together images from different realms of experience, and by their juxtaposition, break out surprising new meanings" (David Buttrick, *Homiletic: Moves and Structures* [Philadelphia: Fortress Press, 1987], 127–28).

21. Buttrick, *Homiletic*, 128.

22. Ibid., 133–35.

23. Ibid., 135–41. Buttrick actually gives six ground rules, but the second—that illustrations must be "on-target"—he concedes merely restates the criteria regarding analogy, shape and appropriateness (136).

24. As will be seen in the case-study sermons in later chapters, one might use a series of illustrations drawn from a movie over the course of a sermon, but each move of the sermon can have only one of those illustrations. For simplicity's sake, I will here develop *Big Fish* as an illustration for a single sermonic move.

25. Charles Puskas, *Introduction to the New Testament* (Peabody, MA: Hendrickson Publishers, 1989), 127.

26. See Eugene L. Lowry, *The Homiletical Plot* (Atlanta: John Knox Press, 1980; rev. and exp. ed., 2000), and *The Sermon: Dancing the Edge of Mystery* (Nashville: Abingdon Press, 1997).

27. See Lowry, *The Sermon*, 54–89.

28. Ibid., 82–84.

29. Box office totals from http://www.the-movie-times.com/thrsdir/top60dir/top60Search.mv?White%20Chicks; accessed August 31, 2006.

30. Paul Scott Wilson, *The Four Pages of the Sermon: A Guide to Biblical Preaching* (Nashville: Abingdon Press, 1999), 17; for his overview of these "pages" and the reasons for them, see 16–18.

31. See especially ibid., 201–5.

32. Ibid., 79–82.
33. Richard L. Eslinger, *Pitfalls in Preaching* (Grand Rapids: Wm. B. Eerdmans Publishing Co., 1996), 12–13, 57–59, and 86–88.
34. Ibid., 58–59.
35. The same point is made by Buttrick, *Homiletic*, 135–36.
36. I will briefly discuss the ways in which Peter Jackson's intercutting of the material differs from Tolkien's novels and his reasons for making these adaptations in my analysis of the film in chapter 5.

Chapter 3: "Heaven's Light"

1. The question takes slightly different form, as we shall see, in the opening song "The Bells of Notre Dame" (music by Alan Menken, lyrics by Stephen Schwartz [©1996 Wonderland Music Company, Inc. (BMI)/Walt Disney Music Company (ASCAP)]) and its reprise that concludes the film. Annalee Ward (*Mouse Morality: The Rhetoric of Disney Animated Film* [Austin: University of Texas Press, 2002], 59) also identifies this question as enunciating the film's major theme. The identification of actors throughout this chapter will be of those who voiced the animated characters. Quotations from lyrics in the songs of this musical will be cited from the motion picture sound track CD recording; quotations of straight dialogue will be from the DVD edition of the film; Gary Trousdale and Kirk Wise, dir., Disney's *The Hunchback of Notre Dame*, © Disney Enterprises, Inc.
2. Classic film versions include the 1923 silent film (dir. Wallace Worsley) starring Lon Chaney; the 1939 black-and-white film (dir. William Dieterle) starring Charles Laughton and Maureen O'Hara; and the 1957 color film (dir. Jean Delannoy) starring Anthony Quinn and Gina Lollobrigida.
3. And introduces significant tensions; see the fine essay by Ward on the resulting moral ambiguities: "*The Hunchback of Notre Dame*: Comically Framing Virtue and Vice," ch. 4 in Ward, *Mouse Morality*, 57–77.
4. Don Hahn, Gary Trousdale, and Kirk Wise, "Audio Commentary by the Producer and Directors," *The Hunchback of Notre Dame*, DVD edition (© Disney Enterprises, Inc.), commentary on ch. 2. They later note artistic conventions employed in the film to suggest to the audience that these gargoyles are perceived as alive only by Quasimodo (and in one instance by Djali, Esmeralda's goat; commentary on ch. 19).
5. Anne Thompson, "*The Hunchback of Notre Dame*: Playing a Hunch," *Entertainment Weekly*, 21 June 1996, 28–33; *Disney's The Hunchback of Notre Dame: Press Kit* (Burbank, CA: Walt Disney Pictures, 1996), 30 (cited in Ward, *Mouse Morality*, 75). See also Mark I. Pinsky, *The Gospel according to Disney: Faith, Trust and Pixie Dust* (Louisville, KY: Westminster John Knox Press, 2004), 167–68.
6. Ward, *Mouse Morality*, 76; see her fuller discussion of the church as characterized by the Cathedral of Notre Dame on 74–76.
7. As the archdeacon sings in "The Bells of Notre Dame," music by Alan Menken, lyrics by Stephen Schwartz (©1996 Wonderland Music Company, Inc. [BMI]/Walt Disney Music Company [ASCAP]).
8. Menken and Schwartz, "Bells" and "Bells (Reprise)."
9. A point underscored by the producer and directors on the DVD's audio commentary (ch. 1).
10. Menken and Schwartz, "Bells."
11. Music by Alan Menken, Latin lyrics adapted by Stephen Schwartz (©1996 Wonderland Music Company, Inc. [BMI]/Walt Disney Music Company [ASCAP]).

12. Music by Alan Menken, lyrics and Latin lyrics adapted by Stephen Schwartz (© 1996 Wonderland Music Company, Inc. [BMI]/Walt Disney Music Company [ASCAP]).

13. At the end of the song Frollo collapses onto the floor face down in cruciform posture. The producer and directors acknowledge the religious significance of the stance ("some more of our ham-fisted symbolism: Frollo falls down in the shape of a crucifix," DVD audio commentary on ch. 17), but other than its religious origins it is difficult to know what to make of the symbolism. Frollo is obviously not a Christ figure in this film.

14. One of the screenwriters, Irene Mecchi, described the theme as "judge not the outcast, for he may possess the greatest worth" (cited in Ward, *Mouse Morality*, 58).

15. Music by Alan Menken, lyrics by Stephen Schwartz (© 1996 Wonderland Music Company, Inc. [BMI]/ Walt Disney Music Company [ASCAP]).

16. Ward, *Mouse Morality*, 76.

17. An admittedly larger group than those who would recognize the Latin prayer of confession in "Heaven's Light/Hellfire," but probably a small group nonetheless.

Chapter 4: "Time to Get On with It"

1. Others reacted to the trailer quite differently. The film grossed $85,734,045 on its opening weekend in the United States, and went on to make $242,589,580 in domestic box office receipts alone (http://www.imdb.com/title/tt0315327/business; accessed August 14, 2006). A sequel built around the character Evan Baxter (Steve Carell), Bruce's rival for anchor at the local news station, is in production for 2007 release.

2. One of the great moments in the movie comes in an exchange between Bruce and God once Bruce has decided to answer "yes" to all the prayer requests. This decision results in riots in the streets when (among other things) 400,000 lottery winners consequently receive only about $17.00 each. Bruce can't understand why people are so angry, since they all got what they asked for, to which God replies that people are clueless about what they really want.

3. Tom Shadyac, "Feature Commentary," *Bruce Almighty*, DVD edition (© 2003 Universal Studios), commentary on ch. 2.

4. Ibid., ch. 7.

5. Ibid., ch. 5.

6. "Interview with Tom Shadyac, Director of Bruce Almighty," http://www.hollywoodjesus.com/bruce_almighty.htm (accessed September 3, 2004; interview no longer online).

7. Ibid.

8. Timothy B. Cargal, "A Share of the Spirit," *Emphasis: A Preaching Journal for the Parish Pastor* 34, no. 1 (May-June 2004): 58–61.

Chapter 5: "The Return of the King"

1. The original drafts of the screenplay for Miramax pictures were divided into two films. Since Miramax would finance only one film, Jackson subsequently pitched the two films to New Line Cinema. It was the president of New Line who then asked why Jackson wanted to make two films if there were three books (the middle volume of Tolkien's triology is, *The Lord of the Rings: The Two Towers*). See "From Book to Script" in part 1 of the appendices to the special extended DVD edition of *The Lord of the Rings: The Fellowship of the Ring*

(© 2001 New Line Productions, Inc; © 2002 New Line Home Entertainment, Inc.).

2. All its awards came in "technical" categories (cinematography, visual effects, makeup, and musical score) even though it garnered nominations in several of the "major" categories (best picture, best director for Peter Jackson, best supporting actor for Ian McKellen [Gandalf], and best screenplay adaptation for Fran Walsh, Philippa Boyens, and Jackson).

3. Five of which were again in "technical" categories, including its awards for sound editing and once again for visual effects. Its only "major" nomination was for best picture, but even that suggests it was not considered an inferior film compared to its predecessor.

4. Although often considered a trilogy itself, Tolkien's work is actually a single novel that was published in something of a serialization in three parts, known as *The Fellowship of the Ring*, *The Two Towers*, and *The Return of the King*, over a period of about a year (July 29 and November 11, 1954, and October 20, 1955). The last volume was delayed by plans to provide indexes that were finally abandoned in the first edition. See Douglas Anderson, "A Note on the Text," in J. R. R. Tolkien, *The Lord of the Rings*, 50th anniv. one-vol. ed. (Boston and New York: Houghton Mifflin, 2004), xi-xii. The structure of the novel is in six books and a set of appendices, with two books included within each part. The secondary nature of these parts is best seen in their titles. Tolkien liked the title *The Fellowship of the Ring* but disliked the publisher's imposed title of *The Return of the King* because it gave too much away. With regard to *The Two Towers*, there is no clear and consistent identification of which two towers are in view. The respective foci of the two books in this part suggest the Tower of Orthanc at Isengard, where Saruman is based, and Cirith Ungol, where Frodo is captured. The white and black towers on the book's original cover might suggest a juxtaposition of good and evil such as would be represented by Minas Tirith, the stronghold of Gondor, and Barad-dûr, the Dark Tower of Sauron. Tolkien himself later suggested that the two towers were the respective seats of power of Saruman and Sauron, and thus the towers of Orthanc and Barad-dûr. See the discussion in "J. R. R. Tolkien: Origins of Middle-earth" in part 3 of the appendices to the special extended DVD edition of *The Lord of the Rings: The Two Towers* (© 2002 New Line Productions, Inc.; © 2003 New Line Home Entertainment, Inc.).

5. The same search in August 2006 yielded 5,328 results.

6. In just the American market, *Fellowship* grossed $313,837,577; *Towers* brought in $340,478,898; and the box office for *Return* was $377,019,252, placing all three films in the top-twenty all-time leaders through mid-2006 (http://www.imdb.com/boxoffice/alltimegross). Worldwide, the films have grossed $2.9 billion, with *Return* ($1.1 billion) behind only *Titanic* ($1.8 billion) [http://www.imdb.com/boxoffice/alltimegross?region=world-wide; both pages accessed August 25, 2006].

7. J. R. R. Tolkien, "Forward to the Second Edition," in *The Lord of the Rings*, xxiii-xxiv.

8. One of the more prominent examples of their additions/expansions of the novel is the development of a plotline about a romance between Aragorn and Arwen. The marriage of Aragorn and Arwen is mentioned in the "Annals of the Kings and Rulers" that comprises Appendix A of the novel in the section on "The Númenórean Kings" (see Tolkien, *Lord of the Rings*, 1062), but Jack-

son and his cowriters drew on another love story between a man and an elf maiden found in the collection of background myths about Middle-earth ("Of Beren and Lúthien," in J. R. R. Tolkien, *The Silmarillion*, ed. Christopher Tolkien [New York: Ballantine Books, 1979], 195–228) in order to flesh out this story line (see "From Book to Script," extended DVD edition of *Fellowship*).

9. Tolkien, *Lord of the Rings*, 50.

10. Ibid., 59.

11. While the novel presents all the exposition regarding the backstory of the Ring in a discussion between Frodo and Gandalf at Bilbo's house in Hobbiton (see Tolkien, *Lord of the Rings*, 46–64), the film divides the exposition between two scenes. As in the novel, the first takes place at Bag End, Bilbo's house, and covers the history of the Ring, how Bilbo had come by it, and how Sauron had learned that it was now associated with "the Shire" and a certain "Baggins" (see the chapter "The Shadow of the Past" on the DVD editions of *Fellowship*). Frodo and Gandalf's discussion about the place of pity in the unfolding of events is held back until the quest to return the Ring to Mordor is already underway and the Fellowship finds itself in the mines of Moria (see the chapter "A Journey in the Dark" on the DVD of *Fellowship*).

12. Tolkien, *Lord of the Rings*, 59. Gandalf's lines in the film version, while an abridgment, are taken almost verbatim from the paragraphs in the novel.

13. Ralph C. Wood, *The Gospel According to Tolkien: Visions of the Kingdom in Middle-earth* (Louisville, KY: Westminster John Knox Press, 2003), 150.

14. Ibid., 151–52.

15. Lord Acton, in a letter to Bishop Mandell Creighton, 1887 (http://www.phrases.org.uk/meanings/288200.html; accessed August 29, 2006).

16. See the chapters "The Shadow of the Past" and "Parth Galen" on the DVD of *Fellowship*.

17. Cf. Tolkien, *Lord of the Rings*, 397–400, with the chapter "Parth Galen" on the DVD *Fellowship*.

18. See Wood, *Gospel According to Tolkien*, 154–55.

19. Indeed in the course of the debate, Éomer of Rohan says directly to Aragorn, "We cannot achieve victory through strength of arms." Aragorn replies, "Not for our selves. But we can give Frodo his chance if we keep Sauron's eye fixed upon us. Keep him blind to all else that moves." At this point Gimli delivers one of the great cinematic lines of the film: "Certainty of death . . . small chance of success . . . what are we waiting for?" (see the chapter "The Last Debate" on the special extended DVD edition of *The Lord of the Rings: The Return of the King* [© 2003 New Line Productions, Inc.; © 2004 New Line Home Entertainment, Inc.]).

20. See the chapter "The Taming of Sméagol" on the DVD *Two Towers*.

21. This is one of the major structural deviations of the films from the novel. Tolkien structured his novel into six books, each focused on only one plotline of the story. Thus all of the story concerning the other members of the Fellowship—from the death of Boromir through the battle at Helm's Deep, the fall of Isengard, and the discovery of the Palantir—is told in book 3 of *Two Towers*, and the story of Frodo and Samwise, from their encounter with Sméagol through Frodo's capture at Cirith Ungol, is taken up in book 4. Jackson chose to intercut the plotlines to establish their relative chronology and maintain the audience's interest in all the characters. Consequently about half of book 4 is intercut into *Two Towers* and about half into *Return of the King*.

22. Gollum's trap of having Frodo caught and eaten by the giant spider Shelob had gone awry when Frodo's paralyzed body was recovered by Orcs and taken into the tower at Cirith Ungol. He then continued his pursuit of the Ring and Frodo into Mordor.

23. Tolkien, *Lord of the Rings*, 946–47.

24. See "From Book to Script: Forging the Final Chapter" in part 5 of the appendices to the special extended edition DVD of *Return of the King*.

25. See Timothy B. Cargal, "What Makes a King?" *Emphasis: A Preaching Journal for the Parish Pastor* 33, no. 6 (March-April 2004): 36–39.

26. Tolkien, *Lord of the Rings*, 59.

Chapter 6: Dialogues with Two Superheroes

1. *Spider-Man* (dir. Sam Raimi, © 2002 Columbia Pictures Industries, Inc.; DVD © 2002 Columbia TriStar Home Entertainment) grossed $114,844,116 on its opening weekend in the United States and went on to earn $403,706,375 in domestic box office receipts and $806,700,000 worldwide (http://www.imdb .com/title/tt0145487/business and http://www.imdb.com/boxoffice/alltimegross ?region=worldwide; accessed August 30, 2006).

2. Marvel Comics-based films have included two *X-men* sequels: *X2* (2003) and *X-Men: The Last Stand* (2006); and one *Spider-Man* sequel: *Spider-Man 2* (2004); along with *The Hulk* (2003), *Daredevil* (2003), *Fantastic 4* (2005), and *Elektra* (2005); DC Comics saw the renewal of its *Batman* franchise with the release of *Batman Begins* (2005) after an eight-year break (four films had been released between 1989 and 1997), and the *Superman* franchise with *Superman Returns* (2006) after an even longer, nineteen-year break (four films had been released between 1978 and 1987). *Spider-Man 3* is currently scheduled for release in 2007, and the *Batman* sequel *The Dark Knight* for 2008.

3. John Ondrasik, "Superman (It's Not Easy)," © 2000 EMI Blackwood Music, Inc. and Five for Fighting Music.

4. The Superman character was actually created by two Jewish men, Joe Shuster and Jerry Siegel, and so some have preferred to find parallels with Moses rather than Jesus. Like Moses in his papyrus basket, set adrift on the Nile by his mother to escape Pharaoh's slaughter of his people (Exod. 2:1–10), the infant who is to become Superman is set adrift in space by his parents to escape the destruction of his home planet Krypton. Both infants are found and raised in cultures alien to their own. It is also noted that the Kryptonian names of both Superman (Kal-El) and his father (Jor-El) can be interpreted as following an Israelite practice of compounding some proper names with the Hebrew word for "God," *El*. It is, however, not clear if any parallels to Moses or Jesus were intended by Shuster and Siegel. See "Cultural influences on Superman" and references cited there at http://en.wikipedia.org/wiki/Cultural_influences_ on_Superman (accessed August 31, 2006).

5. Richard Donner, dir., *Superman: The Movie*, © 1978 Film Export AG; DVD: *Superman: The Movie Expanded Edition*, © 2000 Warner Bros.

6. Bryan Singer, dir., *Superman Returns*, © 2006 Warner Bros. Entertainment Inc.

7. See the scene "Fatherly Advice" on the DVD of *Superman: The Movie*. Interestingly, it is this same concern that Spider-Man's enemies will attack him through those dear to him that Peter Parker expresses through a voice-over in the final scene of *Spider-Man*: "No matter what I do . . . no matter how hard I try . . . the ones I love will always be the ones who pay."

8. A version of this sermon in dialogue with the lectionary reading Acts 2:1–21

for Pentecost was previously published as sections of Timothy B. Cargal, "Spirit-person," *Emphasis: A Preaching Journal for the Parish Pastor* 33, no. 1 (May–June 2003): 40–43.

9. Ondrasik, "Superman (It's Not Easy)."

10. The same is true in *Superman: The Movie*, where Superman literally turns back time so as to be able to foil Luthor's plot, and then quite literally lands him and his partners in jail. The fate of the three villains from Krypton that he confronts in *Superman II* is less clear, for they disappear into the mists of the fortress of solitude never to appear again in the film.

Chapter 7: "Better Days Ahead"

1. The allusion was obviously intentional on the part of the filmmakers since this action is one of several intercut scenes in the chapter of the DVD titled "From the Tree of Knowledge." See Gary Ross, dir., *Pleasantville*, © 1998 New Line Productions, Inc.; © 1999 New Line Home Video, Inc.

2. Given these clear allusions to biblical stories, one might raise the question of why I did not group *Pleasantville* along with *The Hunchback of Notre Dame* and *Bruce Almighty* as a film with "clear and explicit religious themes or elements." The reason I did not is that there is no clear evidence that the filmmakers use these allusions to develop *religious* themes per se. Indeed, one thing strikingly absent from *Pleasantville*, in terms of the 1950s sitcoms so key to its structure, is any mention of church or religion. Additionally, as I will show below, some of the allusions are put to uses quite different from the biblical traditions from which they are drawn. For a similar assessment of the function of these allusions, see Adele Reinhartz, *Scripture on the Silver Screen* (Louisville, KY: Westminster John Knox Press, 2003), 149, in her chapter titled "*Pleasantville* and the Nostalgia for Eden (Revelation)."

3. For a rather technical analysis, in terms of the literary theories it uses, of these different layers and how they create meanings through their interactions, see George Aichele, "Sitcom Mythology," in *Screening Scripture: Intertextual Connections Between Scripture and Film*, ed. George Aichele and Richard Walsh (Harrisburg, PA: Trinity Press International, 2002), 100–19, especially 100–4.

4. In an effort to be clear about my own references, I will use italics to designate the movie *Pleasantville* itself, quotation marks for the television series "Pleasantville" as referenced within the movie, and no textual indices for Pleasantville the city within the sitcom within the movie. Similarly, I will place quotation marks around the names "Bud" and "Mary Sue" as a reminder that these are roles within "Pleasantville" adopted by the characters of David and Jennifer in *Pleasantville*.

5. Somehow it seems that the people on "Pleasantville" are aware that the greys they see are the representations of other colors through the technological limitations of the then-current television medium. This explanation, however, makes little sense because it would require that they know they are in a television show and that there is some other, outside reality. Nevertheless, it is the filmmaker's device to account for the fact that they can recognize not only "real red" but also such hues as the fourteen colors read out by Big Bob (J. T. Walsh), mayor of Pleasantville, in an indictment in the film's trial scene, including distinctions between crimson and oxblood.

6. Jennifer had earlier discovered that nothing is flammable in Pleasantville. Consequently the only duties of the firemen (and, being the 1950s, they are all men)

had been to rescue cats from trees. "Bud's" cries that there is a fire accomplish nothing; only when he plaintively asks, "Cat?" do they jump into action.

7. Reinhartz, *Scripture on the Silver Screen*, 148–49.
8. See ibid., 164–65; and Aichele, "Sitcom Mythology," 115–19.

Chapter 8: "In His Shoes"

1. *In Her Shoes* (dir. Curtis Hanson, © 2005 Twentieth Century Fox; © 2005 Twentieth Century Fox Home Entertainment LLC) grossed $32,880,591 in domestic box office receipts (almost a third of that on its opening weekend), only about 80 percent of the $42 million gross of *Pleasantville* and less than 40 percent of the $84 million gross of *Atlantis*, the only films produced in the United States examined here to gross less than $100 million in domestic box office. Box office figures are those posted on the respective pages of the Internet Movie Database (http://www.imdb.com) and accessed August 31, 2006.

2. Rotten Tomatoes (a Web site that compiles movie reviews from a wide range of sources) gave it a "freshness rating" of 75 percent (meaning that of 147 reviews compiled, 110 were favorable); see http://www.rottentomatoes.com/m/in_her_shoes/ (accessed August 31, 2006).

3. "Story" link on http://www.inhershoes.com; accessed August 31, 2006.

4. The woman in the picture is credited as the model Ivana Milicevic.

5. When I discussed this line at a conference on preaching in dialogue with film at the Cathedral College of Preachers in Washington, DC, the women in the group all commented that they thought this line was nonsense; to the men, however, the line made perfect sense. Interestingly, both the novel on which the film is based and the screenplay were written by women, Jennifer Weiner and Susannah Grant, respectively. Obviously the choice of this metaphor was not the result of a fundamental difference in outlook between the genders.

6. See the "Story" link on http://www.inhershoes.com; accessed August 31, 2006.

7. The shot of Ella loaning the shoes to Rose is immediately followed by a brief and very restrained conversation between Ella and Michael, in which both acknowledge the many apologies they owe each other. Though this relationship isn't yet healed, the process begins.

Chapter 9: Hearing More Than Just the Film

1. Mel Gibson, dir., *The Passion of the Christ*, © 2004 Twentieth Century Fox Film Corp.; © 2004 Twentieth Century Fox Home Entertainment, Inc.

2. For a review of some of the controversy, see Amy-Jill Levine, "Mel Gibson, the Scribes, and the Pharisees," in *Re-viewing The Passion: Mel Gibson's Film and Its Critics*, ed. S. Brent Plate (New York: Palgrave Macmillan, 2004), 137–49. On the film as a whole from cultural, theological, and artistic perspectives, see the other essays in this book as well as those assembled in Kathleen E. Corley and Robert L. Webb, eds., *Jesus and Mel Gibson's The Passion of the Christ: The Film, the Gospels, and the Claims of History* (London: Continuum, 2004).

3. Through August 2006, *Return of the King* had grossed $377 million in the U.S., and *The Passion*, $370 million. Worldwide the totals were $1.129 billion and $611.8 million, respectively. See http://www.the-movie-times.com/thrsdir/alltime.mv?world+ByWG (accessed August 31, 2006).

4. *The Passion* ranks number 52. Only two other films in which the character of Jesus played a significant ancillary role were also on the list, namely, *Ben Hur* (11) and *The Robe* (42). By way of comparison, Cecil B. DeMille's *The Ten Com-*

mandments ranks number 5. See http://www.the-movie-times.com/thrsdir/
alltime.mv?domesticadj+ByAG (accessed August 31, 2006).

5. See in specific connection with *The Passion of the Christ*, John Dominic Crossan,
"Hymn to a Savage God," in Corley and Webb, eds., *Jesus and Mel Gibson's The
Passion*, 8–27, esp. 23–27.

6. Kirk Wise and Gary Trousdale, dirs., *Atlantis: The Lost Empire*, © 2001 Disney
Enterprises, Inc.; © 2002 Walt Disney Video.

7. Mark I. Pinsky, *Gospel according to Disney: Faith, Trust, and Pixie Dust*
(Louisville, KY: Westminster John Knox Press, 2004), 202. A few pages earlier
(199), he offers one possible answer to his question. Citing the work of Clay
Steinman, he suggests that such stories are precisely what is needed for continued commercial success because it permits continuing to tell stories centered
on white heroes (thus appealing to the current majority in America) while at
the same time appealing to both minorities in this country and members of
other cultures that are less sanguine about capitalism and American imperialism (cultural and otherwise), to which Disney markets its products around the
world.

8. See as examples Robert Jewett and John Shelton Lawrence, *Captain America
and the Crusade against Evil: The Dilemma of Zealous Nationalism* (Grand Rapids:
Wm. B. Eerdmans Publishing Co., 2003); and David Ray Griffin, John B.
Cobb, Jr., Richard A. Falk, and Catherine Keller, *The American Empire and the
Commonwealth of God: A Political, Economic, Religious Statement* (Louisville, KY:
Westminster John Knox Press, 2006). In commending much of this second vol-
ume, I must also explicitly reject the theory argued there and elsewhere by
David Ray Griffin that the Bush Administration either "orchestrated" and
"planned, or a least deliberately allowed" the September 11, 2001 attacks (Grif-
fen et al., *American Empire*, 19; see his more extended presentation in David Ray
Griffin, *Christian Faith and the Truth Behind 9/11: A Call to Reflection and Action*
[Louisville, KY: Westminster John Knox Press, 2006]). His arguments exhibit
some of the worst and most basic logical fallacies. Since the mechanisms of the
attacks in the "official" and Griffin's proposed accounts are mutually exclusive
(either al-Qaeda did it, or someone else), the evidence presumed to support the
second proposal cannot also support the possible conclusion that the administration "deliberately allowed" the actions in the "official" account. The fact
that the United States has carried out "false flag" operations in the past offers
no proof one way or the other even with regard to probability as to the question of whether this particular act was such an operation. In the same way, the
explanations of evidence that he offers as more "rational" than the findings of
the 9/11 Commission are anything but. Despite the similarities of the architectural failure of the Twin Towers and World Trade Center 7 to demolition
implosions, it is not more reasonable to assume that operatives managed to rig
every support pillar on every floor of these three buildings without detection.
If they were demolitions, then the destruction of WTC 7 makes no sense (did
someone reason, "If it's just the Towers, that may not have the desired effect,
but if we also include WTC 7 . . ."?). If the damage to the Pentagon is not consistent with impact by American Airlines Flight 77, then what did happen to
that aircraft and those on board? Why would the administration have ordered
United Flight 93 to be shot down if it was headed to a target planned by the
administration? And if its downing was intended to provide cover for the other
operations, why didn't the administration take credit for downing the plane and
thereby foiling the "terrorist" plot (the only conceivable reason for planning to

down the plane in the first place)? What Griffin has succeeded in providing is a prima facie case that some on the Left have become at least as irrational in their accusations against Bush as some on the Right have been against Clinton (suggesting he was responsible for Vincent Foster's death). A serious theological critique of imperialism and militarism of whatever national origin is only harmed by association with such proposals.

9. See Stanley Hauerwas, *After Christendom? How the Church Is to Behave If Freedom, Justice, and a Christian Nation Are Bad Ideas* (Nashville: Abingdon Press, 1991).

10. For an overview of the case, see http://en.wikipedia.org/wiki/Terri_Schiavo (accessed August 31, 2006).

11. Clint Eastwood, dir., *Million Dollar Baby*, © 2004, 2005 Warner Bros. Entertainment, Inc.; Alejandro Amenábar, dir., *The Sea Inside*, © 2004 New Line Productions, Inc.; © 2005 New Line Home Video, Inc.

Conclusion

1. Richard L. Eslinger, *Pitfalls in Preaching* (Grand Rapids: Wm. B. Eerdmans Publishing Co., 1996), 122–24.

2. Augustine, *On Christian Doctrine* 4.12–13, in Philip Schaff, ed., *The Nicene and Post-Nicene Fathers;* vol. 2, *St. Augustine's* City of God *and* Christian Doctrine (Oak Harbor, WA: Logos Research Systems, 1997), CD–ROM. Also available as Philip Schaff, ed., *A Select Library of the Nicene and Post-Nicene Fathers of the Christian Church*, first series, vol. 2, *St. Augustin: The City of God, Christian Doctrine* (Grand Rapids: Wm. B. Eerdmans Publishing Co., 1979), 583. Augustine is drawing on the work of Cicero, one of the great rhetoricians of the classical world.